KINDERGARTEN
MAGIC

KINDERGARTEN
MAGIC

Theme-Based Lessons for
Building Literacy and Library Skills

Kathy MacMillan and Christine Kirker

AMERICAN LIBRARY ASSOCIATION

Chicago   2012

KATHY MACMILLAN is a writer, American Sign Language interpreter, librarian, and storyteller. She is the author of *Try Your Hand at This! Easy Ways to Incorporate Sign Language into Your Programs* (Scarecrow Press, 2005), *A Box Full of Tales* (ALA, 2008), and *Storytime Magic* (with Christine Kirker, ALA, 2009). She holds an MLS from the University of Maryland, and her library career includes work at the Maryland School for the Deaf and Carroll County (Maryland) Public Library. Kathy presents storytelling programs introducing sign language through Stories By Hand (www.storiesbyhand.com) and offers training and resources for enhancing storytimes through www.storytimestuff.net.

CHRISTINE KIRKER is a children's library associate with the Carroll County (Maryland) Public Library. Since joining the library staff in 2005, Christine has developed and presented many programs for children of all ages and is the coauthor of *Storytime Magic* (with Kathy MacMillan, ALA, 2009). Previously, Christine spent ten years at the University of Maryland, Baltimore County (UMBC) as a research analyst for the Office of Institutional Research. She graduated from UMBC in 1992. Christine presents training and programs introducing ways to enhance storytimes through www.storytimestuff.net.

Illustrations by **MELANIE FITZ**

....

The American Sign Language (ASL) graphic images in this book can be found in *American Sign Language Clip and Create 5*, a software product of the Institute for Disabilities Research and Training (IDRT) and are used here with the permission of the publisher. To purchase a copy or learn more about IDRT's other ASL-accessible software, visit www.idrt.com.

Printed in the United States of America

15 14 13 12 11   5 4 3 2 1

While extensive effort has gone into ensuring the reliability of the information in this book, the publisher makes no warranty, express or implied, with respect to the material contained herein.

ISBN: 978-0-8389-1069-6

Library of Congress Cataloging-in-Publication Data

MacMillan, Kathy, 1975–
    Kindergarten magic : theme-based lessons for building literacy and library skills / Kathy MacMillan and Christine Kirker.
        p. cm.
    Includes bibliographical references and indexes.
    ISBN 978-0-8389-1069-6 (alk. paper)
    1. Elementary school libraries—Activity programs—United States. 2. Kindergarten—Activity programs—United States. 3. School librarian participation in curriculum planning—United States. 4. Language arts (Kindergarten)—United States. 5. Library orientation for school children—United States. I. Kirker, Christine. II. Title.
    Z675.S3M19 2012
    027.8'222—dc23   2011018413

Book design by Karen Sheets de Gracia in Candy Randy, Kristen ITC, Georgia, and Helvetica.
Composition by Dianne M. Rooney.

♾ This paper meets the requirements of ANSI/NISO Z39.48–1992 (Permanence of Paper).

Contents

WEB **Flannelboard patterns, craft patterns, and worksheets are available online at alaeditions.org/webextras.**

Acknowledgments

THANK YOU to Melanie Fitz, who once again produced an astonishing number of illustrations and flannelboard patterns in short order.

Gracias to Ashleigh Kirker, our Spanish translation consultant.

Thank you to Corinne Vinopol and the Institute for Disabilities Research and Training for their continued support and dedication to sharing American Sign Language with the library community.

Thank you to all the children who inspire us every day and to the colleagues who constantly challenge us to better our best efforts.

Introduction

LESS TIME, fewer resources . . . and more time with students, along with higher expectations from administrators. Sound familiar? With schools all over the country implementing full-day kindergarten programs, and higher expectations generated by No Child Left Behind, already overtaxed school librarians are doubling the amount of time they spend working with kindergartners. They are expected to provide media lessons that tie into the kindergarten curriculum topics and meet library media curriculum standards, on top of providing lessons for five other grades! What's a busy librarian to do?

Enter *Kindergarten Magic: Theme-Based Lessons for Building Literacy and Library Skills.* This comprehensive resource provides a framework for kindergarten media lessons, emphasizing activities that are fun, interactive, age-appropriate, and based on standard kindergarten benchmarks. Chapter 1 introduces guiding principles for kindergarten lesson planning, and chapter 2 addresses the inclusion of special needs students and nonnative English speakers. The thematic units that follow offer media activities that connect with thirty-six of the most common kindergarten classroom topics, such as sea animals, dinosaurs, and seasons. Each thematic unit includes

> "Kindergarten Speak" (tips on introducing the content in meaningful language for this age group)
> 5 recommended books to read in class with annotations and suggestions for use
> 4 fingerplays/rhymes/movement activities/songs
> 2 flannelboard or prop stories, with patterns
> 1 writing readiness activity
> 1 math activity
> 1 takeaway activity (craft or worksheet)
> 1 library skill–building game
> 1 American Sign Language activity (accompanied by illustrations of the signs)
> 1 Spanish activity (accompanied by a pronunciation guide)
> "Recommend This!" (suggested age-appropriate books related to the theme that kindergartners may enjoy on their own)

Each activity is labeled with the specific skills it enhances, and an index of activities by skill appears at the end of the book, along with a comprehensive index. These skills listings are drawn from Mid-continent Research for Education and Learning's *Content Knowledge: A Compendium of Standards and Benchmarks* (4th edition; available online at www.mcrel.org), as well as from our own experience. Because various school districts use different guidelines, it would be impossible to provide skills benchmarks that match each reader's needs, but we have endeavored to provide skill labels that will best allow each school librarian to align the lesson ideas here with his or her individual teaching needs.

Appendix A offers suggested resources for lesson planning. For further suggestions on developing flannelboards and other props, see appendix B. To make your life even easier, you can print full-sized versions of all the illustrations and flannelboards from the *Kindergarten Magic* Web Extra page: www.alaeditions.org/webextras/. This icon indicates web-only content: **WEB**

Let the kindergarten magic begin!

1

Creating Memorable Library Moments for Kindergartners

• •

FOR MOST kindergartners, school is a brave new world, full of wondrous places—and one of the most wondrous is surely the school library. A new class of kindergartners entering your library is an opportunity for you to inspire a love of books and information in a whole new group of students. With the right approach, media lessons can be like magic for these children! This chapter will address principles of media instruction that is tailored to kindergartners, principles of early literacy, and techniques for effective classroom management in the school library.

Principles of Library Instruction for Kindergartners

Kindergartners can pose special challenges for school librarians. These students often don't know the rules of school yet or might not even know how to sit still or behave in a library. They may require more concentrated attention than other grades. School librarians who focus on multiple grade levels may have difficulty establishing age-appropriate expectations for kindergartners' behavior and level of understanding. The following principles will give you a framework for creating kindergarten media lessons that capture students' interest and enhance learning.

1. Use a variety of materials and stimuli.
Young children learn about their world through their senses. Though kindergartners are beginning to develop a more mature awareness of the world than they had in preschool, they still need to use their senses to understand major concepts. By using a variety of props, games, books, and other materials in lessons, you will not only capture the attention of your students, you will also give them multiple avenues for understanding the topic. Using a variety of materials also gives students with different learning styles an opportunity to connect with the topic.

2. Make your school library welcoming to kindergartners.
In creating effective media lessons, we need to adjust for the physical, emotional, and intellectual needs of kindergartners. Adults can be intimidating to young children, so doing something as simple

as sitting or bending down so that you can meet the child at eye level will do a lot to strengthen your relationship with your students. Make sure the chairs that kindergartners sit in are of an appropriate size; if necessary, have the children sit on the floor instead. If your library tables are too high, consider purchasing plastic trays for students to use as lap desks (Lakeshore Learning's paint and collage trays are ideal: www.lakeshorelearning.com). Also, remember that children at this age do not have the same attention spans as fifth-graders, so don't expect sustained periods of sitting still or silence. Incorporate movement or interaction throughout your lesson to anticipate this behavior.

One of the most difficult tasks for many school librarians is to find child-friendly ways to explain difficult concepts. After all, most of us do not have the same training and experience that kindergarten teachers have. Strive to keep your explanations about library procedures as jargon-free as possible (for example, say "checkout desk" instead of "circulation desk"). If you do want to introduce library-specific terminology, make sure to explain what each term means. Throughout this book, we have included suggestions for introducing each topic in meaningful ways for kindergartners.

3. Use repetition, reinforcement, and smart planning.

Highlight important information through repetition, preferably in fun, interactive ways. Use praise to reinforce desired behaviors. Find out what motivates your students and use it. Games with simple prizes, such as stickers, are often all that's needed to motivate children at this age.

When planning the order of your lesson, start out strong. A welcome song or ritual can get the group together and focused. Do the hardest material (i.e., that which requires the most sustained attention) at the beginning of the class. Save the most active parts of the class for last, as they tend to dispel the group's focus.

4. Work with classroom teachers to coordinate themes.

Depending on the teacher, coordinating themes can be incredibly easy or incredibly difficult—or somewhere in between. Approach kindergarten teachers at the beginning of the school year and ask them for a list of the themes they plan to cover. Let them know that, to provide a more seamless experience for your students, you are planning to reflect the classroom themes in media lessons and that you would like to maintain an open dialogue with the teachers to avoid overlapping or introducing a theme too early. Check in with teachers periodically throughout the year. (And if you have a particularly uncommunicative teacher, we find that bribing him or her with chocolate is often effective!)

5. Make media lessons interactive.

No one likes to be talked at, but kindergartners don't know how *not* to interact with something that interests them. Find ways to include every child in the lesson, whether by asking questions about a story as you read, playing a game in which everyone gets a turn to match a word, signing a rhyme, or choosing a song that everyone can sing together. Many children learn best through *doing,* so give them something to do that will reinforce the concepts you want them to learn. At this age, children are not yet "too cool" to participate, so harness that energy!

6. Use music whether you can sing or not.

Many adults are uncomfortable singing, in a way children rarely are. But children don't judge your voice. So even if you feel like you can't carry a tune in a bucket, don't be afraid to use music with your kindergartners. Music can influence the mood of a class, capture wandering attention, convey directions, or just add joy. And, more important in our standards-focused time, using music effectively with young children can develop their oral fluency and get them excited about reading. When singing a song with your class, make sure the words are visible on the board or screen, and follow along with your finger as you sing. The music will help the children retain the words, and seeing the words will promote early literacy skills. Children learn new skills through practice, and using music is a way to make that practice and reinforcement fun and enjoyable.

Most of the themes in this book include suggestions for songs to use in conjunction with the lessons. We encourage you not to skip over the musical suggestions, whether you think you can sing or not. If you are uncomfortable singing, then select songs that have common tunes; you will have to sing them only once or twice before the children will sing for you. You can also take advantage of recorded music, but we find that this is rarely as effective as the live human voice.

7. Learn about learning styles, and go beyond yours.

Whether verbal or visual, kinesthetic or social, each person favors one or two learning styles above others. (To find out more about learning styles, check out www.learning-styles-online.com.) Unfortunately, we educators tend to favor our own learning styles, leaving our students who have different preferences to fend for themselves. Use information about learning styles to make your lessons appealing to all your students. This is another reason to use a variety of media and stimuli in your lessons; visual learners will respond to pictures, aural learners will appreciate the music, verbal learners will learn best from your narration, kinesthetic learners will gain most from movement and sign language, and social learners will enjoy group activities. (For more information about using American Sign Language in stories, songs, and rhymes, see *Try Your Hand at This: Easy Ways to Incorporate Sign Language into Your Programs* by Kathy MacMillan, Scarecrow Press, 2005.)

8. Support outcomes in other curriculum areas . . .

The school library is often the hub of an elementary school, and so it should be; with information for and from every area, the school library supports them all. This concept can be applied to media lessons as well. By educating ourselves about the standards for areas such as math, science, and language arts at the various grade levels, we can incorporate skills that students need into media lessons. Writing activities, pattern matching, counting activities, and classification are all easy to implement in the school library and will provide students with reinforcement of curricular skills as well as a more integrated education.

9. . . . but don't forget those library and media skills!

Focusing on outcomes in reading, writing, and math is all well and good, but the primary focus of a school librarian should be on the development of library/media skills. This principle can be easy to forget at the kindergarten level, where the focus is so heavy on weekly themes and topics. The activities suggested in this book use common kindergarten classroom themes to introduce and practice important library/media concepts. Make sure to booktalk some titles pertaining to each week's theme so that children see how their library provides them with information on many areas.

10. Encourage a love of reading and an appreciation of literature without constraints.

In so many areas of their school lives, students are told what to read and when to read it. Let the school library be the place where students can choose what *they* are interested in. Reading incentive programs can be very effective, but those that require kids to read books in specific categories or to meet specific criteria undermine the joy of reading—particularly for reluctant readers, who need those programs the most! If a child wants to check out a book that is obviously beyond his or her reading level, don't snatch it away . . . but gently guide the child to *also* pick a book or two at the appropriate level. The kindergartner's experience of the school library can establish expectations and emotions toward reading that will last throughout elementary school, and perhaps a lifetime. Let children's experience of books and libraries be one of joy and discovery, not one of limits and wagging fingers.

Supporting Early Literacy in the School Library

Though school librarians do not teach reading and writing per se, we have many opportunities to incorporate reinforcement of these key curriculum areas in our lessons. In fact, studies show that children learn language best through interactive, functional activities that engage them (Neuman and Roskos 2005). These are just the kinds of activities we can provide in library lessons.

Kindergartners need to develop skills in three key literacy areas:

Oral language: This area includes listening comprehension as well as vocabulary development.
Alphabetic code knowledge: This area includes knowledge of the actual letters as well as the ability to discriminate among sounds in words (phonological/phonemic awareness).

Print knowledge and concepts: This area includes general facts about the function of print (for example, letters represent concepts, text is read from left to right, and a book must be held right side up when reading).

Principles of Early Literacy

1. Provide opportunities for students to hear lots of language.
Through storytelling, songs, poetry, and fingerplays, kindergartners absorb language. The more language they hear, the more fluent their speech becomes. Surround your students with the spoken word. And remember, students need to be exposed to a wide variety of vocabulary so they can develop their own vocabularies (Strickland and Riley-Ayers 2006). Don't shy away from using classic poetry or stories with more advanced language, as long as the basic concepts and meaning are within a kindergartner's grasp.

2. Provide opportunities for students to express themselves orally.
The best early literacy practitioners incorporate lots of interaction into their work with children. Don't just read a story aloud; stop at critical points and ask students to predict what will happen next, or ask their opinion about the story so far. Invite them to help tell or retell parts of the story using their own words. Wordless picture books also provide a wonderful way to elicit commentary from children. All these actions help children develop expressive language fluency, and the interaction with a fluent reader is a key part of the motivation for young children.

3. Provide opportunities for students to develop print awareness.
Many educators attempt to instill print awareness in students by labeling anything that doesn't move, but in fact the quality of text (and interaction with that text) is more important than sheer quantity of words (Czarnecki, Stoltz, and Wilson 2008). Provide the printed word in ways that will be meaningful to students: highlight important library vocabulary, or provide the words to a poem or fingerplay on a whiteboard. Use words in games to motivate students to interact with the text.

4. Banish drills and emphasize language in context.
In response to the growing achievement gap in public schools, many pre-K and kindergarten educators have resorted to flash cards and drills to teach reading skills. Not only is this technique developmentally inappropriate for this age group, but the limited view of reading it inspires may actually undermine students' future literacy development. Study after study shows that students need interactive, meaningful experiences through which they can connect language to other concepts (Neuman and Roskos 2005). Rather than focusing solely on letter sounds or on how to write a specific letter, think about the functionality of language—what will motivate your students to interact with language? Connect the vocabulary to kindergartners' interests by using it to show how things work and how they can use language to help them navigate the world.

5. Provide opportunities for students to develop print knowledge and concepts.
In this area the school library has a special advantage, since many concepts about print (such as how to hold a book, where to find the title and author, reading from left to right) tie in nicely with media curriculum goals. Make the process of reading transparent to students by commenting aloud when you are reading and writing, so that children can begin to understand the logic of starting at the beginning of the book or holding the book right side up. Such moments need not be full-blown lessons but can be incorporated each time you open a book.

6. Use multiple methods and adapt for special needs.
In the next chapter we will discuss specific adaptations for special needs, but if you are already using multiple methods in your lessons, this adaptation will be that much easier. To address different personalities and learning styles, use a variety of materials and stimuli in your lessons: books, big books,

charts, toys, props, puppets, music, games, crafts . . . the possibilities are endless. Anything that will capture students' attention, motivate them to interact with the concepts, or provide a fun emphasis of a topic is a candidate.

7. Utilize all the senses.

Young children learn about the world through their senses, so allow them to use all their senses during lessons. Listening is important, but tactile experiences, such as touching magnetic letters, raised print, or beeswax letters, can also help students understand the shapes of letters. Help them develop large motor skills by drawing large letters in the air. Use sign language to help kinesthetic learners connect concepts to movement. Research shows that simply using the American Sign Language manual alphabet with young children can increase letter recall and comprehension. For more information about this phenomenon, see Marilyn Daniels's extraordinary book, *Dancing with Words: Signing for Hearing Children's Literacy* (Bergin and Garvey, 2001). Give students a variety of visual stimulation by using pictures, puppets, videos, scarves, and other props.

8. Don't overlook the mundane details that can affect students' experience of the school library.

Theory and interactive concepts are all valuable, but if your well-planned lesson, carefully crafted with the principles of early literacy in mind, is presented in such a way that students can't hear, see, or interact with the materials appropriately, all your work will be for naught. Think about sightlines when determining the arrangement of your lesson space; many school libraries, for example, are set up with tables and chairs in rows, whereas a semicircle of chairs, or even a comfortable space where children can group on the floor, might be preferable. When presenting stories, be sure to move the book so that everyone can see the pictures. Tilt the top of the book down toward the listeners to minimize glare. Speak loudly enough so that students can hear. (Studies have shown that boys in particular may have difficulty hearing female teachers, especially from their preferred position in the back of the room, leading to many perhaps false diagnoses of ADHD; Sax 2005, 87–88). Think through the possible logistical issues of your lesson plan beforehand and come up with a clear order of events, and then communicate that order to your students. When using props for your lessons, make sure they are large enough for all the children to see. If playing a game or doing an activity for which the children will need to take turns, provide clear instructions and expectations for how the turn-taking will go: Will you call each child up? Will you go down the rows? Though these kinds of details may seem trivial, they can have a significant impact on students' ability to focus, learn, and retain information.

9. Don't confuse early literacy with lack of literacy.

In recent years, there has been a push to shove phonics and writing skills down the throats of progressively younger children—most of whom are developmentally unready for direct reading instruction. Recognize the important concepts being conveyed via reading stories, allowing children to retell stories, and playing with language. Young children learn best through play, so don't assume that enjoyable, playful learning experiences are inferior to traditional classroom drills and instruction. In fact, children learn and retain concepts more readily when those concepts are conveyed through fun, functional activities—in other words, through play (Lu 2003).

Creative Classroom Management in the School Library

Classroom management involves more than punishment and discipline; in fact, teachers and librarians with good classroom management skills tend to be proactive, setting their students up for success and minimizing distractions that can encourage negative behavior.

1. Be prepared.

The best way to ensure a smooth class is to make sure you have all the pieces you need in place before the class arrives. Know your lesson plan and have everything you will need laid out. This point may seem simple and even obvious, but shoddy planning makes for scattershot lessons, which makes it difficult for students to focus. When you are leading activities, have a plan for how the children will take turns or come forward to get their supplies—and communicate that plan clearly to the students. When dismissing the children to look for books, send them in small groups rather than as a herd. A little bit of planning will make your media lessons calm and controlled.

2. Set expectations.

The number one way to prevent unwanted behaviors is to set your expectations from the beginning. The first time the kindergarten class visits the school library, go over the appropriate behaviors. You can even have the students themselves make suggestions for rules (and you may find their rules stricter than your own!). See chapter 3's lesson plan, "Welcome to the Library," for more specific ideas about expectations.

3. Remind students of expectations.

If you do have a specific recurring issue, give a friendly reminder about that issue at the beginning of class. By making a general announcement, you are not singling out any child in particular, and you are also giving students fair warning that the behavior will not be tolerated.

4. Give specific and reasonable consequences.

When making that general announcement, also remind students what the consequence for the behavior will be. Unless the behavior is egregious (such as hitting or endangering another child), give a warning to allow children to make a better choice before you dole out the consequence. For example, if a child runs in the school library, say something like, "Brian, we don't run in the school library. If I see you run again, you will not be able to check out any books today."

5. Make consequences matter, and make them positive whenever possible.

Many schools use one-size-fits-all consequences such as going to a time-out room, making a trip to the principal's office, or losing recess time. Although all these methods can be effective, you might find it more useful to make the consequence fit the child. What motivates one child to pay attention and behave may not motivate another. Use positive reinforcements to encourage the behavior you want to see. For example, while one child may be motivated by the chance to check out an extra book, another may be motivated by a chance to win a small prize, such as a sticker. Another may be motivated by a chance to have the school librarian sit with him or her at lunch.

6. Keep children involved.

Using interactive strategies throughout your lesson will keep kindergartners involved and therefore less likely to be disruptive. If a child is disrupting the group, find ways to bring that child into the group activity. For example, simply incorporating a child's name into a story can distract her from mischief ("Tara, do you know what that crocodile said? He said . . .").

7. Make your lesson plan age-appropriate.

Remember, even though this age group can sit through longer stories than preschoolers can, their attention spans are still shorter than yours. Don't expect them to sit for too long without wiggling. Be ready to adjust your lesson if necessary in response to their needs. Keep a simple fingerplay or song in the back of your mind for moments when everyone needs a quick wiggle to refocus.

8. Use music as a focusing tool.

Playing music as the group enters is a wonderful way to set the mood. You may have a particular welcome song that you like, or you might play music appropriate to your topic. A hello song with motions is also a wonderful way to begin media time and get everyone focused. Don't be afraid to use your voice without accompaniment, too; it is amazing how children of any age will quiet down and pay attention if someone starts singing or reciting a poem.

9. Use puppets in classroom management.

Kindergartners respond well to puppets and often will respond to requests from puppets that they might ignore from adults! Try using a puppet or stuffed animal consistently in your lessons; you can even give it a lovably grumpy personality and have it say things like, "No jumping in the library! No books for you!" (You can play "good cop" to the puppet's "bad cop.") Using puppets helps keep behavior reminders playful; keeping reminders playful cuts down on nagging and increases the likelihood that your directions will be followed.

10. Use sign language for visual reminders.

A great deal of research has been done about the benefits of using sign language with hearing children in the classroom. Aside from the cognitive benefits of language development, using sign language for classroom management can make for a calmer, quieter classroom. Sign language cues also offer visual and kinesthetic learners a more effective way to grasp concepts, and you may find that students enjoy doing the signs so much that they use them to police each other! When introducing some of the basic signs you want to use throughout the year, you may or may not choose to explain to children that what you are using is American Sign Language, or ASL. (It is a good idea to explain this at some point, so that children understand that ASL is another language with its own rules.) Begin by using the sign every time you say the English word; eventually you will only need to use the sign itself, which means no more nagging. Illustrations of some of the most useful classroom management signs follow.

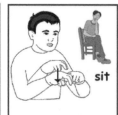

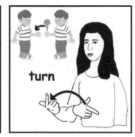

WORKS CITED

Czarnecki, Elaine, Dorothy Stoltz, and Connie Wilson. 2008. "Early Literacy Training for Child Care Providers: A Proven Program for Success." Carroll County (Maryland) Public Library. Paper presented at the annual conference of the American Library Association, Anaheim, California. www.ala.org/ala/mgrps/divs/pla/plaevents/plaatalaannual/past/earlylittrainingppt.pdf.

Lu, Mei-Yu. 2003. *Supporting Early Literacy Development in Family Child Care Settings.* ED477606. Bloomington, IN: ERIC Clearinghouse on Reading English and Communication. www.ericdigests.org/2004-1/early.htm.

Neuman, Susan B., and Kathleen Roskos. 2005. "Whatever Happened to Developmentally Appropriate Practice in Early Literacy?" *Journal of the National Association for the Education of Young Children* (May). http://journal.naeyc.org/btj/200507/02Neuman.asp.

Sax, Leonard. 2005. *Why Gender Matters: What Parents and Teachers Need to Know about the Emerging Science of Sex Differences.* New York: Doubleday.

Strickland, Dorothy, and Shannon Riley-Ayers. 2006. *Early Literacy: Policy and Practice in the Preschool Years.* Preschool Policy Brief. National Institute for Early Education Research (NIEER), Rutgers University. www.readingrockets.org/article/11375.

2

Meeting Special Needs in the School Library

Students with Disabilities

Working with special needs students can take many school librarians aback; after all, most of us do not have specialized training for working with these students and may feel inadequate to the task. Some school librarians may question whether special needs students even receive any benefit from media lessons. In fact, all students need a variety of settings in which to learn and a healthy exposure to a variety of teachers. As a center of the school, the library can help set the tone for inclusion and respect for the diversity of its students.

If working with a self-contained special needs class, you may need to make adjustments to your lesson plan. The classroom teacher is your best resource in this regard. Generally the kinds of lessons that work well with typically developing kindergartners—interactions that make use of props, visuals, and movement—also work well with special needs kindergartners. However, with special needs children the fun elements may be even more necessary to catch and hold attention and foster understanding. The developmental level of your students will determine how much you can cover and in how many different ways. Remember: it is better to teach a single concept well, in a way that children can grasp, than it is to teach many concepts that children are unable to learn all at once. Consult with the classroom teacher to determine what kinds of stories and activities will work best with his or her class and how the teacher and aides can support you during library lessons.

Special needs students mainstreamed into classrooms with their typically developing peers can present more of a challenge, as the needs of these students are more likely to get lost in the crowd. If there is an aide or interpreter working with the child, consult with him or her to find out what, if any, accommodations may need to be made in order for the child to get the most out of library time. Accommodations may include the following:

> *Placement.* Location is particularly important for deaf and hard-of-hearing students, who should be seated near the front of the room for best sightlines. The interpreter should be as close as possible to the teacher (or whoever is speaking) so that the child can follow both. For students with mobility issues, find a place that is easy to get to and will allow for maximum participation on the part of the student.

Getting and keeping students' attention. Some students with special needs may find it difficult to transition from one activity to another—that is, to transfer their attention from one task to another. Getting students' attention may be as simple as using a visual signal, such as raising two fingers in a letter V, flickering the lights, singing a certain song, or repeating a special verse. These sorts of rituals provide great comfort for all students, but are particularly important in helping special needs students make sense of their world. You may also wish to make large, laminated posters representing activities you typically do in the school library ("read a book," "sing a song," "play a game," "look for books," etc.) and create a visual agenda for your students at the beginning of each lesson. Going over the agenda at the beginning of the lesson and referring to it throughout gives students, especially those on the autism spectrum, a comforting sense of foreknowledge. They are participating in the lesson, rather than having it foisted upon them. Agenda-setting is such a simple thing to do that it is easy to underestimate how much benefit students can receive from it.

Assessing understanding. Adults typically assess children's understanding by asking questions. When working with special needs students, you may need to allow additional time for students to process your questions before answering. (Due to differences in learning styles, allowing an extra moment before calling on someone to answer can level the playing field for typically developing children as well. Some children naturally take more time to process than others.) Another simple, effective way to assess your group's understanding is to ask a question and have all the children respond simultaneously via a physical movement or visual symbol. For example, you might say, "If you think the fox will try to eat the grapes, touch your nose. If you think the fox will run away, touch your belly button." The manual alphabet is another easy way to do this. Teach the children the first three or four letters, and then offer a multiple-choice question with a different answer for each letter. Each child should hold up the letter he or she thinks is correct. This technique allows you to get a quick (and quiet) feel for who is following, and it seamlessly includes special needs students who sign. Structuring questions in this way also offers equal access to students who communicate through an interpreter, as the interpreting of your message necessarily means the deaf child will get it slightly later than his or her hearing classmates.

Turn-taking. Many special needs students respond well to visual or tactile prompts, and so a "talking stick," stuffed animal, or other special object that denotes whose turn it is to speak will help keep library time orderly.

Placement of props and materials. Depending on the needs of your students, you may need to keep materials out of reach or even out of sight until needed. Students on the autism spectrum may become easily overstimulated or distracted. Keep your teaching area uncluttered to maximize their focus.

Mobility. Throughout this book, we have included many movement activities. Young children learn best when their senses are engaged, and movement is a valuable way to engage them. These strategies are especially important for special needs students. However, if you have a student with limited mobility, consider choosing movement activities for the entire class based on what that child can do, so that he or she is not left out.

IN ESSENCE, every child is a special needs student, as every child has individual needs. Looking at your students with this attitude means that you accept and include each student. Attitude is the most important factor in working with special needs students. Remember that even if a student is behind peers cognitively, that child is absorbing language and information about the world through interactions with you and other children. Caring and inclusive experiences lay the foundation for self-esteem and further academic development. When in doubt, remember: focus on what a child *can* do, rather than what he or she cannot do.

Nonnative English Speakers

Working with students who speak English as a new language (or not at all) can also pose challenges for the school librarian. Maintaining communication with the student's classroom teacher or aide or both is vital to making sure the student enjoys an inclusive experience in the school library. If the child's experience of literacy is positive at this young age, then he or she will be more motivated to become proficient in English. The following tips are offered in the spirit of making the school library accessible for ENL students.

Use visual aids and props whenever possible. Visual cues will give multiple points of entry to a topic and increase understanding. It is especially important to use pictures when the vocabulary being used goes beyond the child's everyday frame of reference.

Be aware of cultural differences that may influence the way the child communicates. In many Asian cultures, for example, young people are taught to lower their eyes in the presence of elders, while in America, our common refrain is "Look at me while I'm talking to you!"

Make basic concepts about print explicit as you share books with the children. This includes showing where the author and title can be found, showing how to hold a book, and showing how books are read from left to right.

Using basic sign language in the classroom can be a wonderful way to bridge the communication gap. Teaching signs for common objects and actions in the school library gives the children a common language and means to communicate, and because the signs are generally new for everyone, all the students are on equal footing. An excellent resource for teaching basic signs to this age group is *Sign to Learn* by Kirsten Dennis and Tressa Azpiri (Redleaf Press, 2005).

Be sure to model respectful behavior when speaking to students who are nonnative English speakers. Many adults tend to speak loudly to, or speak down to, ENL students without realizing. Speak slowly, clearly, and normally, and patiently rephrase if the student does not understand.

3

Welcome to the Library

· ·

Kindergarten Speak

There are a lot of different words that you may hear in the library, and some can be confusing. To make things easier to understand, I'm going to use some simple words along with what librarians often call things. For example, I'll say "picture storybooks" instead of "easy fiction," "checkout desk" instead of "circulation desk," and "information books" instead of "nonfiction books."

Recommended Books

1 *Can You Guess Where We're Going?* by Elvira Woodruff. New York: Holiday House, 1998.

Jack's grandfather is taking him somewhere special, but Jack has to guess where from a series of outlandish clues. What place has monkeys, mountains, and knights in shining armor that you can take home with you? The library, of course!

    LESSON IDEA: This guessing-game story is a great way to kick off the school year and a fun prelude to a tour of the school library. Pause throughout the story to elicit guesses from the students. To add a writing component to the lesson, keep a list of their suggestions on the board.

SKILLS

▶ Reading for literary experience

▶ Differentiating between text and pictures

▶ Recognizing that print carries a meaningful message

2 *I Took My Frog to the Library* by Eric A. Kimmel. New York: Viking, 1990.

A little girl takes a series of animals to the library, and each trip has disastrous results.

    LESSON IDEA: Follow the story with a game reviewing appropriate and inappropriate behavior in the library. Describe various behaviors (such as running, grabbing books, reading books quietly, or lining up) and ask the students to show a thumbs-up or a thumbs-down to indicate whether the behavior is acceptable in the library.

SKILLS

▶ Reading for literary experience

▶ Understanding the rules and routines of the library

3 *I.Q. Goes to the Library* **by Mary Ann Fraser. New York: Walker, 2003.**

A classroom mouse discovers the various parts of the library each day during Library Week.

LESSON IDEA: This engaging story gives a good basic overview of the parts of the library and is an ideal prelude to a tour of the school library. Follow up by having each child decorate a bookmark.

4 *The Library Dragon* **by Carmen Agra Deedy. Atlanta: Peachtree, 1994.**

Miss Lotta Scales is a dragon librarian who believes her job is to protect books from children, but eventually she realizes that books should be enjoyed and read.

LESSON IDEA: This funny story is a good lead-in to discussion of library rules and book care. Follow up by having each child sign a "contract with a dragon," either by signing his or her name to a list of rules or by decorating a scale with his or her name to add to a bulletin board picture of Lotta Scales, the dragon librarian.

5 *The Library Doors* **by Toni Buzzeo. Fort Atkinson, WI: Upstart Books, 2008.**

The library doors swing open and shut, the children come and go, and the library fun is introduced in this singsong tale that riffs on "The Wheels on the Bus." This book is a fun way to introduce the various parts of the library.

LESSON IDEA: Invite the class to sing each verse with you, then after reading the story, go back through the book and demonstrate where the various library features are in your library. Then, play a game to reinforce the concepts. You sing a random verse of the song, and the children point to the place in your library where that activity happens.

Fingerplays/Songs

6 In the Library
(to the tune of "My Darling Clementine")

In the library, in the library,
We read stories and have fun.
We can check out our favorite books,
And take them home when we're all done.

7 I Like Books Call and Response Chant
(Have the children stand up and clap along, then repeat the lines you call out.)

I like books, oh yes I do, I like books, how about you?
I like books about big cats,
I like books about big hats.
I like books about big dragons,
I like books about big wagons.
I like books to read all day,
I like books in a big way!

8 My Book (adapted traditional)

SKILLS

▶ Recognizing rhyme
▶ Comparing size and volume

I take my book *(hold hands together like a closed book)*
And open it wide *(open hands like a book)*
To see all the stories there inside.

...

(Use a big voice for this verse.)

I take my big book *(hold hands as if holding a giant book)*
And open it wide *(move hands dramatically as if opening a giant book)*
And see the big stories there inside.

...

(Use a tiny, squeaky voice for this verse.)

I take my little book *(hold index fingers together as if holding a tiny book)*
And open it wide *(move fingers apart as if opening a tiny book)*
And see the little stories there inside.

9 It's Library Day (to the tune of "The Farmer in the Dell")

SKILLS

▶ Understanding the rules and routines of the library

It's Library day,
It's Library day.
Bring back our books,
Check new ones out,
On Library day.

Flannelboard/Prop Stories

10 *Book! Book! Book!* by Deborah Bruss. New York: Scholastic, 2001.

SKILLS

▶ Recognizing animals and their sounds
▶ Understanding sequencing

The animals on the farm take turns trying to ask the librarian a question, but only the hen can make her understand what they want. This silly story would also make a great prop story: invite students to take roles as the animals and hold puppets or wear costumes as they act out the sounds. To help students develop the concept of sequencing, follow up the story by inviting them to help you retell it.

11 Marie's Magic Library Binder Ring Story

► Understanding the parts, rules, and routines of the library

► Understanding the role of the school librarian

(Print out each illustration for this story on its own sheet of paper. You may wish to use card stock or construction paper and laminate the papers for durability. Supplement the pictures with clip art or printouts of digital photos to show areas or items specific to your library. Using digital photos of your library is especially effective with special needs students. Punch a hole in the upper left-hand corner of each page and use a binder ring to hook them together. Flip through the pictures as you tell the story. End with a clip art picture of a school librarian or a photo of yourself.)

Marie was a little girl, just your age. Her mother told her that when she went to school, she would visit the school library, a magical place full of things that would help her learn and have fun. Marie was excited.

On the first day that her class went to the school library, she asked the school librarian, Mrs. Stone *(or substitute your own name),* where she could find all the magical things her mother had told her about, the things that would help her learn and have fun. So, Mrs. Stone showed her the many things in the school library. First, they looked at the picture books. "These are fun!" Marie said.

Next, they looked at the information books. "These are fun and will help me learn!" Marie said.

Next, Mrs. Stone showed Marie how to look things up on the computer. "This will help me learn!" said Marie.

Then Mrs. Stone showed her the puppet corner. "These are fun, too!" said Marie.

(Continue the pattern, highlighting items around your school library.)

Mrs. Stone smiled and said, "Do you like the school library, Marie? Did you like seeing all those things that can help you learn and have fun?"

"Yes," said Marie. "But you forgot one. I think there is something here that will help me to learn and help me to have fun more than books, computers, or puppets. Because I couldn't find those things without *you*!"

"Yes," said Mrs. Stone with a smile. "Your school librarian is here to help you find things in the library and to help you learn and have fun, too!"

Writing Readiness Activity

12 Library Letters

► Associating sounds with letters

► Developing spelling knowledge

► Using multiple senses to practice writing

Tell the children you are going to teach them how to write your favorite word in the whole world. Invite them to guess what it is. Then tell them it's the word *library*. Ask if they know what letter *library* starts with. Then sound the word out with the class and write it on the board. Finally, invite the class to write the word in the air with you as you say the following rhyme:

L starts up high and goes straight down, then turns to the side.
I is a straight line up and down, that can't be denied.
B has a straight line at 1 side, add 1 bump, then 1 more.
R has a straight line, and 1 bump, then slides right down toward the floor.
A makes a point up at the top, and then the bar in the middle.
R again, a straight line and a bump, and slide on down, don't wiggle!
1 more letter, can you guess? It's **Y** now, don't you see?
1 straight line, with 2 branches up, and you've spelled **LIBRARY!**

Math Activity

13 Counting Books

Place five books on the flannelboard, then repeat the rhyme and ask the children to help you count the books. Repeat with different numbers of books.

> How many books are on the shelf?
> I can count them by myself.

Takeaway Activity

14 Book Care Worksheet

Pass out the Taking Care of Books worksheet from this book's webpage. In each box, the children should circle the picture that shows proper book care. Then the children can color their worksheets.

Library Skill–Building Game

15 Library Pokey (to the tune of "The Hokey Pokey")

(Introduce your process for selecting and signing out books, and then sing this song with the children to help them remember that process.)

You put your arm in, you put your arm out,
You pick a book off the shelf and you wave it all about,
You do the Library Pokey and you turn yourself around,
That's what it's all about.

…

You put your foot in, you put your foot out,
You walk that book to the desk where you can check it out,
You do the Library Pokey and you turn yourself around,
That's what it's all about.

…

You put your fingers in, you put your fingers out,
You write your name so clearly and you check that book right out,
(Alternate: You hold your card up and you check that book right out)

You do the Library Pokey and you turn yourself around,
That's what it's all about.

…

You put your whole self in, you put your whole self out,
You open up your book and you read what it's about,
You do the Library Pokey and you turn yourself around,
That's what it's all about.

ASL Connection

16 Welcome to the Library (to the tune of "A Bicycle Built for Two")

(Sign the words in capital letters.)

WELCOME, WELCOME,
Come to the LIBRARY, do.
I've been waiting with all these BOOKS for you.
It's fun to READ a BOOK,
So come and take a look,
And you will see it's fun to be
In the LIBRARY with me.

welcome   library   book   read

Spanish Connection

17 Welcome to the Library

The *bibliotecario* (bi-blee-oh-tay-CAH-ree-oh) works in the library. Who do you
  think the *bibliotecario* is?
There are many different types of *libros* (LEE-bros) in the library. What do you
  think *libros* are?
You use your *tarjeta de la biblioteca* (tar-HAY-tah day la bi-blee-oh-TAY-cah) to
  check out your books. What do you think a *tarjeta de la biblioteca* is?

Recommend This!

Maisy Goes to the Library by Lucy Cousins. Cambridge, MA: Candlewick Press, 2005.
Corduroy Goes to the Library by B. G. Hennessy. New York: Viking, 2005.
Max Goes to the Library by Adria F. Klein. Minneapolis, MN: Picture Window Books,
  2006.
A Trip to the Library by Deborah Lock. New York: Dorling Kindersley, 2004.
Tiny Goes to the Library by Cari Meister. New York: Viking, 2000.
It's Library Day by Janet Morgan Stoeke. New York: Dutton, 2008.

4

Welcome to Kindergarten

Kindergarten Speak

Welcome to kindergarten. I'm sure some of you went to preschool, or maybe some went to a child care center or stayed home with a relative. In all those places you learned things. Now you are in school, where you will learn to read, write, do math, and much more. You'll make lots of friends, and you'll have a lot of fun.

Recommended Books

18 *Mouse Views: What the Class Pet Saw* by Bruce McMillan. New York: Holiday House, 1994.

SKILLS

▶ Developing visual discrimination
▶ Understanding multiple perspectives

A classroom mouse escapes and takes a tour of the school in this guessing-game story. Close-up, full-color photos show common classroom items from the mouse's point of view, and readers must guess what the items are. A turn of the page shows each item in a more conventional view.

    LESSON IDEA: Follow the story with a discussion of the importance of using your eyes and paying attention, then show the kids "mouse-eye" views of items in the library and have them guess what the items are. In preparation for this lesson, take ultra-close-up photos of the items using a digital camera, then either print the pictures or connect the camera to a TV screen to share them with the class. For smaller classes, let the children take turns taking close-up pictures of items (with help) and having their classmates guess what the items are. This activity is wildly popular with special needs classes of all ages, and the hands-on component enhances confidence. To extend the lesson, print the pictures and place them on a bulletin board with the close-ups covering the regular views so that others in the school can guess and then lift the top sheet to check their guesses.

19 *A Place Called Kindergarten* **by Jessica Harper.**
New York: Putnam, 2006.

The animals on the farm await Tommy, the little boy who always comes to visit them, only to find out that he has gone off to a place called kindergarten. At the end of the day, his bus drops him off, and he shares all the wonderful things he has learned with the animals.

LESSON IDEA: In the story, Tommy tells the animals the alphabet through the letter H. Follow the story by writing the entire alphabet down the side of a large sheet of paper and working with the children to create an "alphabet of kindergarten": A for alphabet, B for books, C for cutting, and so on.

SKILLS
- ► Reading for literary experience
- ► Associating sounds with letters
- ► Knowing the alphabet

20 *If You Take a Mouse to School* **by Laura Numeroff.**
New York: HarperCollins, 2002.

A little boy takes his mouse to school, and one thing leads to another in this circle story.

LESSON IDEA: Follow the story with a discussion of how the school in the book is similar to or different from your school, and then work with the children to create your own circle story about the school day. You may want to provide common school items, such as books, paper, pencils, and paper clips—or pictures of these items—to prompt ideas.

SKILLS
- ► Reading for literary experience
- ► Developing text-to-self connection

21 *Eliza's Kindergarten Surprise* **by Alice B. McGinty.**
Tarrytown, NY: Marshall Cavendish, 2007.

On the first day of kindergarten, Eliza misses her mother so much that she doesn't want to participate in anything. Instead, she collects items that remind her of her mother and puts them in her pocket. Then, during craft time she realizes she has collected the perfect materials to make a little doll of her mother to keep in her pocket with her all day. This gentle story with a positive conclusion addresses the common emotions of starting kindergarten.

LESSON IDEA: Follow the story with a discussion of feelings about school, and then have each child make a "kindergarten surprise pocket": Give each child a pocket made from two pieces of paper stapled together and provide small pictures cut from magazines. The children can decorate and label their pockets and fill them with pictures that remind them of the people they love.

SKILLS
- ► Reading for literary experience
- ► Developing text-to-self connection
- ► Recognizing emotions

22 *Kindergarten Rocks!* **by Katie Davis.**
San Diego, CA: Harcourt, 2005.

Dexter's big sister, Jessie, has told him all about kindergarten, so he's ready, but he still worries. He has a great time on the first day, but when he loses his stuffed dog, Rufus, only Jessie can help. The quest takes them on a trip all over the school until at last Rufus is found. This bouncy story touches on all the basics of school and addresses the common emotions of the first days.

LESSON IDEA: Follow the story by having the children help you draw a simple map of the important places in the school, such as their classroom, the bathrooms, the library, and the cafeteria.

SKILLS
- ► Reading for literary experience
- ► Developing text-to-self connection
- ► Recognizing emotions

Fingerplays/Songs

23 **I Like School** (to the tune of "Three Blind Mice")

School, school, school,
I like school.

SKILLS
- ► Recognizing rhyme
- ► Developing oral fluency

It is fun,
When we play and run.
I like to learn the ABCs.
We even learn our 123s.
We learn about animals, plants, and bees,
Here at school.

24 Five Little Children

(Hold up your hand and point to each finger as you say the rhyme.)

5 little children went to school.
The 1st one said, "This place is cool!"
The 2nd one said, "Let's read a book!"
The 3rd one said, "Let's pretend to cook!"
The 4th one said, "Let's paint all day!"
The 5th one said, "Let's dance and play!"
Then CLAP went the teacher and they sat right down,
Crisscross applesauce, without a sound.

SKILLS
- ▶ Counting
- ▶ Recognizing rhyme
- ▶ Developing oral fluency

25 Wiggle in My Toe

From *Late Last Night* by Joe Scrugg (Austin, TX: Educational Graphics Press, 1998)

SKILLS
- ▶ Understanding the parts of the body
- ▶ Developing motor skills

26 I Went to School One Morning

From *Sing a Song of Seasons* by Rachel Buchman (Cambridge, MA: Rounder, 1997)

SKILLS
- ▶ Developing motor skills
- ▶ Developing oral fluency

Flannelboard/Prop Stories

27 Packing My School Bag Flannelboard or Prop Story

Place the items on the flannelboard, and then have the children take turns telling you which items do or do not belong in the school bag. If you do not have time to make the flannelboard, you could do this as a prop story with a real backpack, school supplies, and various non-school-related items.

SKILLS
- ▶ Developing text-to-self connection
- ▶ Developing classification and sorting skills

28 B-O-O-K-S Flannelboard Song (to the tune of "B-I-N-G-O")

(Cut large letters out of felt to use as you sing this song. As each letter is replaced with a clap in the song, remove it from the flannelboard.)

Here at school we have some books
That tell us facts and stories.
B-O-O-K-S, B-O-O-K-S, B-O-O-K-S,
Books tell us facts and stories.

(Repeat, gradually replacing each letter with a clap.)

Writing Readiness Activity

29 School Fun

Work with the children to make a list on the board of all the things they like about school.

Math Activity

30 Super Shapes

Have a variety of shapes available for the children to identify. If you have a magnetboard available, attach a magnet to the back of a cardboard shape. Give each child a shape and have her or him place it on the board and tell the class what shape it is.

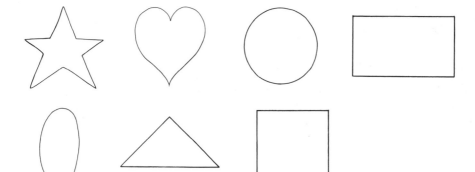

Takeaway Activity

31 Favorite Things about School **WEB**

Pass out Worksheet 4: My Favorite Thing about School from this book's webpage. Ask the children to draw pictures of their favorite things about school and complete the sentence on the worksheet using the list you made in the Writing Readiness Activity section.

Library Skill–Building Game

32 Interview with a Book

Preparation: Find a book puppet, or make your own by attaching googly eyes and a felt face to the front of a discarded book.

Activity: Conduct an interview with the book puppet. Ask the book how it feels when people rip its pages, throw it, write on it, or leave it out in the rain. Have the book respond (in a funny voice) that these things make it very sad. Then ask the book to tell the children how it would like to be treated. Invite the children to question the book as well. End by having the book ask the class to promise to care for its friends.

SKILL

▶ Understanding book care

ASL Connection

33 "Is It at School?" Game

SKILLS

▶ Understanding basic American Sign Language

▶ Developing classification and sorting skills

Teach the children the signs SCHOOL and HOME. Show them pictures of various items and ask them to use the signs to show you whether the items are found at home or at school.

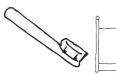
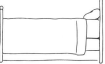

Spanish Connection

34 **Name the Color**

Hold up squares in the following colors and teach the students the corresponding Spanish words. Then read the rhyme below and ask the class to fill in the colors in Spanish.

> Red: *rojo* (ROH-ho)
> Blue: *azul* (ah-ZOOL)
> Green: *verde* (VAIR-day)
> Yellow: *amarillo* (ah-mah-REE-yo)

SKILLS

▶ Understanding basic Spanish vocabulary

▶ Recognizing colors

▶ Recognizing rhyme

▶ Developing attention and response

▶ Developing oral fluency

***De qué color?* (day KAY co-LORE)**

I like my teacher, he's really great,
I brought him an apple of this color, which he quickly ate. *De qué color?*
During recess my teacher takes us outside to play,
When the sky is this color, it's a fun day! *De qué color?*
My teacher is better than all the rest,
Our class pet is a snake of this color, it is the best! *De qué color?*
I like school, but when the day is done,
I run outside to see the bus! *De qué color?*

Recommend This!

Look Out, Kindergarten, Here I Come! by Nancy Carlson. New York: Viking, 1999.

Welcome to Kindergarten by Anne Rockwell. New York: Walker, 2001.

One Happy Classroom by Charnan Simon. New York: Children's Press, 1997.

I Love School! by Philemon Sturges. New York: HarperCollins, 2004.

Tom Goes to Kindergarten by Margaret Wild. Morton Grove, IL: Whitman, 2000.

5

Nursery Rhymes

• •

Kindergarten Speak

Do you know who Mother Goose is? Do you think Mother Goose was a real person? Some people think Mother Goose is an old woman who lived a long time ago and wrote down lots of the nursery rhymes we still say today. But really there were lots of people who wrote them down. So Mother Goose wasn't a real person, but a character people made up to stand for all those people who wrote down our nursery rhymes. What does "nursery rhyme" mean, anyway? A nursery is a place where young children play, and a rhyme is a poem that has words that rhyme, or sound the same at the end. Can you think of a nursery rhyme that you know?

Recommended Books

35 *Hickory Dickory Dock* **by Keith Baker. New York: Harcourt, 2007.**

This story is a new twist on an old classic. The mouse may have run up the clock at 1, but as the hours go by, many other animals visit the clock before the mouse finally goes to bed at 12.

    LESSON IDEA: Read the story through once. Then show a clock that has hands that can move to each position (1 o'clock, 2 o'clock, etc.). As you read the story a second time, have students come up and move the clock hand to the correct time.

SKILLS

▶ Telling time
▶ Reading for literary experience
▶ Recognizing rhyme

36 *You Read to Me, I'll Read to You: Very Short Mother Goose Tales to Read Together* **by Mary Ann Hoberman. New York: Little, Brown, 2005.**

This book is a collection of Mother Goose rhymes color-coded to read with a partner. It is a wonderful way to practice reading with a child.

    LESSON IDEA: Group children and assign each group a rhyme. The children can each take a part and perform the rhyme for the class. (Make sure to assign common nursery

SKILLS

▶ Developing oral fluency
▶ Recognizing that print carries a meaningful message
▶ Reading for literary experience
▶ Recognizing rhyme

rhymes that the students know. Many students will not be able to read the rhymes at this point in the school year, and so this exercise is more about developing confidence and oral fluency.)

37 *To Market To Market* **by Anne Miranda. New York: Harcourt, 1997.**

In this adaptation of the traditional rhyme, a woman goes to the market to buy all kinds of pet animals and vegetables, finally making a soup to feed them all.

    LESSON IDEA: Rhyming is crucial for learning to read and write. Building on the rhyming words in the book, brainstorm other words with the following endings found in the book: -ig, -en, -ow, and -uck.

SKILLS
- ► Recognizing that print carries a meaningful message
- ► Reading for literary experience
- ► Recognizing rhyme

38 *This Is the House that Jack Built* **by Simms Taback. New York: Putnam, 2002.**

This story is a wonderful example of a cumulative rhyme that allows children to practice predicting what will happen next.

    LESSON IDEA: Help children develop an understanding of text patterns and sequencing. Have them help you retell the story, prompting them with questions such as these:

    What was in the house first?
    Who ate the first item?
    What did the cat do?
    Who worried the cat?
    What was wrong with the cow's horn?

SKILLS
- ► Recognizing that print carries a meaningful message
- ► Reading for literary experience
- ► Recognizing rhyme
- ► Understanding sequencing

39 *Over the Moon* **by Rachel Vail. New York: Orchard, 1998.**

This story is a clever twist on the classic nursery rhyme "Hey Diddle Diddle." A frustrated director can't get his cow to understand how to go *over* the moon. The story emphasizes prepositions in a fun way.

    LESSON IDEA: Make a large paper moon and have volunteers help you act out the various ways the cow interacts with the moon. Then, for a surprise, use the "Magic Door to Books" trick found in Carolyn Feller Bauer's *Leading Kids to Books through Magic* (American Library Association, 1996) to actually walk *through* your moon. Review the prepositions in the book at the end.

SKILLS
- ► Recognizing that print carries a meaningful message
- ► Reading for literary experience
- ► Recognizing rhyme

Fingerplays/Songs

40 Pease Porridge Hot (traditional)

Pease porridge hot, *(wave hand, pretend to blow on steam)*
Pease porridge cold, *(wrap arms around self, pretend to be cold)*
Pease porridge in the pot,
9 days old. *(hold up 9 fingers)*
Some like it hot, *(wave hand, pretend to blow on steam)*
Some like it cold, *(wrap arms around self, pretend to be cold)*
Some like it in the pot,
9 days old. *(hold up 9 fingers)*

SKILLS
- ► Recognizing rhyme
- ► Developing oral fluency

41 Before It Gets Dark (traditional)

Down with the lambs, *(bend down low)*
Up with the lark. *(reach up high)*
Run to bed, children, *(run in place)*
Before it gets dark. *(cover eyes)*

42 Early in the Morning (traditional)

Early in the morning at 8 o'clock *(hold up 8 fingers)*
You can hear the postman's knock; *(pretend to knock)*
Up jumps Ella to answer the door, *(jump up)*
1 letter, 2 letters, 3 letters, 4! *(hold up fingers)*

43 Row, Row, Row Your Boat (traditional)

(When dismissing children to choose a book for checkout, ask them to find a book on a topic that makes them happy or makes them feel as though they are reading about a dream. Have them chant this rhyme as they get up to select a book.)

Row, row, row your boat
Gently down the stream.
Merrily, merrily, merrily, merrily,
Life is but a dream.

Flannelboard/Prop Stories

44 One, Two, Buckle My Shoe Flannelboard (traditional)

(Create a flannelboard based on the rhyme and have the children tell you what comes next. This activity will help build their sequencing skills.)

1, 2, buckle my shoe;   7, 8, lay them straight;
3, 4, shut the door;   9, 10, a good fat hen.
5, 6, pick up sticks;

45 Rub-a-dub-dub (traditional)

Rub-a-dub-dub, 3 men in a tub,
And who do you think they be?
The butcher, the baker,
The candlestick maker,
Turn them out, knaves all 3.

(Ask the children to guess what the word *knave* means based on the context of the rhyme. Explain that this nursery rhyme, along with many others, contains words that we no longer use every day. This activity will show children that by reading the rhyme or story, they can often figure out the meaning of a word by seeing how it is used in the text. This practice will help them continue to build deciphering and comprehension skills.)

SKILLS

► Recognizing rhyme
► Understanding sequencing
► Developing comprehension strategies

Writing Readiness Activity

46 Rhyming Words

Give each child an index card with a simple three- or four-letter word. Talk about how rhyming words sound the same at the end. Ask each child to write down two or three words that rhyme with the word on his or her card. To extend this activity, work together as a class to create a nursery rhyme based on the rhyming words the children wrote.

SKILLS

► Recognizing rhyme
► Practicing writing
► Developing vocabulary

Math Activity: Telling Time

(Give each child a clock face, hour and minute hands, and a paper fastener [see illustration] to assemble. Have them practice finding different hours on the clock.)

47 Hickory Dickory Dock

Hickory, dickory, dock,
The mouse ran up the clock.
The clock struck 1,
The mouse ran down,
Hickory, dickory, dock.

SKILLS

► Telling time
► Developing fine motor skills
► Recognizing numbers

Takeaway Activity

48 Jack and Jill Worksheet Craft

Materials: printouts of the Jack and Jill Went Up the Hill worksheets from this book's webpage for each child, scissors, glue, 2 craft sticks for each child, crayons

Directions:

1. Cut a slit in the worksheet along the dotted line.
2. Color Jack and Jill, and then cut them out.
3. Glue Jack and Jill to the craft sticks.
4. Poke the sticks through the slit in the worksheet to act out the rhyme.

SKILLS

▶ Developing fine motor skills
▶ Developing oral fluency
▶ Extending comprehension through dramatic play
▶ Recognizing rhyme

Library Skill–Building Game

49 Library Treasure Hunt

Take the class on a treasure hunt through the library to help them learn about the different parts. Before the lesson, place each clue in an envelope and conceal it in the appropriate place. At each stop, the students need to figure out the nursery rhyme clues. At the final stop, reward students with a sticker or other small prize. Change the wording of the clues to fit your library.

SKILLS

▶ Understanding the parts of the library
▶ Recognizing rhyme
▶ Developing text-to-self connection

Clue 1:

Mary had a little lamb, its fleece was white as snow.
And if her lamb wanted a picture book story, this is where it would go!
(Answer: picture book area)

Clue 2 (to be placed in the picture book area):

A butterfly comes from a caterpillar, a flower comes from a seed.
This is the place with stories for you when you are just learning to read.
(Answer: beginning reader area)

Clue 3 (to be placed in beginning reader area):

Old King Cole was a merry old soul, and a merry old soul was he.
He liked to read from chapter books, where the big kids like to be. (Answer: chapter book area)

Clue 4 (to be placed in the chapter book area):

Hey diddle diddle, the cat and the fiddle wanted a book that was true.
Nonfiction's the word, if you haven't heard, for books of facts for you.
(Answer: nonfiction area)

Clue 5 (to be placed in the nonfiction area):

Jack and Jill went up the hill to get some information.
You'll find some too, that's just for you, at a computer station. (Answer: computer area)

Clue 6 (to be placed in computer area):

> Tom, Tom the piper's son
> Found a book and away he ran.
> It was a reference book
> That he took
> So (librarian's name) brought him back again. (Answer: reference area)

Clue 7 (to be placed in reference area; optional—fill in the blank with a special area of your school library that you want to highlight):

> Little Miss Muffet sat on a tuffet, eating her curds and whey.
> And when she was done, she went to the _____ for some fun, and she stayed
>   there all day.

Clue 8 (to be placed in optional area, or in reference area if clue 7 is not used):

> Humpty Dumpty sat on a wall.
> Humpty Dumpty had a great fall.
> When we gather for stories just so,
> This is the place we always go. (Answer: story/class area)

Clue 9 (to be placed in story/class area):

> Ring a ring o' roses, a pocket full of posies.
> If you can tell me something we've learned, touch your little nosy.

Review the treasure hunt by allowing each child to share something he or she learned. Present a prize to each child as he or she reports.

ASL Connection

50 Two Little Blackbirds (traditional)

(Teach the children the sign for BIRD. As you say the rhyme, sign BIRD with both hands to represent the two blackbirds. When you make the birds fly away, make the right hand fly across to your left, and your left hand fly across to your right, and then back on the same paths. This cross-lateral movement helps develop the connections between the two halves of the brain.)

2 little blackbirds sitting on a hill,
1 named Jack and 1 named Jill.
Fly away, Jack! Fly away, Jill!
Come back, Jack! Come back, Jill!

bird

SKILLS

▶ Recognizing rhyme
▶ Understanding basic American Sign Language

Spanish Connection

51 Counting Elephants

Every culture has nursery rhymes. Share this rhyme from Spain with your students, and they can learn how to count in Spanish.

Cinco Elefantitos (Five Little Elephants)

Cinco elefantitos (SINK-o ele-fan-TI-tose), this one fell down,
Cuatro elefantitos (QUA-tro ele-fan-TI-tose), this one lost its way,
Tres elefantitos (TRACE ele-fan-TI-tose), this one fell sick,
Dos elefantitos (DOSE ele-fan-TI-tose), this one ran away.
Uno elefantito (OO-no ele-fan-TI-toh), I take it away.

Recommend This!

Nursery Rhymes Easy Reader by Emily Clark. Westminster, CA: Teacher Created Resources, 2004.

Mary Had a Little Jam and Other Silly Rhymes by Bruce Lansky. New York: Meadowbrook Press, 2004.

I See the Moon and the Moon Sees Me by Jonathan London. New York: Viking, 1996.

Off to the Sweet Shores of Africa: And Other Talking Drum Rhymes by Uzo Unobagha. San Francisco: Chronicle, 2000.

SKILLS

▶ Counting
▶ Understanding basic Spanish vocabulary
▶ Developing oral fluency

6

All about Me

Kindergarten Speak

You are an amazing and unique person. Yes, we all have arms, legs, hair, and teeth. We all have different moods, and sometimes we have those moods at the same time as someone else! But no one is quite like you. We all have our own interests and things that make us special. Can you think of something that makes you special?

Recommended Books

52 *Parts* **by Tedd Arnold. New York: Dial, 1997.**

A little boy thinks his body is falling apart when his tooth falls out and he loses bits of skin and hair, until he learns that these things are normal.

    LESSON IDEA: Follow up with a discussion about losing teeth. Take a poll to see how many children in the class have lost teeth and make a bar graph to show the number.

53 *Today I Feel Silly and Other Moods That Make My Day* **by Jamie Lee Curtis. New York: HarperCollins, 1998.**

A little girl describes her various moods.

    LESSON IDEA: Write several emotions (such as silly, angry, happy, and excited) on the board and invite the children to suggest things that make them feel each emotion. Write their suggestions under the appropriate emotion.

SKILLS

- ▶ Reading for literary experience
- ▶ Developing text-to-self connection
- ▶ Counting
- ▶ Understanding the parts of the body
- ▶ Understanding that graphs represent information

- ▶ Reading for literary experience
- ▶ Developing text-to-self connection
- ▶ Recognizing emotions

54 *Chrysanthemum* **by Kevin Henkes. New York: Greenwillow, 1991.**

Chrysanthemum's classmates make fun of her unusual name until they find out their favorite teacher's first name is Delphinium.

    LESSON IDEA: Follow this story by writing all the children's names on the board, then counting how many start with A, how many start with B, and so on. Invite the children to identify other similarities, such as names with three letters, long names, or names that end with the same letter. This activity promotes letter identification and sorting and classifying skills.

SKILLS

► Knowing the alphabet
► Developing text-to-self connection
► Recognizing emotions
► Associating sounds with letters
► Reading for literary experience
► Counting

55 *Eyes, Nose, Fingers, and Toes: A First Book All about You* **by Judy Hindley. Cambridge, MA: Candlewick Press, 1999.**

This bouncy rhyming book introduces body parts.

    LESSON IDEA: Follow the story by pointing out some of the rhymes, and then play a rhyming game: write a word on the board, and have the children guess a body part that rhymes with the word. Some suggested rhyming pairs: farm/arm, fly/eye, sand/hand, egg/leg, hose/nose, race/face, tear/ear, snow/toe, bee/knee.

► Recognizing rhyme
► Understanding the parts of the body

56 *Grumpy Bird* **by Jeremy Tankard. New York: Scholastic, 2007.**

Bird wakes up grumpy, but gets cheered up when his friends start copying everything he does.

    LESSON IDEA: Reinforce the sequence in the story by showing pictures of the animals and having the children help you retell the story. Invite volunteers to act out the story for the rest of the class.

SKILLS

► Reading for literary experience
► Understanding sequencing
► Recognizing emotions

Fingerplays/Songs

57 On My Head (adapted traditional)

On my head my hands I place,
On my shoulders, on my face,
On my hips and at my side,
Then behind me they will hide.
I can wave them way up high,
Wiggle my fingers, watch them fly.
I hold them out in front of me,
Then I clap them, 1, 2, 3.
I reach way up then sit right down
On my chair without a sound.

SKILLS

► Recognizing rhyme
► Understanding the parts of the body
► Developing motor skills

58 If You're Happy (adapted traditional)

If you're happy and you know it, clap your hands.
If you're happy and you know it, clap your hands.
If you're happy and you know it, then your face will surely show it.
If you're happy and you know it, clap your hands.

...

If you're sad and you know it, say "boo-hoo" . . .
If you're excited and you know it, jump up and down . . .

SKILLS

► Recognizing emotions
► Developing motor skills
► Developing oral fluency

If you're angry and you know it, say "grrrrr" . . .
If you're calm and you know it, take a seat . . .

59 Feelings

From *Getting to Know Myself* by Hap Palmer. Freeport, NY: Educational Activities, 1972.

60 Toe Leg Knee

From *Jim Gill Sings Do Re Mi on His Toe Leg Knee* by Jim Gill. Oak Park, IL: Jim Gill Music, 1999.

Flannelboard/Prop Stories

61 Joey's Beautiful Name Flannelboard Story

Once upon a time there was a little boy named Joey. At school one day, his teacher showed him how to write his name. Joey practiced and practiced until he got it just right. He wrote his name just like this. *(Write "Joey" on the board.)* He was so proud, he couldn't wait until he got home to show his mother.

On the way home from school, he ran into a police officer. "Hi, I'm Joey," he said. "What's your name?" *(Solicit suggestions from the class for the names of the people and animals Joey meets, or make up your own names throughout.)* "My name is Tony," said the police officer. "Wow, that's a great name!" said Joey Tony. "I am going to add it to my name, and from now on I will be Joey Tony. Bye!" *(Add the police officer's name to Joey's name on the board.)*

Joey Tony continued on his way home. He saw the mail carrier coming up the street and said, "Hi, I'm Joey Tony. What's your name?" "My name is Bob," said the mail carrier. "Wow, that's a great name!" said Joey Tony. "I am going to add it to my name, and from now on I will be Joey Tony Bob. Bye!" *(Add the mail carrier's name to Joey's name on the board.)*

(Repeat the pattern with Joey meeting the dog, cat, rabbit, and bird and adding each of their names to his.)

Finally Joey Tony Bob (etc.) got home and told his mother all about how he had met all the people and animals and changed his name. He was so excited that he forgot all about how he had learned to write his name.

The next day, he went back to school. He told all his friends about his new name, and whenever someone called him Joey, he said, "No! My name is Joey Tony Bob (etc.)!"

Then, after lunch, his teacher said, "All right class, yesterday, we wrote our first names. Today we will write our *whole* names. Would you like to go first, Joey Tony Bob (etc.)?"

Joey gulped and said, "I think I'll just go back to being Joey."

62 I Have Two of These Flannelboard Matching Rhyme

Preparation: Cut out two of each picture. If you have more than twenty-eight children in the class, cut out multiple pairs of eyes, gloves, mittens, socks, and shoes in different colors.

Activity: Give each student one item and then say the following rhyme. Continue until every child has had a turn.

> (Child's name) has 1 (body part/clothing item), as you can see,
> So put it up on the board, 1, 2, 3.
> But I have 2 (body parts/clothing items), so we need another.
> Who in the classroom has the other?

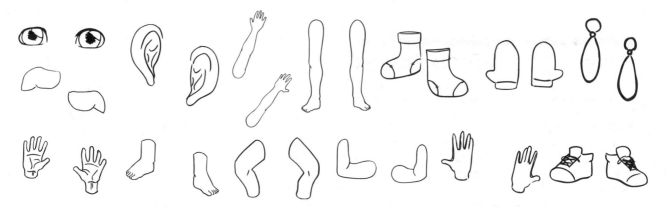

Writing Readiness Activity

63 Name Acrostic

Provide each child with a piece of paper and a pencil or crayon and explain that the children are going to write a poem using their names. Show them an example using your own first name. First, write your name vertically down the left side of the chalkboard. Then write a word that describes you and that begins with each letter of your name. For example:

> Jolly
> Acrobatic
> Merry
> Enthusiastic
> Sporty

Math Activity

64 How Many Letters?

Have each child write his or her first name on the board. Then count the letters in each name and write the number of letters next to each name. Then ask the following questions:

> How many children's names have three letters? (four letters, five letters, etc.)
> Who has the longest name?
> Who has the shortest name?
> How many letters do most of the names in the class have?

Takeaway Activity

65 Name Shapes

SKILLS
▶ Writing one's name
▶ Developing creativity

Materials: a piece of white paper for each child, crayons or markers, scissors

Directions:

1. Fold the paper in half the long way.
2. Put the folded paper in front of you so that the fold faces you.
3. Write your name so that it touches the fold, using as much space on the paper as possible.
4. Keeping the paper folded, cut out the shape made by your name.
5. Unfold the paper, and decorate your shape according to what it looks like. Does your unfolded shape look like a butterfly? A snake? A face? Use the crayons or markers to decorate. Each child's shape will be as unique as he or she is.

Library Skill–Building Game

66 Book Parts Simon Says

SKILLS
▶ Developing attention and response
▶ Understanding the parts of a book

Introduce the following parts of a book by showing a book and giving the hints below to help children locate them:

Front cover: the front of the book, usually has a picture
Spine: the side of the book
Title: usually in large print on the front cover
Author name: usually in smaller print, either above or below the title (the author's name might have the word *by* in front of it, which shows that the author is the person who wrote the book)
Title page: usually two to three pages into the book; shows the title and author's name again
Back cover: the back of the book; may have a picture on it, or sometimes just words

After introducing the parts of a book, hand each child a book. Play "Simon Says," incorporating book parts. For example: "Simon says point to the front cover of your book." Remind students that when you do *not* say "Simon says . . ." they should *not* perform the action.

Once the students have the basic pointing down, make the actions more complicated. For example:

Simon says touch the spine of your book to your knee.
Simon says show your title page to your neighbor.
Simon says hold up your book if it has a letter A in the title.
Simon says touch the back cover of your book to your head.

To finish the game and collect the books, give a series of instructions such as:

Simon says if your book has a blue cover, bring it to me. *(repeat with different colors until all books are collected), or*
Simon says if your book's title has a letter A in it, bring it to me. *(repeat with different letters until all books are collected)*

ASL Connection

67 Feelings (to the tune of "A Bicycle Built for Two")

FEELINGS, FEELINGS
Are different every day.
Sometimes I'm HAPPY and I want to play.
Sometimes I'm SAD and weepy,
Or SCARED when things get creepy.
Let FEELINGS be,
'Cause now I see
My FEELINGS are part of ME.

Spanish Connection

68 How Do I Feel?

Teach the class the following Spanish words for feelings. As you say each word, fill in the blanks with the appropriate feeling.

Happy: *feliz* (fell-EASE)
Angry: *enfadado* (en-fa-DAH-doh)
Sad: *triste* (TREES-tay)
Shy: *timido* (TEE-mee-doh)

When I have a big smile on my face, you know that I am . . . (*feliz*).
When I frown, you know that I am . . . (*enfadado*).
When I am crying, you know that I am . . . (*triste*).
Around strangers I sometimes feel . . . (*timido*)

Recommend This!

Sometimes by Keith Baker. San Diego, CA: Harcourt Brace, 1999.

How to Be by Lisa Brown. New York: HarperCollins, 2006.

Giggle Belly by Page Sakelaris. New York: Scholastic, 2000.

A Head Is for Hats by Mary Serfozo. New York: Scholastic, 1999.

My Friend Is Sad by Mo Willems. New York: Hyperion, 2007.

Quick as a Cricket by Audrey Wood. New York: Child's Play, 1982.

7

Friends and Family

· ·

Kindergarten Speak

We are all part of a family, even if each person's family is different. Some of us may live with a mother and father and brothers and sisters. Others may live with a grandparent. Regardless, we all have people who take care of us. We also have friends. Some of our friends are best friends, whom we do lots of things with. Some friends may just be school friends. We are lucky to be part of a family and have a variety of friends.

Recommended Books

69 *Too Close Friends* **by Shen Roddie. New York: Dial, 1998.**

Hippo and Pig are such good friends that they decide to cut down the hedge separating their houses—but when they learn *too* much about each other, their friendship begins to suffer.

LESSON IDEA: Emphasize sequencing by having the children act out the story after reading it.

70 *What a Treasure!* **by Jane Hillenbrand. New York: Holiday House, 2006.**

Mole sets out to dig for treasure, finds items for others, and finally finds the best treasure of all—a friend.

LESSON IDEA: After reading the story, emphasize sequencing by having the children help you retell the story. For science connections, show pictures of the animals and the items Mole found and have the children match them.

SKILLS

▶ Reading for literary experience

▶ Understanding sequencing

▶ Recognizing days of the week

▶ Extending comprehension through dramatic play

▶ Reading for literary experience

▶ Understanding sequencing

▶ Recognizing animal characteristics

▶ Developing oral fluency

71 *Families Are Different* **by Nina Pellegrini. New York: Holiday House, 1991.**

A little girl who was adopted from Korea tells about her family and how all families are different.

 LESSON IDEA: Follow the story with a discussion of different kinds of families. Emphasize math skills by making a chart showing how many brothers and sisters the children in the class have. Using a white board or flipchart, make two columns labeled "Brothers" and "Sisters." Invite each child to come up and draw stick figures to represent his or her siblings and step-siblings in the appropriate columns. Then count the stick figures together.

SKILLS
▶ Reading for literary experience
▶ Developing text-to-self connection
▶ Counting
▶ Understanding that graphs represent information
▶ Understanding vocabulary relating to families

72 *The Relatives Came* **by Cynthia Rylant. New York: Simon and Schuster, 2005.**

A large group of relatives gets together for a reunion.

 LESSON IDEA: Read the story, and then discuss extended families. Make a family tree on the board to show aunts, uncles, cousins, grandparents, and so on.

SKILLS
▶ Reading for literary experience
▶ Developing text-to-self connection
▶ Understanding vocabulary relating to families

73 *Louanne Pig in the Perfect Family* **by Nancy Carlson. Minneapolis, MN: Carolrhoda, 2004.**

Louanne Pig, an only child, envies her friend's large family—until she spends a weekend at his house and realizes that her family is just perfect for her.

 LESSON IDEA: Follow up with a discussion of the good and bad things about big families, and then about small families. Work with the class to make a list of each.

SKILLS
▶ Reading for literary experience
▶ Developing text-to-self connection
▶ Understanding vocabulary relating to families
▶ Recognizing emotions

Fingerplays/Songs

SKILLS
▶ Developing attention and response
▶ Developing motor skills

74 Suzy's Friends

Once there was a little girl named Suzy. She said, "I only want to be friends with people who DANCE." Can you dance?

 But then she changed her mind. She said, "I only want to be friends with people who JUMP." Can you jump?

 Then she changed her mind again. She said, "I only want to be friends with people who SPIN." Can you spin?

 Then she changed her mind again. She said, "I only want to be friends with people who WAVE." Can you wave?

 Then all her friends said, "We want to do what we feel like doing, but we still want to be your friend!" And Suzy said, "OK!" So some of them DANCED, and some of them JUMPED, and some of them SPUN, and some of them WAVED, but they all had lots of fun!

SKILLS
▶ Developing motor skills
▶ Understanding vocabulary relating to families
▶ Developing oral fluency

75 This Is My Family

This is the mommy kind and dear, *(point to thumb)*
This is the daddy sitting near, *(point to index finger)*
This is the sister tall and strong, *(point to middle finger)*
This is the brother singing a song, *(point to ring finger)*
This is the baby sweet as can be, *(point to pinkie finger)*
All together they are a family!

76 **I Had a Friend**

From *Buzz Buzz* by Laurie Berkner. Two Tomatoes, 1998.

SKILLS

▶ Developing motor skills
▶ Recognizing rhyme

77 **The More We Get Together**

From *Singable Songs for the Very Young* by Raffi. Troubadour Records, 1976.

SKILLS

▶ Developing motor skills
▶ Recognizing rhyme

Flannelboard/Prop Stories

78 *Little Quack's New Friend* **Flannelboard Story**
(Based on the book by Lauren Thompson. New York: Simon and Schuster, 2006.)

Little Quack's enthusiasm for playing with his new frog friend eventually rubs off on his skeptical brothers and sisters. Tell the story with the flannelboard, or read the book first and then have the children help retell the story with the flannelboard pieces.

SKILLS

▶ Counting
▶ Understanding sequencing
▶ Reading for literary experience

79 *Benny's Pennies* **Magnetboard Story**
(Based on the book by Pat Brisson. New York: Dragonfly, 1995.)

Benny has five pennies to spend, and he decides to use them to buy gifts for his mother, sister, brother, dog, and cat. Place the people in a line at the top of the board and put the pennies in a line at the bottom. Each time Benny spends a penny, replace the penny with the item he bought and have the children count the remaining pennies. At the end of the story, remind the children what Benny's family asked for (for example, his brother asked for "something good to eat") and have them help you match the gift to the family member.

SKILLS

▶ Understanding vocabulary relating to families
▶ Developing logic
▶ Counting

Writing Readiness Activity

80 At My House

Have each child make a list of the people who live in his or her house.

SKILLS
- ▶ Developing text-to-self connection
- ▶ Practicing writing

Math Activity

81 Who Would Use This? Matching Game

Present a collection of household objects (mixer, small spade, baby rattle, etc.) and ask the children who would be most likely to use each one.

SKILLS
- ▶ Developing logic
- ▶ Understanding vocabulary relating to families

Takeaway Activity

82 Family Portrait Worksheet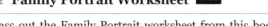

Pass out the Family Portrait worksheet from this book's webpage and have the children draw pictures of the people in their families.

SKILL
- ▶ Developing creativity

Library Skill–Building Game

83 A Book's Family

Preparation: Photocopy the covers of various picture books in your collection, enough so that each child has one (more if you wish to offer additional practice). Make sure you choose books with lighter-color covers that will photocopy clearly, and pick some books that have a single author/illustrator, some with separate authors and illustrators, and a variety of wordings of author and illustrator credits (e.g., some that say "by," some that say "story by," some that say neither of these).

Activity: Tell the children that the people who make a book are like the book's family. Introduce the concept of author and illustrator, and, using example books, share the following hints for finding the author's and illustrator's names:

> **Author:** The author is the person who wrote the story. The author's name is found on the cover, and sometimes you may see the words "by," "written by," or "story by" before his or her name. Sometimes you won't see any of these words at all, just the person's name. The first name you see on the cover is usually the author's name.

> **Illustrator:** The illustrator is the person who made the pictures in the book. The pictures might be watercolor paintings, ink drawings, photographs, oil paintings, collages, or another kind of art. Sometimes you will see the words "pictures by" or "illustrated by" before the illustrator's name, and sometimes you will just see the name. If there are two names on the cover, the second is usually the illustrator's name.

SKILLS
- ▶ Understanding the parts of a book
- ▶ Developing visual discrimination
- ▶ Recognizing colors

If you see only one name on the cover of a picture book, that means the person is both the author *and* the illustrator.

Write cue words (such as "written by" or "pictures by") on the board, along with the following words:

Title (in red)
Author (in blue)
Illustrator (in green)

Divide the children into teams of four to six students each. (Balance the teams so that those students who might need help with the activity are with others who can help.) Give each child a photocopy of a book cover.

First, each child should look at his or her book cover and do the following:

color the title red
color the author blue
color the illustrator green

Next, the teams should share their book covers and make sure that everyone agrees where the title, author, and illustrator are on each cover. When the team members think that all their covers are completed correctly, they should raise their hands. Check their work and explain any mistakes. If mistakes have been made, give the team another book cover to work on (or give each child another cover if you wish to extend the activity). When team members have correctly completed one set of book covers (or their team book cover), dismiss them to find books to check out. To extend this activity, have each child identify the title, author, and illustrator of one of his or her books while checking out.

ASL Connection

84 Friendship Sign Song (to the tune of "Row, Row, Row Your Boat")

Here's the sign for YOU.
Here's the sign for ME.
I put my fingers together like this,
'Cause FRIENDS we'll always be!

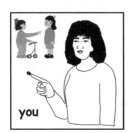

you

me

friend

Spanish Connection

85 Family Simon Says

Mexican families might include

Madre (MAH-dray): mother
Padre (PAH-dray): father
Abuela (ah-BWAY-la): grandmother
Abuelo (ah-BWAY-lo): grandfather
Hermano (er-MAH-no): brother
Hermana (er-MAH-na): sister

Introduce the vocabulary above, and then play a form of "Simon Says." If the *madre, padre, abuela,* or *abuelo* gives a direction, the children have to copy it (for example, "Madre says touch your toes!"). If the *hermano* or *hermana* gives a direction, the children do not have to copy it (for example, "Hermano says jump up and down!").

Recommend This!

My Family Is Forever by Nancy Carlson. New York: Penguin, 2004.

Name That Ed by Laura Driscoll. New York: Grosset and Dunlap, 2002.

The Adventures of Max and Pinky: Best Buds by Maxwell Eaton III. New York: Knopf, 2008.

Best Friends by Anna Michaels. New York: Harcourt, 2001.

Yo! Yes? by Chris Raschka. New York: Orchard, 1993.

Dog and Bear: Two's Company by Laura Vaccaro Seeger. New York: Roaring Brook, 2008.

8 Safety

Kindergarten Speak

There are many people who keep us safe, like our parents, teachers, the principal, police officers, doctors, and more. It's always important to listen to the rules these people tell us. The rules are meant to keep us safe. If you're ever unsure of what the rules are, ask a parent to help you find out.

Recommended Books

86 *Please Play Safe: Penguin's Guide to Playground Safety* **by Margery Cuyler. New York: Scholastic, 2006.**

Animal friends learn how to have safe fun at the playground in this question-and-answer book.

    LESSON IDEA: After discussing the playground safety issues in the book, follow up with a writing activity: as a class, write a story about school and library safety behavior by following the pattern of the text. Assign groups of children pages to illustrate each part of the story, and then staple the pages together to create a class book.

SKILLS

▶ Understanding safe behaviors
▶ Developing creativity
▶ Practicing writing
▶ Developing text-to-self connection

87 *Axle Annie and the Speed Grump* **by Robin Pulver. New York: Dial, 2005.**

Axle Annie the bus driver and the students on her bus are plagued by the unsafe behaviors of Rush Hotfoot, a convertible driver who's always in a hurry.

    LESSON IDEA: Follow the story by discussing automobile safety: wearing seat belts, using a booster seat, not distracting the driver, and so on.

SKILLS

▶ Reading for literary experience
▶ Understanding safe behaviors
▶ Developing text-to-self connection

88 *Officer Buckle and Gloria* **by Peggy Rathmann. New York: Putnam, 1995.**

This funny and engaging story incorporates safety tips into the tale of a police officer and his dog.

LESSON IDEA: After you read the story, play a sorting game. Use a die-cutter to cut out stars, and then write a safety tip on each star. (Use the safety tips on the inside covers of the book for inspiration.) On the board, put headings such as "Safety at Home," "Safety at School," "Water Safety," "Fire Safety," and so on, and ask the children to help you put the tips into the appropriate categories.

SKILLS
► Reading for literary experience
► Differentiating between text and pictures
► Understanding safe behaviors
► Developing classification and sorting skills

89 *Peanut's Emergency* **by Cristina Salat. Watertown, MA: Charlesbridge, 2002.**

A little girl remembers her safety rules when no one comes to pick her up from school one day.

LESSON IDEA: Use this book as a launching point to discuss what an emergency is and the feelings children have during emergencies.

SKILLS
► Reading for literary experience
► Recognizing emotions
► Understanding safe behaviors
► Developing text-to-self connection

90 *Emergency!* **by Margaret Mayo. Minneapolis, MN: Carolrhoda, 2002.**

In rhyming text, this book explores the various types of emergencies that rescue vehicles respond to.

LESSON IDEA: After reading the book, discuss what an emergency is and what children should do in an emergency. Then play a matching game where the children help you match rescue workers to their vehicles (firefighter to fire truck, police officer to police car, etc.).

SKILLS
► Reading for literary experience
► Developing classification and sorting skills
► Recognizing rhyme

Fingerplays/Songs

91 Emergency!

Emergency! Emergency! *(throw hands up in the air)*
What are we going to do? *(spread hands to sides)*
If you see a fire, or someone's hurt, *(wiggle fingers like fire)*
Here's some good advice for you. *(shake index finger)*
Pick up the phone, dial 9-1-1. *(mime picking up phone and dialing)*
Tell them your name and where to come.
Emergency! Emergency! *(throw hands up in the air)*
Now we know what to do! *(nod and point to forehead)*

SKILLS
► Understanding safe behaviors
► Developing motor skills
► Recognizing rhyme

92 I Am a Police Officer

I am a police officer in my car,
Driving near and driving far.
If I see someone speeding past,
Then I drive my car very fast! *(mime driving car fast, make siren noises, and then mime giving a ticket)*

...

I am a police officer in my car,
Driving near and driving far.

SKILLS
► Developing motor skills
► Recognizing rhyme

I keep a watch for danger, you know,
So most of the time I drive my car slow. *(mime driving slowly)*

...

I am a police officer in my car,
Driving near and driving far.
I've kept you safe all day, and so
Now it's back to the station I go!

93 **The Buddy System** (to the tune of "B-I-N-G-O")

When I need to go somewhere, I always take my buddy.
B-U-D-D-Y, B-U-D-D-Y, B-U-D-D-Y,
We use the buddy system.

(Repeat, gradually replacing each letter with claps.)

SKILLS
▶ Recognizing rhyme
▶ Developing spelling knowledge
▶ Developing rhythm

94 **I Like to Play Safe** (to the tune of "Happy Birthday")

I like to play safe.
I want to play safe.
I do not like danger.
I like to play safe.

SKILL
▶ Developing oral fluency

Flannelboard/Prop Stories

95 **Who Keeps Us Safe? Flannelboard Song** (to the tune of "The Farmer in the Dell")

Who keeps us safe? Who keeps us safe?
He wears a hat and a shiny badge.
The police officer keeps us safe.

...

Who keeps us safe? Who keeps us safe?
She puts the fires out.
The firefighter keeps us safe.

...

Who keeps us safe? Who keeps us safe?
She watches over us at school all day.
Our teacher keeps us safe.

...

Who keeps us safe? Who keeps us safe?
They're grown-ups at home who love us so much.
Our parents keep us safe.

SKILLS
▶ Recognizing community helpers
▶ Developing logic
▶ Developing oral fluency

96 Five Fire Trucks Flannelboard Song (to the tune of "Down by the Station")

SKILLS

► Counting
► Recognizing rhyme
► Developing oral fluency

(Pieces needed: fire trucks with numbers 1–5)

Early in the morning, down at the fire station,
5 little fire trucks sitting in a row.
When the fire chief sounds the alarm,
Engine Number 1, off you go.

(Repeat, counting down to zero.)

Writing Readiness Activity

97 SAFE Acrostic

SKILLS

► Developing spelling knowledge
► Understanding safe behaviors
► Developing vocabulary

Work with the class to create an acrostic poem for the word SAFE. Write the letters vertically on the board, and then elicit suggestions from the students for safety-related words that begin with each letter. For more of a challenge, try creating an acrostic for the word EMERGENCY.

Math Activity

98 Fire Truck Shapes

SKILLS

► Recognizing shapes
► Developing creativity

Provide the following shapes cut out of construction paper or felt and have the children help you assemble a picture of a fire truck. First ask them to identify each shape.

    Large red rectangle (body of fire truck)
    2 black circles (wheels)
    Red square (cab of truck)
    White squares (windows)
    Yellow triangle (bell)
    White rectangles with the centers cut out (assemble to create ladder)

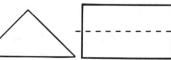

Takeaway Activity

99 My Phone Number Worksheet

SKILLS

► Writing numbers
► Understanding safe behaviors

Give each child a copy of the My Phone Number worksheet from this book's webpage. If the children know their phone numbers, they can write them in the blanks. If they do not, have them take the worksheets home and fill them out with their grown-ups.

Library Skill-Building Game

100 Library Charades

Pass out small paper plates to the children and give them a few minutes to draw a happy face on one side and a sad face on the other. Then act out the following behaviors and have the children show the appropriate side of their plate to let you know whether that behavior is acceptable or not in the library. (You may wish to have some of the children take turns acting out these items. If you do this, either provide picture cards to show them what to act out or take the actors aside and whisper instructions to them.)

running in the library
sitting still
throwing a book on the floor
reading a book nicely
drawing in a book
carefully turning pages
ripping a book
shouting
putting a book back just anywhere on the shelf
putting a book back on the designated cart or in
    the designated bin for reshelving
hitting
paying attention
chewing gum
talking during a story or lesson
lying down and sleeping
lining up and waiting patiently to check out books

Add other behaviors specific to your school library and its procedures.

ASL Connection

101 Safety Signing Game

Teach the children the signs SAFE and DANGEROUS. Then read the following list and have the children sign whether they think the item is SAFE or DANGEROUS.

1. Holding a grown-up's hand when crossing the street
2. Taking candy from strangers
3. Playing with matches
4. Asking for help from a trusted grown-up
5. Running in the hallway
6. Knowing your phone number
7. Playing near construction equipment
8. Playing with your teddy bear
9. Buckling up in the car
10. Throwing things on the school bus
11. Wearing a helmet when riding your bike
12. Climbing up the slide when someone else is trying to slide down

13. Running near the pool
14. Knowing different ways to get out of your house if there is an emergency
15. Crossing in the middle of the street instead of at a crosswalk

Spanish Connection

102 *Cinco Autocamiónes de Bomberos* (Five Fire Trucks)
(to the tune of "Down by the Station")

Early in the morning, down at the fire station,
Cinco (SINK-o) *autocamiónes de bomberos* (ow-toh-cah-me-ON-ays day bom-BEAR-ose)
  sitting in a row.
When the fire chief sounds the alarm,
Engine Number *cinco,* off you go.
Cuatro (QUA-tro) *autocamiónes de bomberos* . . .
Tres (TRACE) *autocamiónes de bomberos* . . .
Dos (DOSE) *autocamiónes de bomberos* . . .
Uno (OO-no) *autocamiónes de bomberos* . . .

SKILLS

► Counting
► Recognizing rhyme
► Understanding basic Spanish vocabulary

Recommend This!

D.W. Rides Again by Marc Brown. Boston: Little, Brown, 1993.

Stop, Drop, and Roll by Margery Cuyler. New York: Simon and Schuster, 2001.

Watch Out! At Home by Claire Llewellyn. Hauppauge, NY: Barron's, 2006.

Yes, No, Little Hippo by Jane Belk Moncure. Mankato, MN: Child's World, 2001.

Fire Engine Man by Andrea Zimmerman. New York: Henry Holt, 2007.

9
Fall

Kindergarten Speak

Fall, or autumn, is a season. In the United States, fall occurs in the months of September, October, and November. In many areas of the United States, the temperatures are lower and often the air is crisp and cool. This is also the time when the leaves change color and drop from the trees.

Recommended Books

103 *Leaf Man* by Lois Ehlert. San Diego, CA: Harcourt, 2005.

The Leaf Man goes where the wind blows in this clever book in which the illustrations are composed of autumn leaves.

LESSON IDEA: Follow up by identifying the different kinds of leaves using the guide in the back inside cover.

SKILLS

▶ Reading for literary experience
▶ Appreciating nature
▶ Differentiating between text and pictures

104 *We're Going on a Leaf Hunt* by Steve Metzger. New York: Scholastic, 2005.

Three children go on a leaf hunt and find various kinds of leaves.

LESSON IDEA: This variation on "Going on a Bear Hunt" is ideal for acting out while reading the story, or you may wish to read the story and then act it out together or in small groups. Another great follow-up activity is to display different kinds of leaves (either real leaves or shapes cut from construction paper) and match them with their names.

SKILLS

▶ Reading for literary experience
▶ Appreciating nature

105 *When Autumn Falls* **by Kelli Nidey. Morton Grove, IL: Whitman, 2004.**

This book talks about the things we see and do in the autumn.

LESSON IDEA: Before reading the story, have the children guess what will be in the book (leaves, apples, pumpkins, etc.) and make a list on the board as they make their suggestions. After reading the story, go through the list and check off the items they guessed correctly. Then count how many they guessed.

SKILLS

▶ Reading for literary experience
▶ Appreciating nature
▶ Developing prediction skills
▶ Counting

106 *The Busy Little Squirrel* **by Nancy Tafuri. New York: Simon and Schuster, 2007.**

A little squirrel is too busy to play with any of his animal friends.

LESSON IDEA: After reading this story, help the students write a list of all the jobs the squirrel was busy with.

SKILLS

▶ Reading for literary experience
▶ Appreciating nature
▶ Understanding sequencing
▶ Practicing writing

107 *Do Cows Turn Colors in the Fall?* **by Viki Woodworth. Plymouth, MN: Child's World, 1998.**

This book explores autumn through silly multiple-choice questions that invite reader participation.

LESSON IDEA: Follow up by dividing the class into small groups and having each group come up with its own question. Students should write out the group's question. Then invite each group forward to present its multiple-choice question to the class. Write the questions on the board.

▶ Appreciating nature
▶ Practicing writing
▶ Developing teamwork skills

Fingerplays/Songs

108 A Song of Fall (to the tune of "Twinkle, Twinkle Little Star")

Let us sing a song of fall.
Leaves are falling for us all.
Rake them up into a pile. *(mime raking)*
Run and jump and laugh and smile. *(run and jump in place)*
Squirrels and apples, pumpkins, too.
Fall is fun for me and you.

SKILLS

▶ Developing oral fluency
▶ Recognizing rhyme
▶ Developing motor skills

109 Little Squirrel

"Hey little squirrel," said I, said I. *(wave)*
"The wind's in the trees and the sun's in the sky. *(wave hands back and forth, point to sun)*
I want to play on this beautiful day." *(spread hands wide)*
But the little squirrel just ran away. *(move index finger away from you)*
"Hey little squirrel, won't you play with me?" *(spread hands wide)*
"I can't," he said. "I'm too busy. *(shake head and move index finger back and forth)*
I cannot play with you in the sun,
For I have nuts to gather before winter comes." *(make index finger wiggle around as if squirrel is looking for nuts)*

SKILLS

▶ Appreciating nature
▶ Developing oral fluency
▶ Developing motor skills

110 Where Is Squirrel? (to the tune of "Frère Jacques")

Where is Squirrel? Where is Squirrel?
In the tree. In the tree.
Searching for some acorns, searching for some acorns.
In the fall. In the fall.

SKILLS

► Appreciating nature
► Developing oral fluency

111 Scarecrow, Scarecrow

Scarecrow, Scarecrow, turn around.
Scarecrow, Scarecrow, touch the ground.
Scarecrow, Scarecrow, shoo the crows.
Scarecrow, Scarecrow, touch your nose.
Scarecrow, Scarecrow, tip your hat.
Scarecrow, Scarecrow, jump like that.
Scarecrow, Scarecrow, flop around.
Scarecrow, Scarecrow, sit right down.

SKILLS

► Developing oral fluency
► Developing motor skills
► Recognizing rhyme

Flannelboard/Prop Stories

112 Where Is My Pumpkin? Flannelboard Song
(to the tune of "Oh Where, Oh Where Has My Little Dog Gone?")

Oh where, oh where has my pumpkin gone?
Oh where, oh where can it be?
I'm searching and singing my pumpkin song.
Oh won't you please help me?
Is it behind the swing set? No, it isn't there.
Is it under my jacket? No, it isn't there.
Is it behind the car? . . .
Is it under the leaf pile? . . .
Is it behind the tree? . . .

(Repeat song, looking under each item in turn.)

Is it there behind the house? Yes, yes, indeed, it's there!
Thank you for helping me find it and searching everywhere!

SKILLS

► Developing oral fluency
► Developing visual discrimination
► Recognizing rhyme

113 **Five Gray Squirrels Flannelboard**

5 gray squirrels outside my door,
1 ran away and that makes 4.
4 gray squirrels climbing a tree,
1 scampered down and then there were 3.
3 gray squirrels knew just what to do,
1 found a nut and then there were 2.
2 gray squirrels in the autumn sun,
1 jumped in a leaf pile and then there was 1.
1 gray squirrel having lots of fun,
He curled up and went to sleep and then there were none.

Writing Readiness Activity

114 **Fall Pictures**

Ask the children if there is something special that makes them think of fall. Have them draw a picture of something that makes them think about fall or something special they do in the fall. Then have them write what it is.

Math Activity

115 **Apple Fractions**

Cut apples from construction paper. Cut some of the apple shapes in half, some in thirds, and some in quarters. Label the halves 1 and 2; the thirds, 1, 2, and 3; and the quarters, 1, 2, 3, and 4. Then have the children put together the apple pieces to create a whole apple.

Takeaway Activity

116 **Leaf Person Craft**

Materials: assorted leaves, construction paper for each child, gluesticks, crayons

Directions:

1. Glue two or three leaves onto the construction paper to create a person shape.
2. Add arms, legs, and so on, using crayons.

Library Skill–Building Game

117 Focus on Fiction

Read *The Little Scarecrow Boy* by Margaret Wise Brown (New York: HarperCollins, 1998). After reading the story, ask the children if they think the story is made up or if they think it really happened. Ask them to support their opinions. Point out the cues in the story that tell you it is made up (for example, the pictures do not look real; the scarecrows move, talk, and have human emotions). Introduce the term *fiction* and tell the children that in a fiction book, the story comes from the author's imagination, not from real life. Show other examples of fiction picture books and point out the characteristics of fiction in the illustrations. Then share the following action song with the class to reinforce the characteristics of fiction books.

118 That's a Fiction Book (to the tune of "Here We Go 'Round the Mulberry Bush")

If your book has monkeys talking, *(scratch like a monkey and point to your mouth)*
Monkeys talking, monkeys talking,
If your book has monkeys talking,
That's a fiction book. *(point to the word FICTION on the board)*
If your book has a sad elephant . . . *(show tears on cheeks, make arm into trunk)*
If your book has a mean race car . . . *(show driving, make a mean face)*
If your book has a walking tree . . . *(put hands up above head for branches and walk in place)*

(Invite the children to suggest other examples and incorporate them into the song.)

Last verse: If your book has a made-up story . . . *(point to head)*

SKILLS

► Understanding the concept of fiction
► Developing motor skills
► Reading for literary experience
► Developing oral fluency

ASL Connection

119 Leaves Are Falling (to the tune of "London Bridge")

LEAVES are falling in the FALL,
In the FALL, in the FALL.
LEAVES are falling in the FALL,
SEE them all!

SKILLS

► Understanding basic American Sign Language
► Recognizing rhyme
► Developing oral fluency

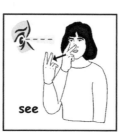

Spanish Connection

120 **Color Guessing Game**

Using the pattern, cut out leaves of red, yellow, green, and brown. Use the leaves to introduce the Spanish words for the colors and then share the guessing-game rhyme with the children to reinforce the color vocabulary.

Red: *rojo* (ROH-ho)
Yellow: *amarillo* (ah-mah-REE-yo)
Green: *verde* (VAIR-day)
Brown: *café* (cah-FAY)
De qué color (de KAY co-LORE)

When leaves of this color hang on the tree,
They look like apples to me. *De qué color?* (*rojo!*)
When leaves of this color hang on the tree,
They look like little suns to me. *De qué color?* (*amarillo!*)
When leaves of this color hang on the tree,
They look like blades of grass to me. *De qué color?* (*verde!*)
When leaves of this color hang on the tree,
They look like chocolate cookies to me. *De qué color?* (*café!*)

Recommend This!

Fresh Fall Leaves by Betsy Franco. New York: Scholastic, 1994.

The Best Fall of All by Laura Godwin. New York: Simon and Schuster, 2002.

Fall Leaves Fall by Zoe Hall. New York: Scholastic, 2000.

Fall Leaf Project by Margaret McNamara. New York: Aladdin, 2006.

Fall Leaves by Mary Packard. New York: Scholastic, 1999.

Mouse's First Fall by Lauren Thompson. New York: Simon and Schuster, 2006.

10

Apples and Pumpkins

Kindergarten Speak

Often the fall season makes you think of apples and pumpkins, especially with Halloween in October. Many people like to go pick their own apples from the orchard or pumpkins from the fields. Have you ever been apple or pumpkin picking?

Recommended Books

121 *The Pumpkin Fair* **by Eve Bunting. New York: Clarion, 1997.**

A little girl celebrates pumpkins in many ways at the pumpkin fair and is thrilled when her little pumpkin wins the prize for "best-loved" pumpkin.

    LESSON IDEA: After the story, help the students write a list of things they can do with a pumpkin.

122 *It's Pumpkin Time!* **by Zoe Hall. New York: Scholastic, 1994.**

Two children grow pumpkins in their patch.

    LESSON IDEA: Use this story to emphasize sequencing. Write the different stages of the pumpkins' growth on index cards, and then have the children put the cards in order. You could also make this a contest by making several sets of cards and letting the children work in groups to see which group can put the cards in the correct sequence first. (If the children will be working independently or in groups, put pictures on the cards along with the words.)

SKILLS

▶ Reading for literary experience
▶ Developing text-to-self connection
▶ Practicing writing
▶ Appreciating nature

SKILLS

▶ Reading for information
▶ Understanding sequencing
▶ Appreciating nature

123 *Russ and the Apple Tree Surprise* **by Janet Elizabeth Rickert. Bethesda, MD: Woodbine House, 1999.**

A little boy picks apples and helps his mother and grandmother bake a pie with them. (Though the text does not mention it, the little boy in the photographs has Down syndrome, making this book an excellent way to incorporate diversity.)

LESSON IDEA: Follow the story with a sequencing activity. Write the steps in making a pie (such as picking the apples, washing the apples, etc.) on sentence strips, and have the children help you put them in order.

SKILLS

► Reading for literary experience

► Appreciating diversity

► Understanding sequencing

► Appreciating nature

124 *Patty's Pumpkin Patch* **by Teri Sloat. New York: Putnam, 1999.**

Rhyming text follows Patty as she plants pumpkins and watches them grow. An alphabet of items found in the pumpkin patch unfurls along the bottom of the pages.

LESSON IDEA: Use this book to introduce or reinforce alphabetical order. After reading the story, review the alphabet and discuss why knowing alphabetical order is important for using the library. Write the words from the book's alphabet on index cards, and then mix them up and give one to each child. Have the children help you put any leftover words in alphabetical order on the board. Then invite each child to come forward and put his or her word in the correct place.

SKILLS

► Reading for literary experience

► Knowing the alphabet

► Understanding alphabetical order

125 *Apples, Apples, Apples* **by Nancy Elizabeth Wallace. New York: Winslow Press, 2000.**

A family of rabbits goes apple picking and learns about the different kinds of apples and what you can make with them.

LESSON IDEA: Follow up by cutting open an apple and showing the different parts or by having the students write a list of the different things that can be made from apples.

SKILLS

► Reading for literary experience

► Developing text-to-self connection

► Practicing writing

► Appreciating nature

Fingerplays/Songs

126 Picking a Pumpkin

I went to the pumpkin patch. *(walk in place)*
I looked all around *(shade eyes with hand and look around)*
For the perfect pumpkin,
And here's what I found. *(mime spying the perfect pumpkin)*
A medium-sized pumpkin *(point to imaginary pumpkin)*
There on the vine.
I reached down and picked it up *(bend down and pick up pumpkin)*
And I felt fine.
I took my pumpkin home *(walk in place, mime carrying pumpkin)*
For my mommy to see,
And she made a pumpkin pie, just for me. *(rub tummy)*

(Repeat with a large pumpkin, using a loud voice and large movements, and then again with a tiny pumpkin, using a squeaky voice and small movements.)

SKILLS

► Developing oral fluency

► Developing motor skills

► Comparing size and volume

► Recognizing rhyme

127 Pumpkin, Pumpkin

Pumpkin, pumpkin, turn around,
Pumpkin, pumpkin, touch the ground,

SKILLS

► Developing motor skills

► Developing oral fluency

Pumpkin, pumpkin, grow on the vine,
Pumpkin, pumpkin, you're all mine.

128 Picking Pumpkins and Apples (to the tune of "Twinkle, Twinkle Little Star")

Picking pumpkins from the vine
Is so much fun every time.
Roll that pumpkin on the ground,
Try to heave it up but it falls right down.
We picked our pumpkin, I'll tell you why:
We'll take it home and make pumpkin pie!

...

Picking apples from the tree
Is such fun for you and me.
Fill our basket to the top,
It's such fun we don't want to stop.
We picked our apples, I'll tell you why:
We'll take them home and make apple pie!

SKILLS

▶ Developing oral fluency
▶ Developing motor skills
▶ Appreciating nature
▶ Recognizing rhyme

129 Nine Little Apples (to the tune of "Ten Little Indians")

1 little, 2 little, 3 little apples,
4 little, 5 little, 6 little apples,
7 little, 8 little, 9 little apples,
Growing on my tree.

...

Pick the apples and put them in my basket,
Pick the apples and put them in my basket,
Pick the apples and put them in my basket,
For my family.

...

Making applesauce and apple butter,
Making apple pie and candy apples,
Making apple juice and apple cider,
Apples are such fun!

SKILLS

▶ Developing oral fluency
▶ Counting
▶ Appreciating nature

Flannelboard/Prop Stories

130 Five Green Apples Flannelboard Song (to the tune of "Ten Green Bottles")

5 green apples growing on my tree,
5 green apples growing on my tree,
And if 1 green apple should fall right down to me,
There will be 4 green apples growing on my tree.

...

4 green apples . . .
3 green apples . . .
2 green apples . . .
1 green apple . . .

SKILLS

▶ Counting
▶ Developing oral fluency
▶ Recognizing rhyme

131 Sarah's Apples Flannelboard Story

Once upon a time there was a little girl named Sarah. She loved the fall because the apple tree in her yard grew such delicious apples. She would eat apples for breakfast, apples for lunch, and apples for dinner. But she saved the 5 biggest, juiciest apples to make a special pie with her grandmother. On the day her grandmother was supposed to come to make the pie, Sarah sat on the porch with her basket of apples, waiting.

Who should come along but a little squirrel? The squirrel said, "Those apples look delicious. Please may I have one to save for the winter?" Sarah thought for a moment. "OK," she said. "I will still have 4 apples left for the pie." "Thank you!" said the squirrel. "You're welcome," said Sarah.

Sarah had been sitting a little while longer when a rabbit hopped into her yard. "Oh!" said the rabbit. "Those apples look delicious. Please may I have one?" Sarah thought for a moment. "OK," she said. "I will still have 3 apples left for the pie." "Thank you!" said the rabbit. "You're welcome," said Sarah.

A little while later a skunk trundled into Sarah's yard. "Those apples look delicious," said the skunk. "Please may I have one?" Sarah didn't really want to give away another apple, but she remembered how skunks can spray stinky stuff when they get angry, and said, "OK. I will still have 2 apples left for the pie." "Thank you!" said the skunk. "You're welcome," said Sarah.

Sarah hadn't been sitting there more than a minute longer when a horse trotted by. Now everyone knows that horses love apples, and this one was no exception. "Neigh!" said the horse. "Do I see some beautiful apples there? Please may I have one, sweet little girl?" Sarah didn't really want to give away another apple, but the horse was polite so she felt she had no choice. "OK," she said. "I will still have 1 apple left for the pie." "Thank you!" said the horse. "You're welcome," said Sarah.

Now Sarah had 1 apple left, and she was determined to keep it. Maybe it wasn't enough for a big apple pie, but they could at least make a tart with it, she thought. But then a big brown bear trundled out of the woods. It was looking for food to eat before it went into hibernation for the winter. It saw Sarah's apple and said, "Please may I have that apple? It's so big it will help keep my tummy full for the long winter." Sarah felt sorry for the bear, and she also felt a little afraid of its big claws, so she gave the apple to the bear. "Thank you," said the bear. "You're welcome," said Sarah sadly.

Now she had no apples left to make a pie. Her grandmother arrived then, and Sarah explained what had happened. Her grandmother laughed and showed her what she had brought with her—a big basket full of shiny red apples!

Sarah and her grandmother went inside and baked a big apple pie, and there was plenty for everyone!

Writing Readiness Activity

132 Picture This!

Have the children draw a picture of something special they do with apples or pumpkins with their family. Maybe they go apple picking or bake a special treat. After they draw the picture, have them write what that special thing is.

Math Activity

133 Matching Jack-o'-Lantern Patterns

Create several different jack-o'-lanterns for the children to match.

Takeaway Activity

134 Paper Bag Pumpkins

Materials: a white paper bag for each child, 6-inch piece of green yarn for each child, scrap paper or old newspapers, crayons

Directions:

1. Color the bag orange.
2. Rip strips of newspaper or scrap paper. Crumple them up and place them in the bag until it is about half full.
3. Gather the top of the bag and tie the green yarn around it.
4. Push down the top of the bag so it smooshes out to a pumpkin shape.
5. Decorate as desired.

Library Skill–Building Game

135 What Is Nonfiction?

Show the children *Pumpkin Harvest* by Calvin Harris (Mankato, MN: Capstone Press, 2008) or *Pumpkins* by Ken Robbins (New Milford, CT: Roaring Brook, 2006). Ask them the following questions:

What do you think this book is about?
What do you already know about pumpkins?
What else do you want to learn about pumpkins?

Read the book. After reading, ask the children if the story answered their questions. Then ask them whether they think the text was made up or real, and why. Point out the characteristics of nonfiction in the book (photographs or drawings look real, objects and animals don't act like people, learning information instead of a story). Ask the children if they remember the word for a story that is made up, then write FICTION on the board. Write

NONFICTION underneath, and explain that *non* means "not," so *nonfiction* means "not fiction." Then show more examples of nonfiction books, pointing out the characteristics of nonfiction in the pictures. Point out that we usually read nonfiction books to learn something and fiction books to enjoy a story (though learning can be enjoyable, and sometimes we learn new things from stories, too!).

Divide the class into teams of four to five students. Give each team six books, all on a similar subject (three fiction, three nonfiction). Each team should work together to decide which three books are fiction and which three books are nonfiction. When everyone on the team agrees, check their answers. Confirm or correct their responses, and then dismiss each group to look for books.

ASL Connection

136 Way Up High (traditional)

Way up high in the APPLE TREE
2 little APPLES SMILED at me.
I shook that tree as hard as I could, *(mime shaking tree)*
Down fell the APPLES and mmmm, they were good. *(rub stomach)*

SKILLS

▶ Appreciating nature
▶ Understanding basic American Sign Language

Spanish Connection

137 Way Up High (adapted traditional)

Way up high in the *manzano* (man-ZAH-no)
2 little *manzanas* (man-ZAH-nas) smiled just so.
I shook that tree as hard as I could, *(mime shaking tree)*
Down fell the *manzanas* and mmmm, they were good. *(rub stomach)*

SKILLS

▶ Understanding basic Spanish vocabulary
▶ Developing oral fluency

Recommend This!

Colleen and the Bean by Kelli C. Foster. Hauppauge, NY: Barron's, 1995.

Max and Mo Go Apple Picking by Patricia Lakin. New York: Simon and Schuster, 2007.

My Pumpkin by Julia Noonan. New York: Children's Press, 2005.

Apples and Pumpkins by Anne Rockwell. New York: Scholastic, 1989.

Apple Farmer Annie by Monica Wellington. New York: Dutton, 2001.

Found an Apple by Harriet Ziefert. New York: Sterling, 2007.

11
Trees

• •

Kindergarten Speak

There are trees all around us. Trees provide a home for wildlife and protect us from the sun, wind, and rain. There are two different types of trees: evergreen trees, which keep their leaves or pine needles all year long, and deciduous trees, which lose their leaves in the fall.

Recommended Books

138 *Little Apple Goat* **by Caroline Jayne Church. Grand Rapids, MI: Eerdmans, 2007.**

A little goat loves to eat the apples, pears, and cherries in the orchard and then spit the seeds over the hedge. After a storm destroys the orchard, a new one grows on the other side of the hedge, thanks to the goat.

    LESSON IDEA: After reading the story, play a game about what grows on trees. Draw a tree on the board. Then show pictures of various items that do and do not grow on trees (such as apples, pumpkins, money, shoes, pears, cherries, books, etc.) and have the children identify which things grow on trees. Attach the items that do grow on trees to your tree.

SKILLS

▶ Reading for literary experience
▶ Developing logic
▶ Appreciating nature
▶ Developing classification and sorting skills

139 *Mighty Tree* **by Dick Gackenbach. San Diego, CA: Harcourt Brace Jovanovich, 1992.**

Three tiny seeds grow into three tall trees with very different destinies.

    LESSON IDEA: After reading the book, discuss the different things that come from trees. Make a list of these things with the class.

SKILLS

▶ Reading for literary experience
▶ Practicing writing
▶ Appreciating nature
▶ Developing text-to-self connection

140 *Red Leaf, Yellow Leaf* **by Lois Ehlert. San Diego, CA: Harcourt Brace, 1991.**

A child describes how her maple tree grew.

    LESSON IDEA: After reading the story, play a sequencing game. Write the major events in the tree's growth on cards and ask the children to help you put them in order.

SKILLS

▶ Reading for literary experience
▶ Understanding sequencing
▶ Appreciating nature

141 *The Seasons of Arnold's Apple Tree* **by Gail Gibbons. San Diego, CA: Harcourt Brace, 1984.**

A little boy enjoys his apple tree in every season of the year.

    LESSON IDEA: Follow up the story with a matching game. Write traits of the apple tree (such as green leaves, buds, and flowers) on sentence strips and ask the children to match the traits to the correct season.

SKILLS

▶ Reading for literary experience
▶ Understanding sequencing
▶ Appreciating nature

142 *Fall Is Not Easy* **by Marty Kelley. Madison, WI: Zino Press, 1998.**

In rhyming text, a tree explains how it feels in various seasons.

    LESSON IDEA: After reading the story, reread it and ask the children to identify the rhyming words.

SKILLS

▶ Reading for literary experience
▶ Recognizing emotions
▶ Appreciating nature
▶ Recognizing rhyme

Fingerplays/Songs

143 Be a Tree

Be a tree! Be a tree!
Hold up your branches and sway with me.
Reach your branches up to the sun,
Now shake your leaves out 1 by 1.
A tree stands in 1 place and does not wiggle,
But when a squirrel runs up your trunk, I bet it tickles!

SKILLS

▶ Developing motor skills
▶ Appreciating nature
▶ Recognizing rhyme

144 Trees, Trees, Trees (to the tune of "Three Blind Mice")

Trees, trees, trees, I love trees.
Trees, trees, trees, I love trees.
They're big and leafy and sway in the breeze,
They're homes for animals, birdies, and bees,
They make great shade for you and for me,
Yes, I love trees.

SKILLS

▶ Developing oral fluency
▶ Appreciating nature
▶ Recognizing rhyme

145 Five Little Monkeys Swinging from a Tree (adapted traditional)

5 little monkeys swinging from a tree, *(wiggle 5 fingers)*
Teasing Mr. Crocodile, "Can't catch me!" *(put thumbs in ears, wiggle fingers, and stick out tongue)*
Along came Mr. Crocodile, quiet as could be *(hold palms together in front of you)*
And SCARED a monkey right out of that tree! *(clap hands together loudly)*

...

SKILLS

▶ Counting
▶ Developing oral fluency
▶ Recognizing rhyme

4 little monkeys . . .
3 little monkeys . . .
2 little monkeys . . .
1 little monkey . . .

146 Shakin' Like a Leafy Tree

From *Racing to the Rainbow* by The Wiggles. Koch Records, 2007.

Flannelboard/Prop Stories

147 *A Tree for Me* Flannelboard (Based on the book by Nancy Van Laan. New York: Knopf, 2000.)

In this bouncy rhyming story, a child looks for the perfect tree, but keeps finding that his chosen trees are taken by various animals. Invite the children to join you on the refrain: "Big one, small one, skinny one, tall one, / Old one, fat one, I choose *that* one."

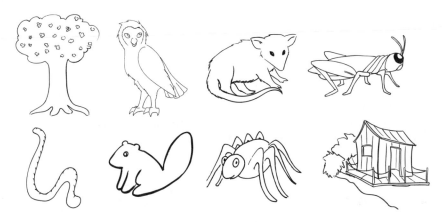

148 The Lonely Tree Flannelboard Story

Once there was a lonely tree. He wished that he had friends to talk to, but he stood all alone in a field. Then one day a bird landed on the tree's branch and said, "May I build my nest here? My eggs need a safe place to hatch." "Yes," said the tree. "Please do!" And so the bird built her nest there. All throughout the spring the tree happily watched the little birds hatch and learn to fly. And then in the fall, the birds flew away, and the tree was lonely again. But then one day the tree felt a tickling on his trunk. It was a little squirrel. "May I take your acorns and store them up for the winter? And may I make my home in the hollow in your trunk?" "Yes," said the tree. And the little squirrel did, and the tree was happy all winter, knowing he was keeping the little squirrel safe and warm. In the springtime, the squirrel left to see the world, and the tree was lonely again. But do you know what? The little bird came back in the spring and built a new nest, and then in the fall the squirrel came back and made his winter home in the tree. And so it continued each year, and the little tree was not lonely anymore.

Tree top

Writing Readiness Activity

149 Tree Lore

Invite the children to take turns writing different characteristics of trees on the chalkboard. Headings could include Pine Trees, Deciduous Trees, Trees That Flower, and Trees That Fruit. Discuss what all trees have in common and what some of the differences are.

Math Activity

150 Tree Shapes

Make a tree with different shapes. Hand out rectangles, triangles, squares, semicircles, and circles and let the children create a tree of their choice.

Takeaway Activity

151 Handy Tree Worksheet

Pass out the Handy Tree worksheet from this book's webpage. Have each child trace a hand and wrist onto the worksheet to create a tree, and then decorate it with crayons or small pieces of tissue paper for leaves. Then ask each child to write a sentence about his or her tree.

Library Skill–Building Game

152 Fiction versus Nonfiction

Preparation: Print the Fiction vs. Nonfiction Book Cover Sheets from this book's webpage.

Activity: Review the characteristics of fiction and nonfiction and explain that fiction and nonfiction books are kept in different parts of the library. Show an example of a fiction book about trees and a nonfiction book about trees. Tell the children that you will play a game where they will become library books, and they must help you sort them into fiction and nonfiction. Place a sign on one side of your class area that says FICTION and a sign on the other side of your class area that says NONFICTION. Pass out one book sheet (from the website) to each child and have the children line up at the center of the class area. As each child reaches the front of the line, read the title and author on his or her paper to the class (or have the child read it, if able). Ask the class to point to show whether the "book" should go in the fiction or the nonfiction section. "Shelve" each book by directing the child to a chair on the appropriate side of the room.

When all the children are seated, explain that you need to organize the books. Ask the children for ideas on how you should organize the fiction books. ("Should all the blue books be together? Should all the tall books be together? But wait, suppose I really like stories by a certain author. What would make it easier for me to find all of her books in one place?") Explain that fiction books are organized by the author's last name, and show an example of the call letters used in your library. Ask each child in the fiction section to look at the author's name on his or her page and then move to specific tables according to the author's last name. ("If your author's name starts with A, sit here.")

Now go to the nonfiction side of the room and ask if the same arrangement would work there. ("Suppose I need to find lots of books about apple trees. If the books all have different authors, they will be all over the library.") Explain that nonfiction books are grouped by what they are about and that you use a number system to put them in order. Show an example of the call numbers used in your library. Ask the nonfiction children to sit at certain tables, depending on what their book is about. ("If your book is about pine trees, sit here.") Then ask a series of questions, such as:

> If I want to find a book about branches, where would I look?
> I want to find a storybook by Joe Smith. Which table should I visit?

Finish by pointing out where fiction and nonfiction books are housed in your library.

ASL Connection

153 The Tree

There was a TREE so straight and tall *(sign TREE)*
People came to see it from miles around.
But one day the winds blew it to and fro, *(make TREE sign move as in the wind)*
And knocked it to the ground. *(show TREE falling to the ground)*
But an acorn fell off of the tree,
Tumbled to the soil, and then
The sun and rain helped it to GROW
And a tree stood there again! *(sign GROW and TREE)*

SKILLS

▶ Appreciating nature
▶ Understanding basic American Sign Language
▶ Developing oral fluency

tree

grow

Spanish Connection

154 *El Arbol* (The Tree)

Introduce the following vocabulary, and then have students tell you which season it is by the leaf description.

Tree: *el arbol* (el ARE-bol)
Summer: *el verano* (el vay-RAH-no)
Autumn: *el otoño* (el o-TONE-yo)
Winter: *el invierno* (el in-vee-AIR-no)
Summer: *la primavera* (la pri-ma-VAIR-ah)

SKILL

▶ Understanding basic Spanish vocabulary

El arbol (el are-BOL) is full of leaves.
El arbol has begun to drop its leaves.
El arbol has no leaves.
El arbol has flowers and budding leaves.

Recommend This!

What Good Is a Tree? by Larry Dane Brimmer. New York: Children's Press, 1998.

The Oak Tree by Laura Jane Coats. New York: Macmillan, 1987.

The Acorn's Story by Valerie Greeley. New York: Macmillan, 1994.

The Searcher and Old Tree by David McPhail. Watertown, MA: Charlesbridge, 2008.

A Tree Is Nice by Janice May Udry. New York: HarperCollins, 1956.

12

Spiders

Kindergarten Speak

How many of you like spiders? Although some of you may think they are creepy, others may like them and be amazed by their webs. Spiders are not bugs, but rather are part of the arachnid family. Spiders are known for their eight legs.

Recommended Books

155 ***The Very Busy Spider*** **by Eric Carle. New York: Scholastic, 1984.**

All the animals on the farm want to play, but the very busy spider is just too busy.

LESSON IDEA: After reading the story, invite the children to take the parts and act it out. This dramatic play activity builds comprehension, reinforces story sequencing, and allows the children to learn through multiple senses.

SKILLS

▶ Reading for literary experience
▶ Understanding sequencing
▶ Extending comprehension through dramatic play

156 ***Diary of a Spider*** **by Doreen Cronin. New York: HarperCollins, 2005.**

This funny book presents a spider's diary with comic situations and illustrations.

LESSON IDEA: Before reading the story, discuss what a diary is. Build on the concept after reading the story by working with the class to write a diary of the Itsy-Bitsy Spider.

SKILLS

▶ Reading for literary experience
▶ Practicing writing
▶ Understanding literary genres

157 *Itsy Bitsy the Smart Spider* by Charise Mericle Harper. New York: Dial, 2004.

This rhyming story builds on the familiar song as Itsy Bitsy uses her brain to figure out how to keep from getting wet again.

LESSON IDEA: Pause at appropriate points during the story to ask the children how they think Itsy Bitsy will solve her problem. Then invite them to apply their problem-solving skills to other well-known songs and rhymes, such as "Little Miss Muffet" ("How could the spider have avoided scaring Little Miss Muffet?"), "Jack and Jill" ("How could they have kept from falling down the hill?"), and "Little Bo Peep" ("How could she find her sheep?").

SKILLS

▶ Reading for literary experience

▶ Recognizing rhyme

▶ Developing prediction skills

▶ Developing problem-solving skills

158 *Anansi and the Moss-Covered Rock* by Eric Kimmel. New York: Holiday House, 1990.

Anansi the trickster spider finds a strange rock that causes animals to fall asleep, and he uses it to trick the other animals out of their food. He gets his comeuppance, though, when quiet Little Bush Deer uses the rock on him.

LESSON IDEA: As you read the story, invite the children to join you on the refrain ("My, what a strange moss-covered rock"). Then have the children take the parts in the story and act it out.

SKILLS

▶ Reading for literary experience

▶ Developing prediction skills

▶ Developing problem-solving skills

▶ Extending comprehension through dramatic play

▶ Understanding sequencing

159 *The Spider Who Created the World* by Amy MacDonald. New York: Orchard, 1996.

In this pourquoi tale, Nobb the spider needs a place to set her egg, and when the sun, moon, and cloud refuse to help her, she creates the world to keep her egg safe.

LESSON IDEA: Though this original story does not draw from any particular culture, it is a good way to introduce the concept of pourquoi tales. Explain that this book is an example of a pourquoi tale, and then tell the children that *pourquoi* means "why" in French. Ask the children why they think this type of story would be called a "pourquoi tale."

SKILLS

▶ Reading for literary experience

▶ Understanding literary genres

Fingerplays/Songs

160 Miss Muffet, Silly Style

(Present the following rhyme as if you think it is the real version, and let the children correct you after each line. Kindergartners find this wildly hilarious.)

Little Miss Muffet sat on an . . . easy chair,
Eating her . . . pepperoni pizza,
Along came a . . . monkey,
And sat down beside her . . . and asked her out to dinner!

SKILLS

▶ Developing oral fluency

▶ Recognizing rhyme

161 Ten Little Spiders (to the tune of "Ten Little Indians")

(Hold up a finger each time you count a spider. On the last line, wiggle all 10 fingers to show the spiders spinning.)

1 little, 2 little, 3 little spiders,
4 little, 5 little, 6 little spiders,
7 little, 8 little, 9 little spiders,
10 little spiders spinning their web.

SKILLS

▶ Counting

▶ Developing oral fluency

162 If You're a Spider (to the tune of "If You're Happy and You Know It")

If you're a spider and you know it, wave your legs.
If you're a spider and you know it, wave your legs.
If you're a spider and you know it, then you really ought to show it,
If you're a spider and you know it, wave your legs.

...

. . . spin a web.

163 Do the Daddy Long Legs

From *Racing to the Rainbow* by The Wiggles. Koch Records, 2007.

SKILLS

▶ Developing oral fluency
▶ Developing motor skills

SKILL

▶ Developing motor skills

Flannelboard/Prop Stories

164 Abigail's Surprise: A Draw-and-Tell Story

(Draw the picture on a flipchart or a blackboard as you tell the story. Begin at the middle of the spider's face, then draw one-half of the face, and go down a leg each time Abigail goes down a street. Each time the children go back to the main road, draw the second side of the leg. When the girls cross over to the boys' houses, draw the rear of the spider, and then repeat the pattern on the other side. When the children walk back to Abigail's house, draw the final half of the face.)

SKILLS

▶ Developing prediction skills
▶ Developing listening skills
▶ Developing visual discrimination

Once upon a time there was a little girl named Abigail. One day when Abigail was outside in her backyard, she saw something so exciting she had to show it to her friends. So, after her mother said it was okay, she went down the street to her friend Bella's house. "Bella!" she said. "You have to come see what I found in my backyard."

"Well, if it's that exciting, we'd better get Carly, too," said Bella. So Abigail and Bella walked back up to the main street, and then turned down Carly's street.

When they got to Carly's house, Carly said they should ask Debbie and Ellen to come too, so the girls walked up to the main street, and down to Debbie's house, then all the way back so they could turn down the street to Ellen's house.

Ellen thought they should show Abigail's surprise to some of the boys in their class, too, so the girls crossed the main street and went down the street to Frankie's house. Then they all went up to the main road and turned off to get George. Then they had to go up to the main road, and down to Harry's house, and then back to the main road, and down to Ivan's house.

Finally, Abigail had gathered all her friends. "Come on!" she said. "Let's go see the cool thing I found in my backyard."

So all the children skipped down the sidewalk until they got to Abigail's house. They couldn't believe their eyes when she showed them what she had found.

A GIANT SPIDER!

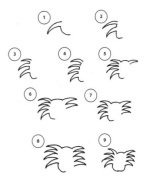

165 The Spider Went Over the Mountain Prop Song
(to the tune of "The Bear Went Over the Mountain")

(Pass out two rhythm sticks, straws, or chopsticks to each child. As you sing the song, hold the sticks vertically to represent long spider legs, and make them "walk.")

The spider went over the mountain,
The spider went over the mountain,
The spider went over the mountain
To see what he could see.

...

SKILLS

▶ Developing motor skills
▶ Developing oral fluency

He saw another mountain,
He saw another mountain,
He saw another mountain,
And that's what he could see.

Writing Readiness Activity

166 Web Words

SKILLS

▶ Practicing writing
▶ Developing vocabulary
▶ Developing oral fluency

Ask the children to think of some words that describe a spider and its web and write their words on the board.

Math Activity:

167 Match the Spider Webs

SKILL

▶ Understanding patterns

Print a variety of spider webs and have the children find the matches.

Takeaway Activity

168 Spider's ABC Web Worksheet WEB

SKILLS

▶ Knowing the alphabet
▶ Understanding alphabetical order

Pass out the Spider's ABC worksheet from this book's webpage and ask each child to connect the dots in alphabetical order.

Library Skill–Building Game

169 Alphabet Web

SKILLS

▶ Knowing the alphabet
▶ Understanding alphabetical order

This simple game reinforces the concept of alphabetical order in preparation for future lessons building on this skill.

Preparation: Get a ball of white or black yarn.

Activity: Seat the class in a circle on the floor. Hold up the ball of yarn and explain that the students will be making their own alphabet spider web during the game. Begin the game by holding the loose end of the yarn and tossing the ball to someone across the circle from you. As you toss the ball, say "A." The child you threw the ball to should hold on to the yarn, then say "B" and throw the ball to someone else. (Emphasize to the children that they should make eye contact with the person they are throwing to before they toss the ball, so that no one gets taken by surprise. If you feel your group is too rambunctious to handle tossing the yarn, limit them to rolling it instead. Also, tell them that giving the ball to the person next to them is not allowed, as it makes for a much less exciting spider web!)

When you reach Z, start through the alphabet again if not all the children have had a turn. When everyone has had a turn, play another round, only make it more challenging: instead of saying the next letter in order, the children must say a word that begins with that letter. When everyone has had a turn in this round and you have reached Z again, ask the last child to toss the yarn ball back to you. Then dismiss the class alphabetically by first names to find books. "If your first name starts with an A, go pick out books . . . ." Leave the spider web in place for the rest of the class and let them admire their handiwork.

ASL Connection

170 The Eensy Weensy Spider

(For the first verse, have the children sign normally. For the second verse, sign everything using very large gestures and sing in a loud voice. For the third verse, sign everything very small and sing in a small voice. If you prefer to use a CD, an excellent recording of this version can be found on *Mainly Mother Goose* by Sharon, Lois, and Bram [Elephant Records, 1984].)

The eensy weensy SPIDER went up the water spout. (*show spider sign climbing upward*)
Down came the RAIN and washed the spider out.
Out came the SUN and dried up all the rain,
And the eensy weensy SPIDER went up the spout again. (*show spider climbing upward*)

...

spider   rain   sun

The big, fat SPIDER went up the water spout . . .
The teensy-weensy SPIDER went up the water spout . . .

Spanish Connection

171 *La Araña Muy Pequeña* (The Eensy Weensy Spider)

La araña muy pequeña (la a-RAHN-ya moy pay-KAY-nia)
Climbed up the waterspout.
Down came the rain
And washed *la araña* out.
Out came the sun
And dried up all the rain.
La araña muy pequeña
Climbed up the spout again.

Recommend This!

Spiders Are Not Insects by Allan Fowler. New York: Children's Press, 1996.

Miss Spider's Tea Party by David Kirk. New York: Scholastic, 1994.

Spin, Spider, Spin! by Dana Meachen Rau. Tarrytown, NY: Marshall Cavendish, 2008.

Squash the Spider! by Nick Ward. New York: Random House, 2003.

A Spiderling Grows Up by Pam Zollman. New York: Scholastic, 2005.

13

Nocturnal Animals

. . . .

Kindergarten Speak

Nocturnal animals are active at night and sleep during the day. Many of these animals have special adaptations that make it easier for them to hunt at night and that protect them from predators that would normally hunt them during the day. Some nocturnal animals are bats, raccoons, owls, and wombats.

Recommended Books

172 ***The Very Lonely Firefly*** **by Eric Carle. New York: Philomel, 1995.**

The lonely firefly flies toward different kinds of lights until finally he finds a group of fireflies and is not lonely anymore.

    LESSON IDEA: After reading the story, have the children take the parts and act the story out. This activity reinforces comprehension and allows children to learn through multiple senses.

173 ***Animals of the Night*** **by Merry Banks. New York: Scribner, 1990.**

After the sun sets, the nocturnal animals come out.

    LESSON IDEA: After reading the story, play a movement game. Explain that you will say the names of various animals. Each time you say the name of a nocturnal animal, the children should stand up.

SKILLS

▶ Reading for literary experience
▶ Recognizing emotions
▶ Understanding sequencing
▶ Extending comprehension through dramatic play

▶ Reading for information
▶ Appreciating nature

174 *Baby Bat's Lullaby* by Jacquelyn Mitchard. New York: HarperCollins, 2004.

A mother bat sings a sweet lullaby to her baby.
    LESSON IDEA: After reading the story, go through it again to point out the rhymes. Then work with the class to write a lullaby poem to another nocturnal animal, such as a baby owl or wolf. First, make a list of words about the animal, and then use those words to make a poem.

SKILLS
- ▶ Reading for literary experience
- ▶ Recognizing rhyme

175 *A Promise to the Sun: An African Story* by Tololwa M. Mollel. New York: Little, Brown, 1994.

This pourquoi tale explains why bats live in caves and only come out at night—a long-ago bat broke a promise to the sun, and bats have been hiding during the day ever since.
    LESSON IDEA: Discuss the features of a pourquoi tale (starts in the distant past, ends in the present, explains something about the natural world), and then work with the class to create and act out their own pourquoi tale explaining a feature of another nocturnal animal.

SKILLS
- ▶ Reading for literary experience
- ▶ Understanding literary genres

176 *Whooo's There?* by Mary Serfozo. New York: Random House, 2007.

A grumpy owl meets other nocturnal animals.
    LESSON IDEA: Use this story to emphasize rhymes. After reading it for content, read the story again and ask the children to raise or lower their arms each time they hear a rhyme.

SKILLS
- ▶ Reading for literary experience
- ▶ Recognizing rhyme

Fingerplays/Songs

177 I Am a Bat

I am a bat,
I fly just like that. *(flap arms)*
I soar through the night,
I am quite a sight.
I can't see so well, *(squint eyes)*
So I use sounds to tell
If you're near or far
And where the mice are.
When the sun starts to rise, *(raise arms in circle over head)*
I fly home and close my eyes! *(close eyes)*

SKILLS
- ▶ Developing motor skills
- ▶ Recognizing rhyme

178 Animals of the Night

Oh, we are the animals of the night.
We don't mean to cause a fright.
Some of us are owls and say "Who, who."
Some of us are wolves who say "Arooooo!"
Some of us are bats and we swoop and soar,
And some of us are lions and we let out a roar!

SKILLS
- ▶ Developing motor skills
- ▶ Recognizing rhyme

179 Bats Are Flying (to the tune of "Frère Jacques")

Bats are flying, bats are flying,
In the sky, in the sky.
Only in the nighttime, only in the nighttime,
Bats fly by, bats fly by.

180 Animals of Nighttime (to the tune of "The More We Get Together")

Animals of nighttime, of nighttime, of nighttime,
Oh, animals of nighttime are called nocturnal.
They sleep in the daytime,
And play in the nighttime.
Oh, animals of nighttime are called nocturnal.

Flannelboard/Prop Stories

181 How the Raccoon Got His Mask Flannelboard Story (a Seneca folktale)

Long ago, Raccoon had no mask. One winter, it was so cold, and there was so much snow on the ground that Raccoon could not find any berries or nuts or vegetables to fill his belly. So he took to following the people around, hoping they would share their food. But the people were also hungry, trying to get through the winter, so they shooed him away. Raccoon hid by the longhouse until the people went to sleep. Because it was so cold, they had left the fire burning. Raccoon waited until the longhouse was silent, and then he crept inside on careful feet. The fire had just gone out, and it was dark in the longhouse. So Raccoon put his nose right down to the ground to sniff for the food. He sniffed around on the floor, but, oh no! He went too close to the firepit and put his nose right into the hot, black ashes. How it stung and burned! He yelped and raced outside to cool his nose in the snow. But from that day on the ashes stuck to Raccoon's face, and now everyone knows him for the bandit he is.

Snow

182 Five Little Bats Flannelboard Song (to the tune of "Six Little Ducks")

5 little bats flew out 1 night
Underneath the moon so bright.
Mama Bat called, "Squeak, squeak, squeak."
4 little bats came home to sleep.

...

4 little bats . . .
3 little bats . . .
2 little bats . . .

...

1 little bat flew out 1 night
Underneath the moon so bright.
Mama Bat called, "Squeak, squeak, squeak."
No little bats came home to sleep.
Mama Bat called, "SQUEAK SQUEAK SQUEAK!"
5 little bats came home to sleep.

Writing Readiness Activity

183 Nighttime Animals

SKILLS

► Developing creativity
► Practicing writing

Have the children draw a picture of their favorite nocturnal animal, write its name, and describe some of its special characteristics.

Math Activity

184 Owl Eggs

SKILL

► Counting

Print a variety of owls and write different numbers on their chests. Place each owl in its own nest. Have the children place the appropriate number of eggs, corresponding to the owl's number, in its nest.

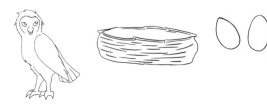

Takeaway Activity

185 Handy Bat Puppets

SKILLS

► Developing creativity
► Developing fine motor skills

Materials: a piece of construction paper for each child, a craft stick for each child, gluestick, scissors, crayons, stickers, other decorating materials

Directions:

1. Fold the construction paper in half.
2. Place one hand on the paper with your thumb along the fold. Keep your other four fingers together.
3. Trace your hand.
4. Keeping the paper folded, cut out the handshape. Do not cut along the fold.
5. Unfold the paper to reveal your bat shape.
6. Draw the bat's face at the center.
7. Glue a craft stick to the back.
8. Decorate as desired.

Library Skill–Building Game

186 Alphabet Animals

Preparation: Make several sets of alphabet playing cards, using index cards. At the top of each index card, write one letter of the alphabet. Each set should include one card for each letter of the alphabet. Make one set of playing cards for every four students in your class.

Activity: Review alphabetical order by singing the alphabet song. Then show the following list of nocturnal animals on sentence strips. (Make sure they are not in alphabetical order when you show them to the class.)

fox	owl
cat	raccoon
bat	wolf

Ask the children if they remember how fiction books are arranged in the library (alphabetically by author's last name). Explain that when you put names or words in alphabetical order, you don't need to have a name or word for each letter, but it's important to remember the order of the alphabet. Draw their attention to the first letter of each word in the list, and ask them which letter comes first in the alphabet. (Sing the alphabet song slowly, stopping at B if needed to prompt them.) Move "bat" to the top of the list, and then proceed to alphabetize the entire list with their help.

Next, divide the class into teams of four and explain that they will play a game to help them remember alphabetical order. Give each team a shuffled set of alphabet playing cards and instruct each child to take six cards without looking at them. Each child should hold his or her cards so the other players can't see them. The player who has A should start. The player to his or her right should go next, putting down any letter that comes after A in the alphabet. The next player puts down a letter after that, and so on. When everyone has put down all the letters they can, start again with the player who has the letter closest to the beginning of the alphabet. The player who runs out of cards first is the winner.

For an easier version of this game, have the students put down all their cards in order, and see how fast they can get to Z. When a team has finished, they should all raise their hands. Check the accuracy of their pile. The team that accurately gets to Z the fastest wins.

ASL Connection

187 The Owl

The OWL is a friendly sight.
We see him in the woods at night.
He looks to the left and he looks to the right, *(turn head to left and then right while signing OWL)*
And flies home to sleep before it's light.

Spanish Connection

188 Can You Name the Animals?

Introduce the Spanish words for the following nocturnal animals, and then give the clues and have the children respond in Spanish. To help children with recognition, show a picture of the animal labeled with its Spanish name.

Owl: *el buho* (el BOO-ho)
Raccoon: *el mapache* (el mah-PAH-chay)
Lion: *el leon* (el lay-OWN)
Bat: *el murciélago* (el moor-see-AY-lah-go)

1. I'm easy to recognize because I say "whooo."
2. I look like a bandit with a mask on my face.
3. I hunt at night and let out a mighty roar.
4. I fly silently and eat lots of bugs.

Recommend This!

Stellaluna by Janell Cannon. San Diego, CA: Harcourt, 1993.

Wake-Up Kisses by Pamela Duncan Edwards. New York: HarperCollins, 2002.

Henry the Owl by Wendy Kanno. Provo, UT: Aro, 1993.

Firefly Friend by Kimberly Wagner Klier. New York: Scholastic, 2004.

Owl at Home by Arnold Lobel. New York: HarperCollins, 1975.

Little Hoot by Amy Krouse Rosenthal. San Francisco, CA: Chronicle, 2008.

14

Thanksgiving

Kindergarten Speak

Thanksgiving is a time to give thanks for all we have and to remember the first Thanksgiving that the pilgrims and Native Americans celebrated. Thanksgiving in the United States is celebrated on the fourth Thursday in November each year. Friends and family usually gather together to celebrate with a Thanksgiving dinner.

Recommended Books

189 *The Firefighters' Thanksgiving* by Maribeth Boelts. New York: Putnam, 2004.

A group of firefighters attempts to make a Thanksgiving dinner, but emergency calls and injuries threaten to derail it—until grateful community members show up with a feast.

LESSON IDEA: Before reading the story, ask the children to describe how their families celebrate Thanksgiving. Then ask if any of them have family members who are doctors, nurses, police officers, firefighters, or another profession that means they have to work on Thanksgiving. Explain that today's story is about people who don't get the day off for Thanksgiving—firefighters. After reading the story, have the children make Thanksgiving cards (or make a large one as a class) to send to your local fire station.

SKILLS

- ▶ Reading for literary experience
- ▶ Practicing writing
- ▶ Developing text-to-self connection
- ▶ Recognizing community helpers

190 *A Turkey for Thanksgiving* by Eve Bunting. New York: Clarion, 1991.

Mr. Moose tries to persuade a turkey to come for Thanksgiving dinner, and only when the turkey arrives does he realize he is to be a guest, not an entrée.

LESSON IDEA: Before reading the story, ask the children what the title means. After reading the story, discuss how words can have multiple meanings (some examples to consider: *run, break, right*). Ask the children to suggest other words or phrases that can mean different things in different situations. Make a list of these as a class.

SKILLS

- ▶ Reading for literary experience
- ▶ Developing prediction skills
- ▶ Developing vocabulary

191 *The Very First Thanksgiving Day* by Rhonda Gowler Greene. New York: Atheneum, 2002.

SKILLS

▶ Reading for literary experience
▶ Practicing writing
▶ Developing compare and contrast skills

This lovely book tells the story of the first Thanksgiving in a cumulative rhyme, from the land where it all began to the ocean journey of the *Mayflower* to meeting the Indians and sharing a grateful feast.

LESSON IDEA: After reading the story, work with the class to compare and contrast the first Thanksgiving, as presented in the book, with the holiday as we celebrate it today. Make a list of the ways our current holiday is the same as and different from the first Thanksgiving. An alternate lesson idea is to work with the class to write a cumulative story following the pattern of the text, but applying it to our current celebration of Thanksgiving.

192 *I Know an Old Lady Who Swallowed a Pie* by Alison Jackson. New York: Dutton, 1997.

SKILLS

▶ Reading for literary experience
▶ Developing oral fluency
▶ Developing vocabulary
▶ Recognizing rhyme

In this delightfully silly variation on "I Know an Old Lady Who Swallowed a Fly," the old lady doesn't die—she merely becomes a giant balloon in the Thanksgiving parade after eating too much.

LESSON IDEA: After reading the story, play a matching game with the students. Write the names of the items the old lady swallows on one set of index cards, and print out clip art pictures of the items on another set. (Make multiple copies of each item if you have a large class.) Give each child either a word or a picture card, and then instruct the children to find the person who has the card that matches theirs. Once they have found their match, the two children should sit down next to each other. Once all the matches have been found, sing through the story again, with each pair standing up when the class sings about its item.

193 *Thanks for Thanksgiving* by Julie Markes. New York: HarperCollins, 2004.

SKILLS

▶ Reading for literary experience
▶ Developing text-to-self connection
▶ Understanding literary genres

In a simple, rhyming text, children express thanks for the people and things in their lives.

LESSON IDEA: After reading the story, invite each child to tell about something or someone he or she is thankful for. List the suggestions on the board, and then work as a group to put them into a poem that mirrors the format of the book.

Fingerplays/Songs

194 The Turkey

SKILLS

▶ Recognizing rhyme
▶ Developing motor skills
▶ Developing oral fluency

The turkey is a silly bird, *(spread hands to sides)*
One might even say absurd. *(make a silly face)*
2 spindly legs, a bright red wattle, *(hold pinkie fingers down to show legs, then point to chin)*
And oh my goodness! Hear that gobble! *(cover ears)*
Gobble! Gobble! Gobble! *(place fist of right hand against palm of left hand to represent turkey and wiggle fingers to shake tail feathers)*

195 Thanksgiving, Thanksgiving

SKILLS

▶ Recognizing rhyme
▶ Developing oral fluency

Thanksgiving, Thanksgiving, come on in.
Sit right down and let the meal begin.
Thanksgiving, Thanksgiving, time to say
Thanks to everyone we love today.
Thanksgiving, Thanksgiving, have some pie
And have fun till it's time to say goodbye.

196 I'm a Little Turkey (to the tune of "I'm a Little Teapot")

I'm a little turkey, hear me gobble,
Here is my tail, and here is my wattle.
The rest of the year I'll stay and play,
Thanksgiving comes, and I run away!

SKILLS

► Recognizing rhyme
► Developing motor skills
► Developing oral fluency

197 The Turkey Pokey (to the tune of "The Hokey Pokey")

You put your right leg in, you put your right leg out,
You put your right leg in and you shake it all about.
You do the Turkey Pokey and you start to swing and sway,
Happy Thanksgiving Day!

•••

You put your left leg in . . .
You put your wattle in . . .
You put your tail feathers in . . .
You put your whole self in . . .

SKILLS

► Recognizing rhyme
► Developing motor skills
► Developing oral fluency

Flannelboard/Prop Stories

198 The First Thanksgiving Flannelboard Song (to the tune of "Ten Little Indians")

1 little, 2 little, 3 little Indians,
4 little, 5 little, 6 little Indians,
7 little, 8 little, 9 little Indians,
On the first Thanksgiving Day.

•••

1 little, 2 little, 3 little Pilgrims,
4 little, 5 little, 6 little Pilgrims,
7 little, 8 little, 9 little Pilgrims,
On the first Thanksgiving Day.

•••

Eating and drinking with their new friends,
Playing and sharing with their new friends,
Loving and caring with their new friends,
On Thanksgiving Day.

SKILLS

► Recognizing rhyme
► Developing oral fluency
► Counting

199 Thanksgiving Day Flannelboard

Mashed potatoes on my plate,
Turkey, stuffing, this is great!
Green beans, sweet potatoes too,
Here are some corn and rolls for you.
We gather 'round the table to say
Thanks for everything on Thanksgiving Day!

SKILLS

► Recognizing rhyme
► Developing oral fluency

Writing Readiness Activity

200 **Thanksgiving Acrostic**

Print out the Thanksgiving Acrostic worksheet from this book's webpage. Ask the children to write a word for each letter of the word *Thanksgiving* that is something they are grateful for.

SKILLS

▶ Practicing writing
▶ Developing text-to-self connection
▶ Developing vocabulary

Math Activity

201 **Favorite Thanksgiving Food Graph**

Make a graph of the children's favorite Thanksgiving foods. Along the bottom of a poster-board or chalkboard, list Thanksgiving foods: turkey, mashed potatoes, sweet potatoes, pumpkin pie, and so on. Ask each child which food is his or her favorite, and mark it in the appropriate column. After all the children have revealed their favorite food, discuss which food was most liked and which was least liked.

SKILLS

▶ Counting
▶ Understanding that graphs represent information

Library Skill–Building Game

202 **Alphabetizing Ourselves**

Pass out sentence strips or index cards on which each child should write his or her last name. Then ask the children to pretend that they are fiction books and the cards are their spine labels showing the author's last name. Work with the class to create an alphabetical line by last name, talking through the steps and explaining as you go. For example: "We start at the beginning of the alphabet. Which letter comes first? Yes, A. Whose last name starts with A?" If some students' last names begin with the same letter, ask the class for ideas about which should come first, then explain how, when the first letter is the same, we move on to the second letter. If both the first and second letters are the same, we look at the third letter, and so on. Continue until you have alphabetized the entire class.

Next, separate the class into groups of five to six students. Pass out paper turkey feathers (from the pattern) on which each child should write his or her first name. Then give each group a turkey body (from the pattern) and read the poem aloud. Each group should then work together to place the feathers in alphabetical order left to right and glue them on the turkey's tail. Group members should raise their hands when they are finished so you can check their work. Hang the completed turkeys in the library to decorate for Thanksgiving!

SKILLS

▶ Knowing the alphabet
▶ Understanding alphabetical order

I'm an alphabetical turkey,
I like things to be just so.
So let's sort our names by the ABCs.
From left to right we'll go.
And on this Thanksgiving
I hope you won't think me a bore
Because alphabetical order
Is what I am thankful for!

Takeaway Activity

203 **Thankful Collage**

Materials: magazines, scissors, glue, crayons, and so on

Directions:

1. Have the children cut out or draw pictures of things they are thankful for and glue the pictures on a piece of construction paper.
2. Encourage students to share the collage during their Thanksgiving feast at home.

SKILLS

▶ Developing creativity
▶ Developing fine motor skills

ASL Connection

204 We Are Thankful   (to the tune of "Happy Birthday")

(Before singing the song, work with the class to make a list of the things they are thankful for. Use those items to fill in the blanks in the song. Then teach the signs and sign the words in capital letters as you sing the song.)

We are THANKful for _____.
We are THANKful for _____.
We are THANKful for _____.
HAPPY THANKSGIVING DAY!

thank   happy   Thanksgiving   day

Spanish Connection

205 *Nueve Peregrinos Pequeños* (Nine Little Pilgrims)

(Introduce the following vocabulary, and then sing the song in Spanish.)

1: *uno* (OO-no)
2: *dos* (DOSE)
3: *tres* (TRACE)
4: *cuatro* (QUA-tro)
5: *cinco* (SINK-o)
6: *seis* (SASE)
7: *siete* (see-ET-tay)
8: *ocho* (OH-cho)
9: *nueve* (noo-WAY-vay)
Little: *pequeño* (pay-KAY-nio)
Pilgrim: *Peregrino* (pay-ray-GREE-no)
On the first Thanksgiving Day: *En el primero Día de Acción de gracias*
    (en el pre-MAY-ro DEE-ah day ac-SEE-on de GRA-see-as)

Nueve Peregrinos Pequeños (Nine Little Pilgrims)

Uno pequeño, dos pequeños, tres Peregrinos pequeños,
Cuatro pequeños, cinco pequeños, seis Peregrinos pequeños,
Siete pequeños, ocho pequeños, nueve Peregrinos pequeños,
En el primero Día de Acción de gracias.

•••

1 little, 2 little, 3 little Pilgrims,
4 little, 5 little, 6 little Pilgrims,
7 little, 8 little, 9 little Pilgrims,
On the first Thanksgiving Day.

Recommend This!

Minnie and Moo and the Thanksgiving Tree by Denys Cazet. New York: Dorling Kindersley, 2000.

More Snacks! A Thanksgiving Play by Joan Holub. New York: Aladdin, 2006.

Happy Thanksgiving by Margaret McNamara. New York: Scholastic, 2005.

I Am the Turkey by Michele Sobel Spirn. New York: HarperCollins, 2005.

The Know-Nothings Talk Turkey by Michele Sobel Spirn. New York: HarperCollins, 2000.

Thanksgiving Is for Giving Thanks by Margaret Sutherland. New York: Penguin Putnam, 2000.

15

Nutrition and Food Groups

• •

Kindergarten Speak

Our bodies work very hard each day. To keep our bodies strong, it's very important to eat good foods. We're going to learn about the food groups, which will help you make the right food choices each day.

Recommended Books

206 *Showdown at the Food Pyramid* **by Rex Barron. New York: Putnam, 2004.**

Disaster strikes when junk food and candy overtake the food pyramid, causing it to collapse. But members of the various food groups work together to rebuild, using the Great Food Guide.

LESSON IDEA: Before reading the book, ask if the children know what a pyramid is. Show pictures of Egyptian pyramids and discuss how the stones must be perfectly balanced so the pyramid doesn't collapse. Then compare this concept to the food pyramid—you can't eat too much of certain foods, or your body will "collapse" (become unhealthy). Read the story, and then draw a diagram of the food pyramid on the board. Ask the children to help you label each group. Then pass out pictures (or printed words on cards) of various foods, and invite each child to come forward and place his or her card in the correct level of the pyramid.

SKILLS

▶ Reading for information

▶ Developing vocabulary

▶ Developing text-to-self connection

▶ Classifying foods and food combinations according to the food groups

207 *Lunch* **by Denise Fleming. New York: Henry Holt, 1992.**

A hungry mouse eats his way through a rainbow of healthy foods.

LESSON IDEA: After reading the story, discuss how foods of different colors provide different nutrients and why it is important to eat foods from the various food groups. (See www.choosemyplate.gov for extensive information on the food groups.) Post a large piece of white paper on the wall, and then use red, orange, yellow, green, blue, purple, brown, and black markers to draw a large rainbow. Give each child a crayon in one of these colors, then invite the children to come forward one at a time to draw (or write the name of) a healthy food of that color on the appropriate band of the rainbow. If a child can't think of a food, he or she can ask a classmate for help. Label the rainbow "Our Rainbow of Healthy Foods" and the class's name and display it in the school library or classroom.

SKILLS
▶ Reading for literary experience
▶ Recognizing colors
▶ Developing text-to-self connection
▶ Knowing that some foods are more nutritious than others

208 *The Beastly Feast* **by Bruce Goldstone. New York: Henry Holt, 1998.**

A host of animals brings foods that rhyme with their names to the beastly feast.

LESSON IDEA: As you are reading the story, pause before each of the food names to see if the children can guess the rhyme. After the story, play a rhyming matching game. Divide the class into two lines facing each other. Give each child in one line a card with the name of an animal on it. Give each child in the other line a card with the name of a food on it. Pick children at random, or choose names from a hat, to determine the order. When it is a child's turn, he or she should say, "I am a(n) (animal) and I will bring . . ." and guess a food that rhymes with the animal, or "I will bring (food), because I am a(n) . . ." and guess an animal that rhymes with his or her food. If the child guesses a rhyming animal or food that another child is holding, the two children put their cards together for a match and sit down. As each pair is matched, hold up the cards and point out the rhyming parts of the words. Continue until all cards have been matched.

Rhyming pairs for the cards:

bear/pear	bunny/honey
parrot/carrot	moose/juice
antelope/cantaloupe	mice/rice
puffin/muffin	flea/pea
mosquito/burrito	fly/pie
fish/knish	fox/lox
bee/tea	

SKILLS
▶ Reading for literary experience
▶ Recognizing rhyme

209 *Alphabet Soup: A Feast of Letters* **by Scott Gustafson. Shelton, CT: Greenwich Workshop Press, 1994.**

This alphabet book features animals and foods for each letter of the alphabet.

LESSON IDEA: After reading the story, reinforce alphabetical order with this game. Give each child an index card with the name of a food on it. If the class is new to the idea of alphabetical order, then review the alphabet and explain that you are going to alphabetize the cards as a group, just like the picture books are arranged in alphabetical order. Then invite each child to come up and place his or her card on the board so that it is in the right spot in relation to the others.

If your class is already familiar with alphabetical order, try one of these variations:

Divide the class into groups and have a contest to see which group can put its cards in correct alphabetical order first.

Challenge the class to line up in alphabetical order with their cards. Tell them where A should stand and where Z should stand, and then let them line up in order. When they have finished lining up, go down the line and have each child read his or her card out loud. Correct the line order where needed.

SKILLS
▶ Reading for literary experience
▶ Knowing the alphabet
▶ Understanding alphabetical order

210 *Yoko* **by Rosemary Wells. New York: Hyperion, 1998.**

The other children make fun of the sushi that Yoko brings to school for her lunch, until one of the other children tries it and likes it.

LESSON IDEA: After reading the story, discuss the importance of trying new foods before deciding you don't like them. Then reinforce math concepts by making a bar graph as a class. Write the names of the foods from the story (*sushi, red bean ice cream, enchiladas, coconut crisps, nut soup, Brazil nuts, Irish stew, potato knishes, mango smoothies, spaghetti, franks and beans*) along the bottom of the chart, and write numbers up the left side. Then survey the class and make a bar in one color to show how many people have tried these foods and a bar in another color to show how many would like to try them. When you have finished making the chart, ask questions such as "How many people would like to try mango smoothies?" to help the children learn to read it. When one child answers a question correctly, invite him or her to pose a question to the next child.

SKILLS

▶ Reading for literary experience
▶ Understanding other cultures
▶ Developing text-to-self connection
▶ Appreciating diversity
▶ Developing oral fluency
▶ Understanding that graphs represent information

Fingerplays/Songs

211 Crazy Food

Popcorn, popcorn *(jump up and down)*
Mashed potatoes, mashed potatoes *(swish feet)*
Boiling water, boiling water *(run in place)*
Spaghetti, spaghetti *(wave arms loosely)*
Fruitcake *(sit down heavily)*

SKILLS

▶ Developing oral fluency
▶ Developing motor skills
▶ Developing vocabulary

212 Food Groups Song (to the tune of "The More We Get Together")

(Before singing this song, ask the class to help you think of foods from each of the food groups. Write their suggestions on the board and use them in the appropriate verses.)

The more we eat our veggies, our veggies, our veggies,
The more we eat our veggies, the healthier we'll be.
Like carrots and tomatoes and broccoli and asparagus, *(or insert class suggestions here)*
Oh, the more we eat our veggies, the healthier we'll be.

...

The more we eat our fruits . . .
The more we eat our grains . . .
The more we eat our protein . . .
The more we eat our dairy . . .

SKILLS

▶ Developing vocabulary
▶ Developing text-to-self connection
▶ Classifying foods and food combinations according to the food groups
▶ Developing oral fluency

213 If You're Hungry (to the tune of "If You're Happy and You Know It")

If you're hungry and you know it, eat some food.
If you're hungry and you know it, eat some food.
If you're hungry and you know it, then you really ought to show it.
If you're hungry and you know it, eat some food.

...

If you're thirsty and you know it, take a drink . . .

SKILL

▶ Developing oral fluency

214 Buffet Ballet

From *Jim Gill's Irrational Anthem and More Salutes to Nonsense* by Jim Gill. Jim Gill Music, 2001.

Flannelboard/Prop Stories

215 *Stop That Pickle!* Flannelboard Story
(Based on the book by Peter Armour. Boston: Houghton Mifflin, 1993.)

A pickle flees through the city streets, chased by hungry people and other foods. Kids will enjoy the silly ending: after consuming the sandwich, pretzel, apple, almonds, grape juice, raisins, doughnut, and ice cream that are chasing the pickle, a little boy leaves the pickle alone, because who would want to eat a pickle after ice cream?

Almond

Grape juice

Raisin

216 My Pizza (to the tune of "Dreidel")

I made myself a pizza with all my favorite food,
And maybe you can have a bite if you are in the mood.
I looked in the pantry to see what I could see,
And I thought that cheese pizza would be perfect for me.

...

I made myself a pizza with all my favorite food,
And maybe you can have a bite if you are in the mood.
I looked in the pantry to see what I could see,
And I thought that ice cream–cheese pizza would be perfect for me.

(Continue, gradually adding more toppings.)

Ice cream

Popcorn

Yogurt

Writing Readiness Activity

217 Picture Perfect Food

Have the children draw a picture of their favorite food and write what it is.

Math Activity

218 Favorite Food Graph

Make a graph of the children's favorite foods. Along the bottom of a posterboard or chalkboard list typical favorite foods: pizza, ice cream, chicken nuggets, french fries, hamburgers, and so on. Ask each child which food is their favorite, and mark it in the appropriate column. After all the children have revealed their favorite food, discuss which food was most liked and which was least liked.

Takeaway Activity

219 Going on a Picnic WEB

Print the Going on a Picnic worksheet from this book's webpage and ask the children to draw the foods they would pack in their picnic baskets.

Library Skill-Building Game

220 Cracking the Secret Code—Fiction

Preparation: Pull thirty to forty picture books or beginning readers related to food or nutrition. File them by call number on a cart. Write the call number of each book on a separate index card. (Write large so that the call number takes up the whole card.)

Activity: Begin by reviewing alphabetical order and reminding students that the fiction books are filed alphabetically by author. Take one index card from the pile and show the students that the upper portion of the call number shows what kind of book it is (easy, beginning reader, etc.) and the bottom of the call number shows the beginning of the author's last name. Explain that the call numbers in the library are like a secret code, and if you know how to read the code, you can find any book you want!

Then invite each child to take a turn being a "call number detective" by taking one card and finding the book that matches it on the cart. (For extra fun, let the child hold a large magnifying glass as he or she looks for the book.) As the children find their books, send them back to their seats and tell them to look at the cover and the pictures in the book and see if they can guess what the story is about and whether they would like to read it. When all the children have found their books, ask for a few volunteers to share their books and what they guessed about them. Ask whether they think the books would be good ones to check out and why, emphasizing that they should ask themselves the following questions:

Do I like the pictures?
What does the story seem like: happy, sad, funny, serious? Do I like that?
Are there too many words? Not enough words?

Then let the children know that they may check out the books they chose, or place them in a designated spot if they don't want to check them out.

ASL Connection

221 **I Like to Eat** (to the tune of "Apples and Bananas")

I LIKE to EAT, EAT, EAT yummy yummy APPLES,
I LIKE to EAT, EAT, EAT yummy yummy APPLES.

(Repeat with other foods.)

SKILLS

▶ Understanding basic American Sign Language
▶ Developing oral fluency

Spanish Connection

222 Food Guessing Game

Share the book *My Food/Mi Comida* by Rebecca Emberley (LB Kids, 2002). Read the Spanish words to the children and see if they can tell you the English word by looking at the pictures. Then write all the Spanish words for the foods on the board, and play a game. Give clues about a food from the book and ask the children to guess which food you are describing by telling you the Spanish word. When a child guesses correctly, let him or her come forward and give clues about another food for the class.

SKILLS

▶ Understanding basic Spanish vocabulary

▶ Developing oral fluency

▶ Differentiating between text and pictures

▶ Developing attention and response

Recommend This!

Pancakes, Crackers, and Pizza by Marjorie Eberts and Margaret Gisler. New York: Children's Press, 1984.

Mary Clare Likes to Share by Joy Hulme. New York: Random House, 2006.

A Lunch with Punch by Jo S. Kittinger. New York: Scholastic, 2003.

Pizza for Sam by Mary Labatt. Tonawanda, New York: Kids Can Press, 2003.

The Lunch Line by Karen Berman Nagel. New York: Scholastic, 1996.

Eat Your Peas, Louise! by Pegeen Snow. New York: Children's Press, 1985.

16

Holidays and Traditions

· ·

Kindergarten Speak

We all have different holidays we celebrate and traditions we observe. Some holidays are specific religious events, while others are celebrated within the country or area you live in. Often traditions are started surrounding these holidays, but sometimes a tradition can be something special and unique that your family does, like watching movies on Friday nights or getting ice cream when you lose a tooth.

Recommended Books

223 *Feast for Ten* by Cathryn Falwell. New York: Clarion, 1993.

An African American family cooks and shares a meal in this counting book.

LESSON IDEA: Before reading the story, ask the children how their families celebrate special occasions. Since most special celebrations involve sharing a meal, this will lead into the story. After reading the story, go back through it and have the children identify the ways the family members worked together. Ask the children to give examples of how their families work together to prepare for the holidays.

224 *Light the Candle! Bang the Drum! A Book of Holidays Around the World* by Ann Morris. New York: Dutton, 1997. WEB

This brightly illustrated, nonfiction book takes readers through the year featuring holidays from around the world, each accompanied by a brief, engaging description. The punchy text and bold illustrations make this an ideal nonfiction read-aloud.

LESSON IDEA: After reading the story, pass out the Comparing Holidays worksheet from this book's webpage. Read the book again and have the children place a check in the appropriate boxes for each holiday. (You may also wish to share more information about

SKILLS

▶ Reading for literary experience

▶ Counting

▶ Developing text-to-self connection

▶ Developing teamwork skills

▶ Reading for information

▶ Understanding that graphs represent information

▶ Counting

▶ Understanding the concept of nonfiction

▶ Developing compare and contrast skills

each holiday, such as the countries where it is celebrated, from the additional notes at the back of the book.) When the children have finished their worksheets, ask them questions to help them interpret the data (for example, "How many of the holidays use candles?"). Make a bar graph on the board to show this information as they answer your questions. Emphasize how the nonfiction book, the chart, and the graph are all different ways of showing the same information.

225 *Mrs. Muddle's Holidays* **by Laura F. Nielsen. New York: Farrar, Strauss and Giroux, 2008.**

The neighbors on Maple Street celebrate lots of different holidays, but they've never seen anything like Mrs. Muddle, who celebrates Earthworm Appreciation Day, Watermelon Bash, the Ice Spectacle, and many others.

LESSON IDEA: Before reading the story, ask the class to define the word *holiday*. Then tell them their idea of a holiday might change after they hear the story. After the story, revisit the definition and ask if they think it needs changing. As a class, make a list of the ways Mrs. Muddle celebrates her holidays. Then separate the class into groups of three to five children and give each group an index card with an unusual holiday written on it. (Check out http://holidayinsights.com/moreholidays/index.htm for ideas.) Have each group write or draw a description of how they would celebrate their holiday.

SKILLS

► Reading for literary experience
► Appreciating diversity
► Practicing writing
► Developing text-to-self connection

226 *The Always Prayer Shawl* **by Sheldon Oberman. Honesdale, PA: Boyds Mills Press, 1994.**

A little boy named Adam receives a prayer shawl from his grandfather, and when he grows up, he passes it on to his own grandson. Set against a backdrop of political upheaval, this gentle story of family traditions acknowledges the difficulties of life but focuses on the positive message of hope.

LESSON IDEA: In the story, Adam's grandfather says, "Some things change. And some things don't." After reading the story, draw a Venn diagram on the board. Label one circle "Grandfather" and one circle "Adam." Ask the children what changed in the story and write these items in the outer circles. Ask the children what things didn't change (such as the name, the prayer shawl) and write these items in the overlapping parts of the circle.

SKILLS

► Reading for literary experience
► Appreciating diversity
► Developing compare and contrast skills

227 *Cherry Pies and Lullabies* **by Lynn Reiser. New York: Greenwillow, 1998.**

A little girl explores how four different traditions have been passed down in her family.

LESSON IDEA: Follow up the story by making a chart with the class showing how the traditions are the same and different with each generation. Share something that has been passed down in your family, and then ask the class to share traditions that have been passed down in their families.

SKILLS

► Reading for literary experience
► Developing compare and contrast skills
► Developing text-to-self connection

Fingerplays/Songs

228 Traditions

My family means so much to me,
I love them, every one. *(hug arms to chest)*
Each family has its special ways
To be together and have fun. *(2 thumbs up)*
We have traditions we do again and again
One year after another. *(mime pulling pages off a calendar)*

SKILLS

► Recognizing rhyme
► Developing oral fluency
► Developing motor skills

Our traditions are part of our family's life
And our love for one another! *(hug arms to chest)*

229 On This Holiday (to the tune of "Ten Little Indians")

SKILL

▶ Developing oral fluency

Eating and drinking with friends and family,
Playing and sharing with friends and family,
Loving and caring with friends and family,
On this holiday.

230 Giving Presents (to the tune of "Frère Jacques")

SKILLS

▶ Recognizing rhyme
▶ Developing oral fluency

Giving presents, giving presents
Is such fun, is such fun.
Let's give out our presents,
And open up our presents,
Everyone, everyone.

231 Light the Candles (to the tune of "My Darling Clementine")

SKILLS

▶ Developing oral fluency
▶ Recognizing rhyme

Light the candles, light the candles
So we all can celebrate
On this holiday, on this special day
With friends and family, it's so great.

Flannelboard/Prop Stories

232 The Best Gift Prop Story

SKILLS

▶ Appreciating diversity
▶ Developing compare and contrast skills

(Cut out a small heart from red construction paper or felt and wrap it in a small box. Place the box in a larger box and wrap it. Then place that box in a larger box and wrap it. Continue until you have five to eight boxes-in-boxes.)

When I was little, my mother gave me a present. She told me this was a very important present, one that had been passed down for many years in my family. "Is it a bike?" I asked. "No," she said. "Your great-grandmother didn't have a bike, and she still had fun every day." I thought some more. "Is it a remote-controlled airplane?" I said. "No," said my mom. "Your grandmother didn't have a remote-controlled airplane, and she still had fun every day." I thought some more. "Is it a video game?" I asked. "No," said my mother. "I didn't have video games when I was a little girl, and I still had fun every day." What do you think it could be?

Wow, those are all great suggestions. Let's open the present and see. (Open each box in succession, building the suspense. When you finally reach the last box, open it slowly and reveal the heart.) "That is the best gift anyone can give you, and it's something that has been passed down in our family for generations," said my mother. Do you know what it is? Love!

233 Five Balloons Flannelboard

SKILLS

▶ Counting
▶ Recognizing rhyme

5 balloons on this holiday,
I took 1 and gave it away.
I gave it to *(child's name)* for some fun,
I thought she/he would really like 1.

...

4 balloons . . .
3 balloons . . .
2 balloons . . .
1 balloon . . .

Writing Readiness Activity

234 Family Traditions WEB

Print the Family Traditions worksheet from this book's webpage. Ask the children to share some of their special family traditions. Then ask each child to draw a picture of his or her favorite tradition and write a sentence about it on the worksheet.

SKILLS

► Developing creativity
► Developing text-to-self connection
► Practicing writing

Math Activity

235 Holiday Flag

Create a celebration flag for the holiday of your choice.

Materials: a sheet of construction paper for each child, a variety of shapes (rectangles, stars, squares, circles, hearts, etc.) cut from construction paper, crayons, glue

Directions:

1. Ask the children to think of their favorite holiday.
2. Have each child create a flag for his or her favorite holiday, gluing a variety of shapes on the flag to make the decoration.

SKILLS

► Recognizing shapes
► Developing fine motor skills
► Appreciating diversity
► Developing creativity

Takeaway Activity

236 Celebration Candle

Materials: card stock, a flame (from pattern) for each child, tape or stapler, gluesticks, crayons

Directions:

1. Fold a piece of card stock in half. Cut along the fold.
2. Roll one of the halves into a tube and tape or staple the tube closed. (These first two steps can be done ahead of time.)
3. Glue the flame to the top of the tube.
4. Decorate as desired.

SKILL

► Developing fine motor skills

Library Skill–Building Game

237 Holiday Feast Counting Memory Game

Have the children sit in a circle. Explain that the Number family is having a holiday feast and everyone is invited to bring their favorite food or toy—but the Number family only likes things to be in the pattern of counting 1–10. Begin the game by saying, "I will bring one banana to the feast." (Replace "banana" with your favorite food!) The child to your right should then say, "I will bring one banana and two apples to the feast" (replacing "apples" with his or her favorite food or toy). The next child should then repeat the first two and add another item onto the list, and so on around the circle. When you get to ten, have the children begin again at one. (Don't be surprised if your students remember the list better than you do!)

SKILLS

▶ Counting
▶ Understanding numerical order
▶ Developing memory
▶ Developing attention and response
▶ Developing oral fluency

ASL Connection

238 Celebration Song (to the tune of "If You're Happy and You Know It")

It's the HOLIDAYS again, so CELEBRATE.
It's the HOLIDAYS again, so CELEBRATE.
We will see our friends and family and we'll have a great big party.
It's the HOLIDAYS again, so CELEBRATE.

SKILLS

▶ Understanding basic American Sign Language
▶ Developing oral fluency

holiday

celebrate

Spanish Connection

239 *Bate, Bate, Chocolate*

In Mexico, children often drink chocolate with breakfast. They stir their chocolate with a *molinillo*, which is held between the palms and rotated by rubbing the palms quickly back and forth. Invite your class to stir their imaginary chocolate with imaginary *molinillos* as they say this rhyme. Repeat the verse faster, then slower, and then challenge the children to do it as quickly as possible.

SKILLS

▶ Developing oral fluency
▶ Developing motor skills
▶ Understanding basic Spanish vocabulary
▶ Developing compare and contrast skills

Bate, bate, chocolate, (BAH-tay, BAH-tay CHO-co-LAH-tay)
Bate, bate, chocolate,
Uno (OO-no), *dos* (DOSE), *tres* (TRACE), *CHO!*
Uno, dos, tres, CO!
Uno, dos, tres, LA!
Uno, dos, tres, TE!
Chocolate, chocolate! Bate, bate, chocolate!
Bate bate bate bate, bate, bate, CHOCOLATE!

...

Stir, stir the chocolate, stir, stir the chocolate,
1, 2, 3, CHO!
1, 2, 3, CO!
1, 2, 3, LA!
1, 2, 3, TE!
Chocolate, chocolate! Stir, stir the chocolate!
Stir stir stir stir, stir, stir the CHOCOLATE!

Recommend This!

Holiday! Celebration Days Around the World by Deborah Chancellor. New York: DK, 2000.

The Dumb Bunnies' Easter by Sue Denim. New York: Scholastic, 1995.

My First Kwanzaa by Karen Katz. New York: Henry Holt, 2003.

Eloise and the Big Parade by Lisa McClatchey. New York: Aladdin, 2007.

It's Hanukkah! by Jeanne Modesitt. New York: Holiday House, 1999.

Mousekin's Special Day by Jane Belk Moncure. Mankato, MN: Child's World, 2001.

17
Gingerbread

- -

Kindergarten Speak

How many of you have had gingerbread cookies? A lot of people make gingerbread in the winter or for the Christmas holiday. Often people use gingerbread to make houses decorated with icing and candy or to make gingerbread people.

Recommended Books

240 *Gingerbread Baby* **by Jan Brett. New York: Putnam, 1999.**

When the gingerbread baby he makes escapes from the house, Matti comes up with a clever way to catch him—he builds a little gingerbread house for the baby to live in.

    LESSON IDEA: After reading the story, go back through the book and point out the sidebar illustrations, which show Matti carefully planning and building the gingerbread house while his family runs about chasing the gingerbread baby. Discuss the importance of making a plan before doing a big job, and then tell the class they will build their own gingerbread house out of paper. Work with the group to make a list of the things they will need (brown paper, tape, construction paper in various colors, etc.) and then have the students assist in writing a step-by-step plan on the board. Provide precut pieces of construction paper to represent various types of candy, and have the group work together to build a gingerbread house by layering the brown paper over a book cart or small table, then decorating it. Make sure that the students follow the plan they have written together.

SKILLS

▶ Reading for literary experience
▶ Developing logic
▶ Setting and managing goals
▶ Practicing writing

241 *The Gingerbread Boy* by Richard Egielski. New York: HarperCollins, 1997.

This modern version of the classic folktale is set in a city, and the gingerbread boy's pursuers include a rat, construction workers, and a policeman.

LESSON IDEA: After reading the story, go back through and point out how the city setting appears throughout the story. Show other versions of the folktale as well. Invite the children to help you create a version of the gingerbread boy story that takes place at your school and act it out.

SKILLS

▶ Reading for literary experience

▶ Understanding literary genres

▶ Developing text-to-self connection

▶ Developing compare and contrast skills

242 *The Gingerbread Girl* by Lisa Campbell Ernst. New York: Dutton, 2006.

The Gingerbread Girl has learned a lesson from the fate of her older brother, who was eaten by a fox, and she uses her smarts to outwit her pursuers and make a happy ending for everyone.

LESSON IDEA: After reading the story, place a cutout of the Gingerbread Girl on the board. Pass out stickers, pieces of yarn, or candy cut from construction paper. Invite each child to come up to the board and identify a way the story is either the same as or different from the classic tale, and then put his or her decoration on the Gingerbread Girl.

SKILLS

▶ Reading for literary experience

▶ Understanding literary genres

▶ Developing compare and contrast skills

243 *The Gingerbread Man* by Eric A. Kimmel. New York: Holiday House, 1993.

This straightforward version of the classic folktale is a great read-aloud and has pictures large and colorful enough to share with a big class.

LESSON IDEA: After reading the story, reinforce sequencing and narrative structure by having the children help you retell the story, either using puppets or acting it out.

SKILLS

▶ Reading for literary experience

▶ Understanding literary genres

▶ Understanding sequencing

▶ Extending comprehension through dramatic play

244 *The Gingerbread Cowboy* by Janet Squires. New York: HarperCollins, 2006.

The Gingerbread Cowboy escapes from the ranch kitchen and is pursued by hungry javelinas, a roadrunner, and a horned lizard, before being tricked by a coyote.

LESSON IDEA: After reading the story, make a compare and contrast chart with the class to show how the story both follows and differs from the original version.

▶ Reading for literary experience

▶ Understanding literary genres

▶ Developing compare and contrast skills

Fingerplays/Songs

245 Gingerbread Rhyme

Mix the gingerbread as fast as you can. *(mime mixing batter in a bowl)*
Pour that gingerbread in the pan. *(mime pouring batter into pan)*
Cut out a shape of a little cookie man. *(mime using cookie cutter)*
Now put it in the oven and wait if you can. *(mime placing pan in oven)*
Gingerbread, gingerbread bakes in the heat. *(fan face)*
Gingerbread, gingerbread smells so sweet. *(point to nose)*
Open up the oven and put it on the plate. *(mime opening oven)*
Take the first bite now, we can't wait! *(mime taking a bite of a cookie)*

SKILLS

▶ Recognizing rhyme

▶ Developing oral fluency

▶ Developing motor skills

246 Do You Know the Gingerbread Man? (to the tune of "Do You Know the Muffin Man?")

Oh do you know the gingerbread man,
The gingerbread man, the gingerbread man?
Oh do you know the gingerbread man
Who ran on down the lane?

. . .

He ran away from the man and woman,
The cow and horse, the pig and dog.
He ran away from everyone
Until the fox tricked him!

. . .

Oh did you know the gingerbread man,
The gingerbread man, the gingerbread man?
Oh did you know the gingerbread man
Who ran on down the lane?

247 Making Gingerbread (to the tune of "The Farmer in the Dell")

Oh, we're making gingerbread,
We're making gingerbread,
We'll mix it up and eat it up,
We're making gingerbread.

. . .

We're mixing up the dough . . .
We're rolling out the dough . . .
We're cutting out the shapes . . .
We're putting it in the oven . . .
We're taking it out of the oven . . .
We're waiting while it cools . . .
We're eating gingerbread . . .

248 I'm Bringing Home a Little Gingerbread Man
(to the tune of "Bringing Home a Baby Bumblebee")

I'm bringing home a little gingerbread man. *(mime holding cookie)*
I'll take him home as quickly as I can.
I'm bringing home a little gingerbread man.
Hey! He ran away!

. . .

I'm chasing that little gingerbread man. *(run in place)*
He ran away, shouting, "Catch me if you can!"
I'm chasing that little gingerbread man.
Hey! I caught him!

. . .

I'm eating up that little gingerbread man. *(mime eating)*
He's so tasty, fresh out of the pan.
I'm eating up that little gingerbread man.
Yum! Delicious!

Flannelboard/Prop Stories

249 Gingerbread Man File Folder Story

SKILLS
► Recognizing colors
► Understanding literary genres
► Understanding sequencing

(Trace the gingerbread man shape onto one side of a manila file folder, and the fox shape on the other side. Cut out both shapes. Then tape the bottom and sides of the folder together, leaving the top open. Cut strips of blue, pink, yellow, green, and orange construction paper and tape them together to make a rainbow sheet the same size as a regular sheet of paper. Place construction paper sheets in the folder in the following order: red, rainbow, orange, green, yellow, pink, blue, brown. Make sure that the red paper shows through the fox cutout, and the brown paper shows through the gingerbread man cutout. As the gingerbread man changes colors, remove the top sheet from the gingerbread man side to show the new color. As the gingerbread man drips the food coloring onto the parts of the fox, slowly ease out the red sheet from the fox's side so that his tail, then back, then head and nose become rainbow colored.)

Once upon a time there was an old woman who made a little gingerbread man. She cut him out of the dough carefully and put him in the oven to bake. But when he was all browned in the oven, and she reached in to take him out, the gingerbread man popped up out of the pan and hopped out of the oven. On his way out of the kitchen, he grabbed some food coloring off the counter. The old woman chased him, shouting, "Come back here, little brown gingerbread man!" But the gingerbread man ducked behind the house and opened up the little jar of blue food coloring. Drip drip drop, he poured it over his head, and in no time at all, he was a little blue gingerbread man. He popped up right in front of the old lady and said, "Run, run, as fast as you can. It's not me you want—I'm the blue gingerbread man!" The old woman looked at him, and sure enough, he was blue. "Oh," she said, "sorry to bother you." And she set off down the road to look for the brown gingerbread man.

The blue gingerbread man started walking in the other direction, and soon he ran into a pig. Now everyone knows that pigs love gingerbread. The pig started to chase him, shouting, "Oink! Come back here, little blue gingerbread man!" The gingerbread man ducked behind the pigsty and uncorked the second jar of food coloring. Drip drip drop, he poured it over his head, and in no time at all, he was a little pink gingerbread man. He popped up right in front of the pig and said, "Run, run, as fast as you can. It's not me you want—I'm the pink gingerbread man!" The pig looked at him, and sure enough, he was pink. "Oh," said the pig, "sorry to bother you." And he set off down the road to look for the blue gingerbread man.

(Repeat pattern with a dog, a man, and a duck as the gingerbread man turns yellow, green, and orange.)

So the gingerbread man, now orange, came to the river. He only had a little bit of each color left, not enough to dye himself again, and so he was nervous when he saw the red fox. But how would he get across the river? "Oh, little orange gingerbread man, I am the red fox," said the red fox in sly tones. "Hop on my red tail and I will carry you across."

Now, the gingerbread man didn't trust the red fox, but he didn't have much choice. He jumped onto the fox's tail, and the fox started paddling across the river, licking his lips. After awhile he said, "Gingerbread man, the water is getting deeper. You had better climb up onto my red back." So the little gingerbread man did, but as he climbed, he let a little bit of the food coloring from each jar dribble onto the fox's tail and back.

A little while later, the fox said, "Oh, gingerbread man, the water is getting deeper, you'd better climb up onto my red head." The gingerbread man did, but as he climbed, he let a little bit of the food coloring from each jar dribble onto the fox's head.

They were almost at the far shore when the fox said, "Oh, gingerbread man, the water is getting deeper, you'd better climb up onto my red nose." The gingerbread man did, but as he climbed, he let a little bit of the food coloring from each jar dribble onto the fox's nose.

The fox laughed. "Oh, silly gingerbread man, don't you know that red foxes love to eat gingerbread?"

"What red fox?" said the clever little gingerbread man. "Why, I only see a rainbow-colored fox."

The fox whipped his head around in surprise and stared at his rainbow-colored fur. The little gingerbread man took advantage of his distraction to jump to shore. The air whooshed past him and blew off the pink coloring, and he was back to being a little brown gingerbread man. He ran away in the woods and lived happily ever after.

250 Five Gingerbread Men in the Bakery Shop Flannelboard

5 little gingerbread men in the bakery shop,
The ones with the sugar and the icing on top.
Along comes a child with a nickel to pay.
He/She buys a gingerbread man and takes it away.

4 little gingerbread men . . .
3 little gingerbread men . . .
2 little gingerbread men . . .
1 little gingerbread man . . .

SKILLS

▶ Counting
▶ Recognizing rhyme
▶ Developing oral fluency

Writing Readiness Activity

251 My Gingerbread House 🌐WEB

Print the My Gingerbread House worksheet from this book's webpage. Ask the children to draw pictures of gingerbread houses and then list the items they drew to decorate the houses.

SKILLS

▶ Practicing writing
▶ Developing creativity

Math Activity

252 Gingerbread Men Counting Game

Using the gingerbread man pattern, cut out fifty gingerbread men from various colors of construction paper. Place between two and ten gingerbread men of various colors in brown paper lunch bags, enough for each group of four to five children to have one. Have each group sit in a circle and give each a bag. As a group, the children should count their gingerbread men. Then ask each group to report how many gingerbread men they have and write the numbers on the board. Then ask questions such as these:

Which group has the most gingerbread men?
Which group has the fewest?
How many red gingerbread men does each group have? Blue? Yellow?
Which group has the most red gingerbread men? Which group has the most blue?

SKILLS

▶ Counting
▶ Recognizing colors
▶ Understanding the terms more than, less than, and same as for comparing quantity

Takeaway Activity

253 Gingerbread Cookie Matching Game **WEB**

Pass out the Gingerbread Cookie Matching worksheet from this book's webpage. Have the children draw lines to identify the matching pairs and then color their gingerbread cookies.

SKILLS

► Developing compare and contrast skills

► Understanding patterns

Library Skill–Building Game

254 Gingerbread Race

Preparation: Using the patterns, print and cut out each of the following:

1 Gingerbread Man	13 cows	17 horses
10 cats	14 pigs	18 birds
11 dogs	15 ducks	19 roosters
12 mice	16 goats	20 farmers

SKILLS

► Counting

► Understanding numerical order

► Understanding sequencing

Now, write a large number on each piece. Number the cats 1–10, the dogs 1–11, and so on. Group the pieces by type and place each group in an envelope or plastic bag. Keep the Gingerbread Man separate.

Activity: Divide the class into ten teams. Explain that the Gingerbread Man is running away, but all the animals on the farm are chasing him. Give each team an envelope or bag of pieces and instruct them to lay the pieces out in numerical order, and then count how many pieces they have. When all the teams have completed this task, tape the Gingerbread Man to one end of the board and begin the story:

"The Gingerbread Man was running away, but he only made it 1, 2, 3, 4, 5, 6, 7, 8, 9 steps when he saw 10 animals standing before him. Do you know what they were? Which team has 10 animals?" When the cat team identifies itself, have those children come forward and tape their cats to the board. Count the cats with the class, and then resume the story:

"He ran past those 10 cats, but then guess how many animals he saw? What number comes after 10? That's right, 11! Which team has 11 animals?" Invite the dogs forward to tape their animals on the board.

Continue with this pattern until all the pieces are on the board. Continue the story with this:

"And then the Gingerbread Man said, 'Wait, everyone! Let's play a game. Close your eyes and count to 20, and you will have a big surprise!'" Encourage the children to close their

eyes and count to 20 with you. While their eyes are closed, remove the Gingerbread Man from the board and hide him. When the children open their eyes, finish the story with:

"Surprise! The Gingerbread Man was gone! And all the animals and the farmers heard him laughing in the distance as he ran away."

ASL Connection

255 Gingerbread Jam

MIX up the gingerbread, MIX it up, MIX it up.
BAKE up the gingerbread, BAKE it up, BAKE it up.
EAT up the gingerbread, EAT it up, EAT it up.

SKILLS

▶ Understanding basic American Sign Language
▶ Developing oral fluency

Spanish Connection

256 *Cinco* Little Gingerbread Men

Cinco (SINK-o) little gingerbread men lying on a tray,
Uno (OO-no) jumped up and ran away,
Shouting, "Catch me, catch me, catch me if you can . . .
I run *rapido* (RAH-pee-do), I'm a gingerbread man!"

...

Cuatro (QUA-tro) little gingerbread men . . .
Tres (TRACE) little gingerbread men . . .
Dos (DOSE) little gingerbread men . . .
Uno (OO-no) little gingerbread man . . .

SKILLS

▶ Counting
▶ Understanding basic Spanish vocabulary
▶ Recognizing rhyme

Recommend This!

The Gingerbread Man by Eric Blair. Minneapolis, MN: Picture Window, 2005.

Maisy Makes Gingerbread by Lucy Cousins. Cambridge, MA: Candlewick Press, 1999.

The Little Cookie by Margaret Hillert. Cleveland, OH: Modern Curriculum Press, 1981.

The Gingerbread Kid Goes to School by Joan Holub. New York: Grosset and Dunlap, 2002.

The Truth about Hansel and Gretel by Karina Law. Minneapolis, MN: Picture Window, 2002.

The Gingerbread Boy by Harriet Ziefert. New York: Puffin, 1995.

18
The Five Senses

Kindergarten Speak

We have five senses. They are the sense of sight, touch, hearing, taste, and smell. These senses help us recognize things in our world.

Recommended Books

257 *The Black Book of Colors* **by Menena Cottin. Toronto, Ontario: Groundwood Books, 2006.**

This unique book features raised, black illustrations on a black background, with text in braille as well as print. The story invites readers to consider how they would experience colors if they were blind.

LESSON IDEA: Before reading the story, ask the children to name the five senses, and then explain that today you will discuss what it would be like to be without sight. Tell them the title of the book and then open it to show the illustrations, explaining that this book is meant to be experienced through the sense of touch instead of sight. As you read each page, invite a small number of children to come forward to touch the illustrations, making sure each child gets at least one turn.

258 *Forest Friends' Five Senses* **by Cristina Garelli. New York: Knopf, 2001.**

A group of forest animals tells stories about how they use their five senses.

LESSON IDEA: After reading the story, make a chart with the class showing the things one can see, hear, taste, touch, and smell in the forest.

SKILLS

▶ Reading for literary experience

▶ Appreciating nature

▶ Developing text-to-self connection

▶ Developing classification and sorting skills

▶ Knowing that people use their senses to find out about their surroundings and themselves and that different senses provide different information

▶ Reading for literary experience

▶ Appreciating nature

▶ Developing text-to-self connection

▶ Developing classification and sorting skills

▶ Knowing that people use their senses to find out about their surroundings and themselves and that different senses provide different information

259 *You Smell and Taste and Feel and See and Hear* **by Mary Murphy. New York: DK, 1997.**

A little dog describes the way he uses his five senses all day long.

LESSON IDEA: After reading the story, give each child a picture of an eye, a nose, a tongue, a hand, or an ear. Then list adjectives relating to the senses (such as *fuzzy, delicious, stinky, beautiful,* and *loud*) and ask the children who have the picture of the appropriate body part to hold it up.

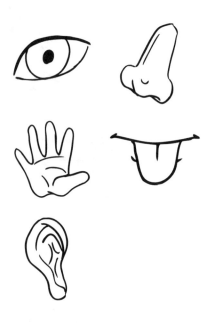

SKILLS

► Reading for literary experience

► Developing classification and sorting skills

► Knowing that people use their senses to find out about their surroundings and themselves and that different senses provide different information

260 *Senses at the Seashore* **by Shelley Rotner. Minneapolis, MN: Millbrook, 2006.**

A group of children experiences a day at the beach through their senses.

LESSON IDEA: After reading the story, write your own story as a class about senses at school. Following the pattern of the book, ask each child in turn to suggest something at school that he or she can see, hear, smell, touch, or taste.

SKILLS

► Reading for literary experience

► Appreciating nature

► Developing text-to-self connection

► Developing classification and sorting skills

► Knowing that people use their senses to find out about their surroundings and themselves and that different senses provide different information

261 *Rain* **by Manya Stojic. New York: Crown, 2000.**

The animals of the African savannah use their senses to determine that rain is coming.

LESSON IDEA: After reading the story, play a senses game. Make five cards and write the name of one of the senses on each. Turn the cards over and have each child take a turn choosing a card and naming something he or she can experience by using that sense (for example, smelling a flower or hearing music).

► Reading for literary experience

► Appreciating nature

► Developing text-to-self connection

► Developing classification and sorting skills

► Knowing that people use their senses to find out about their surroundings and themselves and that different senses provide different information

Fingerplays/Songs

262 Five Special Senses

5 special senses just for me. *(show 5 fingers)*
My eyes help me to see the tree. *(point to eyes)*
My nose helps me smell the flowers so sweet. *(point to nose)*
My ears help me hear the birds say "tweet." *(point to ears)*
My fingers touch the apple so smooth. *(point to fingers)*
My tongue helps me taste it, mm, mm, mm. *(point to tongue)*

▶ Recognizing rhyme
▶ Developing oral fluency
▶ Developing classification and sorting skills
▶ Knowing that people use their senses to find out about their surroundings and themselves and that different senses provide different information

263 I Have Five Senses

I have 2 eyes that help me see, *(point to eyes)*
2 ears to hear my mom call me, *(point to ears)*
1 little nose to smell flowers so sweet, *(point to nose)*
1 little tongue to taste the things I eat.*(point to mouth)*
10 little fingers help feel things smooth and rough. *(wiggle fingers)*
My 5 senses are just enough!

▶ Recognizing rhyme
▶ Developing oral fluency
▶ Developing classification and sorting skills
▶ Knowing that people use their senses to find out about their surroundings and themselves and that different senses provide different information

264 Five Senses Guessing Game

You have 5 senses, so let's have fun.
Listen to the clues and guess each one!

...

If something is sweet, or stinky, or yummy,
This sense helps me know it, though it might sound funny.
My little nose always does so well
Because it gives me my sense of . . . (smell!)

...

If something is silky, or smooth, or rough,
I know it with this sense, it's not so tough.
I feel with my fingers and skin and such,
And that's how I use my sense of . . . (touch!)

...

I like candy, I like fruit.
I like broccoli and I like soup.
My tongue helps me know which things to eat with haste.
I decide what I like with my sense of . . . (taste!)

...

I know if music is soft or loud,
If 1 person's talking, or maybe a crowd.
My ears tell me if something is moving away or if it's nearing,
And that is called my sense of . . . (hearing!)

...

▶ Recognizing rhyme
▶ Developing logic
▶ Developing classification and sorting skills
▶ Developing attention and response
▶ Knowing that people use their senses to find out about their surroundings and themselves and that different senses provide different information

Blue and red and green and brown,
My eyes show me things all over town.
Is it a red, yellow, or green traffic light?
I can find out with my sense of . . . (sight!)

265 My Five Senses

From *Circle Time Activities* by Georgiana Stewart. Kimbo Educational, 2004.

SKILLS

► Recognizing rhyme
► Developing oral fluency
► Knowing that people use their senses to find out about their surroundings and themselves and that different senses provide different information

Flannelboard/Prop Stories

266 What Sound Does It Make? Flannelboard

With my ears, I can hear
Things that are far and things that are near.
A fire truck just raced by,
Its siren let out a loud cry!
In my kitchen, pans and pots
Bang and clatter quite a lot.
When my doorbell starts to ring,
I hear it go "ding-a-ling."
The helicopter flies without a stop,
And its blades go chop-chop-chop.
The birds in the trees sound so sweet
When they sing tweet-tweet-tweet.
When we pet the kitty's fur,
She curls up and lets out a purr.
When it's time to sit back down,
I take my seat without a sound.

SKILLS

► Recognizing rhyme
► Developing classification and sorting skills
► Knowing that people use their senses to find out about their surroundings and themselves and that different senses provide different information

267 Touchy-Feely Bag Activity

Create a touchy-feely bag with an assortment of objects, some hard, some soft, some large, some small, and so on. Have the children put their hands in the bag and describe what they are feeling and see if they can guess the object before they pull it out to look at it. Some items that could go in the bag are a small car, a block, a ball, a scarf, or a small stuffed animal.

SKILLS

► Recognizing rhyme
► Developing oral fluency
► Developing logic
► Knowing that people use their senses to find out about their surroundings and themselves and that different senses provide different information

Writing Readiness Activity

268 Senses

Present an object to the class that can be seen, smelled, tasted, touched, and heard. (Good examples are an apple, a carrot, ice, or a rain stick.) Draw an eye, a nose, a tongue, a hand, and an ear across the top of the board. Work with the class to make a list of words under each picture that describe that sense's perception of the object. (For example, for an apple, you might write "red, shiny, round" under the eye.) Then have each child write a sentence for each sense using some of the words from the board.

SKILLS

► Practicing writing
► Developing vocabulary
► Developing classification and sorting skills
► Knowing that people use their senses to find out about their surroundings and themselves and that different senses provide different information

Math Activity

269 "Math Claps" Game

Play a clapping game in which the students must listen to and repeat the patterns you clap. Vary the number of claps each time you clap a pattern. Once the children have practiced repeating the pattern, build a pattern of several clap types in a series (for example, two fast claps followed by two slow claps), and ask the children to predict what kind of clap will come next. This activity engages multiple senses to identify and produce patterns.

SKILLS

► Understanding patterns
► Developing prediction skills

Takeaway Activity

270 My Texture Book Craft

Materials: a booklet for each child (from pattern), feathers, fake fur, sandpaper, plastic wrap, aluminum foil, crayons

Directions:

1. Glue the items onto the appropriate pages to create a texture book.
2. Decorate as desired.

SKILLS

► Knowing that people use their senses to find out about their surroundings and themselves and that different senses provide different information

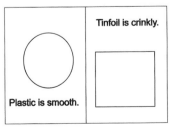

Library Skill–Building Game

271 Ordering Numbers

Preparation: Place a set of magnetic numbers in a bag. Then number forty index cards 1–40, writing the numbers large enough to fill the whole card. Stick a bit of adhesive magnet strip on the back of each card.

Activity: Begin by counting 1–20 with the class, and then explain that just like they learned how to put words in alphabetical order, they can also learn how to put numbers in order, which will help them find things in the library. Draw ten blank lines on the board. Then invite each child forward to reach into the number bag and try to guess the number he or she chooses from its shape alone. Then have the child pull the number out and place it on the board on the correct line. If a child has trouble, encourage him or her to think about whether the number is larger or smaller than other numbers already on the board. When you reach ten, put the magnets back into the bag and begin again until each child has had a turn. Then remove the magnets, erase the board, and tell the children they will have an even bigger challenge. Write the numbers 1–40 on the board in rows of ten, and show them how the number pattern works. Then give each child an index card. Have the children take turns coming forward to place their card over the correct number. Emphasize how thinking about number patterns will help them find the correct place.

SKILLS

► Counting
► Understanding numerical order
► Knowing that people use their senses to find out about their surroundings and themselves and that different senses provide different information

ASL Connection

272 Mirror Game

Teach the signs for DEAF and HEARING and discuss what each one means. Then invite the children to think about how, in sign language, we listen with our eyes rather than our ears. Have the students pair off and play a mirror game. Each pair should face one another. The leader should begin a movement, such as raising her hands above her head, and the "mirror" should copy the movement exactly. Encourage the leaders to move slowly enough that the mirrors can follow. After a few minutes, have the children switch so that everyone has a turn being the leader.

SKILLS

► Understanding basic American Sign Language
► Appreciating diversity
► Developing visual discrimination
► Developing motor skills
► Developing teamwork skills
► Developing attention and response

deaf

hearing

Spanish Connection

273 The Five Senses

Introduce the Spanish words for the senses and write them on the board:

Sight: *vista* (VEE-sta)
Smell: *olfato* (ol-FAH-toh)
Hearing: *oido* (oh-ee-DOH)
Touch: *toque* (TOH-kay)
Taste: *sabor* (sah-BORE)

Now play a game asking students to say in Spanish which of their senses they use for various activities. Remember more than one sense can often be used to answer the questions.

What sense do you use to listen to the radio?
What sense do you use to check for stinky sneakers?
What sense do you use when you are eating?
What sense do you use when you're at the beach?
What sense do you use to find out if something is too cold?

SKILLS

▶ Understanding basic Spanish vocabulary

▶ Developing oral fluency

▶ Developing classification and sorting skills

▶ Knowing that people use their senses to find out about their surroundings and themselves and that different senses provide different information

Recommend This!

You Can't Smell a Flower with Your Ear! by Joanna Cole. New York: Grosset and Dunlap, 1994.

Seeing by Helen Frost. Mankato, MN: Capstone, 2000.

Tasting by Helen Frost. Mankato, MN: Capstone, 2000.

Touching by Sharon Gordon. New York: Scholastic, 2001.

Nosy Rosie by Holly Keller. New York: HarperCollins, 2006.

19

The New Year

Kindergarten Speak

New Year's Day is celebrated on January 1 each year. New Year's Day provides us an opportunity to make new goals or resolutions for the year, a list of things we hope to accomplish. Many people stay up until midnight on December 31 to count down and welcome in the New Year.

Recommended Books

274 *My Love for You All Year Round* **by Susan L. Roth. New York: Dial, 2003.**

A mouse parent and child describe their love for each other in terms of the things they see and do all year long.

   LESSON IDEA: After reading the story, introduce the concept of adjectives (describing words). Go back through the book and ask the children to help make a list of other words to describe the objects and events associated with each month.

SKILLS

▶ Reading for literary experience

▶ Developing vocabulary

275 *Shante Keys and the New Year's Peas* **by Gail Piernas-Davenport. Morton Grove, IL: Whitman, 2007.**

A little girl visits everyone in her neighborhood trying to find black-eyed peas for her family's New Year's celebration and learns about New Year's traditions around the world. This wonderful multicultural story features an African American family and is a great discussion starter.

   LESSON IDEA: Read through the story again and have the class help you make a chart on the board identifying the features of the different traditions.

SKILLS

▶ Reading for literary experience

▶ Appreciating diversity

▶ Understanding other cultures

▶ Developing compare and contrast skills

▶ Organizing information

276 *Month by Month a Year Goes Round* **by Carol Diggory Shields. New York: Dutton, 1998.**

This rhyming story celebrates the fun things we do in each month of the year.

LESSON IDEA: After reading the story, invite the children to play a matching game. Write the names of the months on the board, and then pass out cards showing pictures or words about holidays and seasonal activities throughout the year. Invite each child to come forward and match his or her card to the correct month.

SKILLS

▶ Reading for literary experience

▶ Recognizing rhyme

▶ Developing classification and sorting skills

▶ Developing vocabulary

277 *This Next New Year* **by Janet S. Wong. New York: Farrar, Strauss and Giroux, 2000.**

A Korean American boy describes his family's celebration of Chinese New Year.

LESSON IDEA: After reading the story, explain that Chinese New Year is celebrated at different times each year, because it is based on the lunar year instead of the solar year. Using the background information provided in the book, write the number of days in a lunar year on the board alongside the number of days in a solar year. Ask the children to help you figure out which type of year has more days and which has fewer. Then repeat this process comparing lunar and solar months.

SKILLS

▶ Reading for literary experience

▶ Understanding other cultures

▶ Appreciating diversity

▶ Counting

▶ Developing compare and contrast skills

▶ Knowing basic patterns of the sun and moon

278 *First Night* **by Harriet Ziefert. New York: Putnam, 1999.**

Amanda Dade leads the New Year's parade in this rhyming story.

LESSON IDEA: After reading the story, tell the children they will identify the rhymes with their whole bodies. Read the story again, and tell the children that the first time they hear a rhyme, they should stand up. The next time they hear a rhyme, they should sit down. Continue through the end of the story.

SKILLS

▶ Reading for literary experience

▶ Recognizing rhyme

▶ Developing listening skills

Fingerplays/Songs

279 New Year's Eve

(Begin this rhyme in a very soft voice, then gradually increase your volume on the countdown, ending with a joyful shout on the last line.)

It's (current year), the very last night.
The sun's gone down, it's quiet tonight. *(press finger to lips)*
We watch and wait and stay up late. *(press palms together in anticipation)*
Soon it will be time to celebrate.
The hands are sweeping 'round the clock. *(circle index finger around an imaginary clock)*
Hear them move: tick tock tick tock.
It's 11:59 and then
We start to count backward from 10,
9, 8, 7, 6, 5, 4, 3, 2, 1 . . . *(hold up fingers to show numbers)*
Happy New Year! It's time for fun! *(throw imaginary confetti and blow a noisemaker if you have one)*

SKILLS

▶ Recognizing rhyme

▶ Counting

▶ Developing oral fluency

▶ Developing motor skills

▶ Comparing size and volume

280 Fireworks, Fireworks

Fireworks, fireworks, in the sky, *(throw fingers into the air to represent fireworks)*
Fireworks, fireworks, lights so high,

SKILLS

▶ Recognizing rhyme

▶ Developing oral fluency

▶ Developing motor skills

Fireworks, fireworks, boom boom boom, *(clap hands on each boom)*
The New Year will be here soon!

281 Happy New Year (to the tune of "Frère Jacques")

SKILLS
▶ Developing oral fluency
▶ Recognizing rhyme

Happy New Year, Happy New Year.
Celebrate, celebrate.
Goodbye to the old year,
Hello to the new year.
It will be great. It will be great.

282 New Year Song (to the tune of "My Darling Clementine")

SKILLS
▶ Recognizing rhyme
▶ Developing oral fluency

Happy New Year, Happy New Year
To our friends and family.
May this new year be a great year
For you and for me.

Flannelboard/Prop Stories

283 The New Year Flannelboard (to the tune of "Happy Birthday")

SKILL
▶ Developing oral fluency

(Make large numbers out of felt for the new and old years.)

2011, 2011
Goodbye to the old year, 2011.
2012, 2012,
Hello to the new year, 2012.

284 What Do I Need for My New Year's Eve Party? Game

SKILLS
▶ Developing logic
▶ Developing classification and sorting skills

Explain to the children that you are going to have a New Year's Eve party and want their help to pack all the things you need. Show each piece and ask if it is something you would use for a party on New Year's Eve. If so, place it on the board.

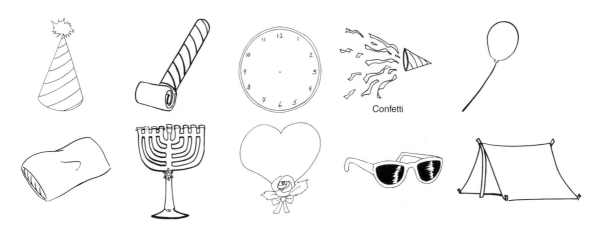

Confetti

Writing Readiness Activity

285 New Year's Resolutions

Introduce the concept of New Year's resolutions, and then work with the class to make a list of New Year's resolutions on the board. Some examples might be doing your chores, following directions, or returning library books on time.

SKILLS

▶ Developing text-to-self connection

▶ Developing vocabulary

Math Activity

286 Match the Fireworks

Go to http://images.google.com and search for "fireworks." Print a variety of pairs of fireworks pictures. Have the children match the various fireworks patterns.

SKILLS

▶ Understanding patterns

▶ Developing classification and sorting skills

Takeaway Activity

287 Countdown Clocks

Materials: a paper plate and a paper fastener for each child, pencils, construction paper, crayons, stickers, other decorating materials

Directions:

1. Cut out two arrows from construction paper, one slightly larger than the other. (These may be provided precut to students to save time.)
2. Push a pencil through the center of the paper plate to make a hole.
3. Fasten the two arrows (the clock hands) to the paper plate using the paper fastener.
4. Write the numbers 1–12 around the outside edge of the plate.
5. Decorate as desired.

SKILLS

▶ Telling time

▶ Developing fine motor skills

▶ Counting

Library Skill-Building Game

288 New Year Relay Race

Preparation: Select five picture books from various years. Make sure you pick some brand-new books as well as old favorites (such as *Where the Wild Things Are* by Maurice Sendak). Make several sentence strips with years on them, and place a magnetic strip on the back of each. Include

the new year
the previous year
the year(s) in which most of your students were born
the year you were born (if you are comfortable revealing it!)
the publication years of the five books you selected

SKILLS

▶ Understanding numerical order

▶ Developing teamwork skills

▶ Developing fine motor skills

▶ Understanding calendar time

Now make five or six sets of index cards for the relay race. Each set should include five cards showing a variety of years. Place each set in an envelope.

Set up a wide open space for the relay, with tables at one end and a space for the children to line up at the other end. You will also need a set of chopsticks for each team. (If you cannot get chopsticks, straws make a nice cheap alternative.)

Activity: Begin by asking the children what year it is. Show the sentence strips of the new year and the old year, and explain how the last number in the year usually gets bigger when the year changes. Ask the children which number is larger.

Now explain that each book tells you when it was published. Show the children where to find the publication date in books. Show a brand-new book and point out how its publication date matches the year on the board. Then ask if only new books are worth reading. Show an old favorite (such as *Where the Wild Things Are*) and ask the children to guess when it was published. Then show them the sentence strip with the book's publication year on it. Show the other books and repeat this process. Follow up by showing the children your year of birth, if desired.

Next, ask the children to help you put the numbers in order. Explain how to look at each number in the year in turn to put the years in the correct order, and emphasize that the children are following the number patterns just like they did with smaller numbers.

For the relay race, divide the class into teams of five. Give each team an envelope full of cards and a pair of chopsticks or straws. On your signal, the first child in line should pick up one card with the chopsticks (holding the chopsticks like a pencil) and carry it to the table. (The rule is that cards can *only* be carried with chopsticks. If a child drops a card, he or she should pick it up and put it in the chopsticks again before moving. For special needs students, you may wish to adapt the race: instead of carrying the cards with chopsticks, students have to balance the cards on their heads or on a flat hand.) When the child reaches the table, he or she should place the card on it and walk quickly back to the next child in line. When the last child has delivered the last card to the table, the entire team should go to the table and work together to put their year cards in the correct order. When the cards are in order, the whole team should call out "Happy New Year!" to signal you to check their work.

ASL Connection

289 Happy New Year (to the tune of "Good Night Ladies")

SKILLS

HAPPY NEW YEAR,
HAPPY NEW YEAR,
HAPPY NEW YEAR,
Today is NEW YEAR'S DAY.

...

Hello, new year, *(wave)*
Goodbye, old year, *(wave)*
HAPPY NEW YEAR,
Today is NEW YEAR'S DAY.

▶ Understanding basic American Sign Language
▶ Developing oral fluency

Spanish Connection

290 Countdown to the *Año Nuevo!*

Diez! (DEE-ez)
Nueve! (noo-WAY-vay)
Ocho! (OH-cho)
Siete! (se-ET-tay)
Seis! (SASE)
Cinco! (SINK-o)
Cuatro! (QUA-tro)
Tres! (TRACE)
Dos! (DOSE)
Uno! (OO-no)
Feliz año nuevo! (fell-EASE AHN-yo noo-WAY-vo)

SKILLS

▶ Understanding basic Spanish vocabulary

▶ Understanding other cultures

Recommend This!

A Year of Fun by Susan Blackaby. Minneapolis, MN: Picture Window Books, 2005.

Babar's Busy Year by Laurent de Brunhoff. New York: Abrams, 2005.

New Year's Day by Kathryn A. Imler. Chicago: Heinemann, 2003.

New Year's Day by David F. Marx. New York: Children's Press, 2000.

Just in Time for New Year's! by Karen Gray Ruelle. New York: Holiday House, 2004.

20
Winter

• •

Kindergarten Speak

Winter in the United States is during the months of December, January, and February. During these months, we have shorter days. Some days might be cold and snowy, and often the days are gray. Most trees are usually bare in the winter. What are some activities you do with your family in the winter?

Recommended Books

291 *Time to Sleep* **by Denise Fleming. New York: Henry Holt, 1997.**

Each animal hurries to tell another that winter is arriving, until the word spreads through the forest.

    LESSON IDEA: After reading the story, have the children help retell it using a flannelboard.

SKILLS

▶ Reading for literary experience

▶ Appreciating nature

▶ Understanding sequencing

292 *In the Snow: Who's Been Here?* **by Lindsay Barrett George. New York: Greenwillow, 1995.**

Two children find evidence of the presence of a variety of animals on a snowy day.

LESSON IDEA: After reading the story, discuss how people and animals leave tracks in the snow. Play a matching game to see if the children can match the animals to the tracks. Print out pictures of mammal and bird tracks from Beartracker's Animal Tracks Den (www .bear-tracker.com), as well as clip art or photos of the animals that made the tracks, and ask the children to guess which animal made which tracks.

293 *The Winter Visitors* **by Karel Hayes. Camden, ME: Down East, 2007.**

In this twist on the story of the three bears, a trio of bears enjoy themselves at a deserted summer house during the winter.

LESSON IDEA: Because this book has limited text, it is excellent for eliciting communication and description from the students. On each page, read the text, and then have each child take a turn giving you a sentence about one of the panels.

294 *A Little Bit of Winter* **by Paul Stewart. New York: HarperCollins, 1998.**

Forgetful Rabbit tries hard to keep his promise to his hibernating friend Hedgehog: that he will save him a little bit of winter.

LESSON IDEA: After reading the story, teach the children how to make paper snowflakes, and then let each child create a snowflake. This is a "little bit of winter" they can keep all year long. (Easy-to-follow instructions can be found at www.kinderart.com/seasons/snowflake9.shtml.)

295 *Sleep, Black Bear, Sleep* **by Jane Yolen and Heidi E. Y. Stemple. New York: HarperCollins, 2007.**

The lilting, rhyming text of this book celebrates animals that hibernate in the winter.

LESSON IDEA: After reading the story, play a sorting game. On the board, write "Hibernates" and "Does Not Hibernate" at the head of two columns. Then divide the children into groups of two or three, and give each group a card with a picture or the name of an animal on it. Group members should decide if their animal hibernates or not, and then place the card in the correct column. Follow up by discussing each list as a class.

Fingerplays/Songs

296 Snowman

Who has a black hat *(touch head)*
And a carrot nose, *(touch nose)*
2 eyes of coal *(touch eyes)*
And frozen toes? *(touch toes)*
Who wears a scarf *(toss imaginary scarf over shoulder)*
And has 2 sticks for arms and hands, *(hold arms out straight to sides)*
And doesn't even shiver *(shake head)*
As in the snow he stands?
It's our snowman!

297 Winter Transportation Guessing Game

SKILLS
▶ Recognizing rhyme
▶ Developing logic
▶ Developing attention and response

(Recite the following rhymes, pausing to allow the children to guess the final rhyme.)

There are so many ways to get around
When winter snow is on the ground.
Listen carefully to the clues and see
If you can guess these ways with me.

...

Snow day! School's out! Oh what fun!
I know what to bring when outside I run.
I wear my coat and boots and scarf of red
And slide down the snowy hill on my . . . (sled!)

...

The snow's piled high on the roads around town.
The cars can't move, and people can't get around.
I'll help clear the roads, and I'll tell you how:
I'll push the snow aside with my big . . . (snowplow!)

...

When winter snows fall from the sky,
These make me feel like I can fly.
I put on special boots when I wear these
And go down the slopes when wearing my . . . (skis!)

...

If I want to go far on a snowy night,
I need something to carry me over the snow so white.
To get to the North Pole so far away,
I'll hook up my reindeer to my . . . (sleigh!)

298 Snow, Snow, Snow (to the tune of "Three Blind Mice")

SKILLS
▶ Recognizing rhyme
▶ Developing oral fluency

Snow, snow, snow. I like snow.
Snow, snow, snow. I like snow.
I like how it flutters and blows on the breeze,
I like how it falls down and covers the trees,
I like when the icicles start to freeze,
'Cause I like snow.

299 I'm a Little Snowman (to the tune of "I'm a Little Teapot")

SKILLS
▶ Recognizing rhyme
▶ Developing oral fluency
▶ Developing motor skills

I'm a little snowman short and fat. *(hold hands out to sides)*
Here is my scarf and here is my hat. *(mime putting on scarf and hat)*
When the snow is falling, come and play. *(wiggle fingers to show snow falling)*
Sun comes up, I melt away. *(droop body as though melting)*

Flannelboard/Prop Stories

300 So Many Snowflakes Flannelboard Rhyme

- ▶ Counting
- ▶ Recognizing rhyme
- ▶ Developing oral fluency

So many snowflakes falling down
To the ground without a sound.
Count them with me, please, my friends:
1, 2, 3, 4, 5, 6, 7, 8, 9, 10!
10 little snowflakes danced with me
Whirling, twirling merrily.
Then the snowflakes melted in the sun:
10, 9, 8, 7, 6, 5, 4, 3, 2, 1!

301 Did You Ever See a Snowflake? (to the tune of "Did You Ever See a Laddie?")

- ▶ Recognizing rhyme
- ▶ Developing oral fluency
- ▶ Developing motor skills
- ▶ Recognizing shapes

(Pass out paper snowflakes from the pattern before the song.)

Did you ever see a snowflake, a snowflake, a snowflake,
Did you ever see a snowflake blow this way and that?
Blow this way and that way, and that way and this way,
Did you ever see a snowflake blow this way and that?

•••

Does your snowflake have a circle, a circle, a circle?
If your snowflake has a circle, then wave it like that.
Wave it out the side if your snowflake has a circle.
If your snowflake has a circle, then wave it like that.

•••

Does your snowflake have a square, a square, a square?
If your snowflake has a square, then wave it like that.
Wave it high in the air if your snowflake has a square.
If your snowflake has a square, then wave it like that.

•••

Does your snowflake have a triangle, a triangle, a triangle?
If your snowflake has a triangle, then wave it like that.
Wave it way down low if your snowflake has a triangle.
If your snowflake has a triangle, then wave it like that.

•••

Did you ever see a snowflake, a snowflake, a snowflake,
Did you ever see a snowflake blow this way and that?
Wave your snowflake in a circle, now a square, now a triangle.
Did you ever see a snowflake blow this way and that?

Writing Readiness Activity

302 Picturing Winter

Ask the children to describe their favorite part of winter. Have them draw a picture of something they like about winter, and then write what the activity is and why they like it.

SKILLS
► Practicing writing
► Developing text-to-self connection

Math Activity

303 Counting Snowflakes

Have an assortment of snowflakes available. Have the students count them by ones, twos, fives, and tens.

SKILL
► Counting

Takeaway Activity

304 Unique Name Snowflakes

Materials: a square piece of white paper for each child, scissors, crayons

Directions:

1. Fold the paper into quarters.
2. Fold the resulting square in half to make a triangle.
3. Write your name along one of the folded edges of the paper, taking up as much space as you can.
4. Cut along the contours of your name, making sure not to cut the folded corner.
5. Open up your snowflake. Each child's snowflake will be different.
6. Decorate as desired.

SKILLS
► Developing creativity
► Developing fine motor skills
► Appreciating diversity
► Writing one's name

Library Skill–Building Game

305 "Dewey" Like Winter?

Preparation: Print the Dewey Categories pages from this book's webpage and tape each page to a bookend so that it stands up straight. Pull thirty to forty nonfiction books about winter (enough for each child to have one and for you to have five or six to use for examples). The books should come from all areas of the nonfiction collection and can be peripherally related to winter if needed. (For example, you can select encyclopedias or books about snow, winter holidays, winter sports, animals in winter, snow-covered mountains, or snowmobiles.) Try to select books that make their subjects clear in the cover illustrations and titles. Tape a small piece of paper over the call number label of each book.

Activity: Place the bookends in a jumbled pile on a table. Ask the children if it would be easy or hard to find a specific picture in the pile. Then line the bookends up in order along a table, and point out how much easier it is to see them. Explain that a man named Melvil Dewey thought that the same thing was true of books—if they are all jumbled up, it's difficult to find the one you are looking for. So he invented a system to put books about the same things

SKILLS
► Understanding the parts of a book
► Developing classification and sorting skills
► Understanding that books can be classified using the Dewey Decimal Classification

together on the shelf. His system is called Dewey Decimal Classification. Explain that Dewey Decimal Classification is like a secret code to help you find the kind of books you want. Then ask the children if they would like to learn this secret code.

Show a nonfiction book, and point out that the call number has three numbers in the beginning, and sometimes more numbers after a decimal point. Tell the children that the three numbers at the beginning tell you which category the book is in. The very first number tells you the general category, and each number after that gives more details. Explain that there are ten general categories in the Dewey Decimal system, and then show each of the bookends and explain what the numbers and categories mean. Be sure to give several examples of the kinds of books that might fall into each category. Mention the topics of the books you have pulled without naming the books specifically.

Once you have explained the ten categories, ask the children where a book about winter might go. Then show five or six examples of winter books with specific subtopics, and ask the children to guess where they go. Place each book in front of the correct bookend and explain why it fits into that category. Then pass out a book to each child. The children should think about where the book belongs, and then, as you call each table or row forward, they should place their books in front of the bookend for that category.

When all the books have been placed, go through each pile and remove the papers covering the call numbers. Read the call number for each book aloud and ask the class if it is in the right spot. If not, discuss why and give hints until the students can tell you where it belongs.

If you like, you can create an additional motivator for the class by setting a class goal and reward before the game (for example: "Our goal is to have fifteen books in the right spot. If we reach that, then everyone can pick a bookmark."). Then keep a count on the board as you go through the piles together.

ASL Connection

306 Winter Signs for Wintertime

In the WINTERtime
When it starts to SNOW,
I put on my HAT and COAT
And I am ready to go!

SKILLS
▶ Understanding basic American Sign Language
▶ Recognizing rhyme
▶ Developing oral fluency

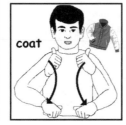

Spanish Connection

307 *Diez Copos de Nieve* (Ten Snowflakes)

Diez copos de nieve, (DEE-ez KO-pose day nee-AY-vay)
Uno, dos, tres copos de nieve, (OO-no, DOSE, TRACE)
Cuatro, cinco, seis copos de nieve, (QUA-tro, SINK-o, SASE)
Siete, ocho, nueve copos de nieve, (see-ET-tay, OH-cho, noo-WAY-vay)
Diez copos de nieve bailando alrededor de mi cabeza. (DEE-ez KO-pose day nee-AY-vay
    BAH-lahn-doh al-RAY-day-dor day mee kah-BAY-zah)

...

10 snowflakes,
1, 2, 3 snowflakes,
4, 5, 6 snowflakes,
7, 8, 9 snowflakes,
10 snowflakes dancing around my head.

Recommend This!

Footprints in the Snow by Cynthia Benjamin. New York: Scholastic, 1994.

Max and Mo Make a Snowman by Patricia Lakin. New York: Aladdin, 2007.

The Big Snowball by Wendy Cheyette Lewison. New York: Grosset and Dunlap, 2000.

Henry and Mudge and the Sparkle Days by Cynthia Rylant. New York: Simon and
    Schuster, 1998.

I Love Snow! by Hans Wilhelm. New York: Scholastic, 2006.

Please Let It Snow by Harriet Ziefert. New York: Sterling, 2006.

SKILLS

▶ Understanding basic Spanish vocabulary
▶ Counting

21
Health

- -

Kindergarten Speak

Our bodies are made to protect us and keep us healthy, but sometimes we still get sick. Usually when we get sick it is because of a germ. Germs are living things that we can't see with our eyes because they are so small. Germs are what cause us to get colds, sore throats, and other illnesses.

Recommended Books

308 *Throw Your Tooth on the Roof* **by Selby Beeler. New York: Houghton Mifflin, 1998.**

This book shares a variety of tooth traditions from around the world.

    LESSON IDEA: Before reading the book, show the cover and read the title to the children. Ask them to predict what the book is about and whether it is fiction or nonfiction. Then share a few traditions from different countries or regions. Ask the children what they think of the various traditions or if anyone has done something similar.

309 *I Lost My Tooth in Africa* **by Penda Diakite. New York: Scholastic, 2006.**

While visiting relatives in Africa, Amina loses her tooth. This book discusses a range of customs in the Mali culture, including receiving a chicken when you lose a tooth!

    LESSON IDEA: Ask the children to tell some of the things they noticed in the book that were different from what they experience here. Ask them what their traditions are when losing a tooth. Would they like to receive a chicken for losing a tooth? Did they notice any similarities to their life here (for example, playing games, sharing meals, etc.)?

SKILLS

▶ Developing prediction skills

▶ Reading for information

▶ Understanding other cultures

▶ Developing text-to-self connection

▶ Appreciating diversity

▶ Reading for literary experience

▶ Developing compare and contrast skills

▶ Understanding other cultures

▶ Appreciating diversity

310 *Germs! Germs! Germs!* **by Bobbi Katz. New York: Scholastic, 1996.**

Rhyming text and great pictures introduce children to ways germs enter the body and make us sick, and things we can do to protect ourselves against them.

LESSON IDEA: Have the children draw what they imagine a germ looks like. Then have the children either write or tell a story about their germ: what the germ's name is, how it makes us sick, and what we can do to stay well.

SKILLS

▶ Reading for information
▶ Developing creativity
▶ Practicing writing
▶ Knowing how to maintain and promote personal health

311 *Wash Your Hands!* **by Tony Ross. New York: Kane/Miller, 2000.**

Little Princess learns the many reasons she needs to wash her hands.

LESSON IDEA: Have the children help retell the story of Little Princess. Ask them prompting questions, such as these: "What was Little Princess playing in first that made her so dirty? What did she want to eat when the Queen reminded her to wash her hands?" Can the children think of any other things that would make their hands dirty? Write their list on the board for the class.

SKILLS

▶ Reading for literary experience
▶ Understanding sequencing
▶ Developing text-to-self connection
▶ Knowing how to maintain and promote personal health

312 *How Do Dinosaurs Get Well Soon?* **by Jane Yolen. New York: Scholastic, 2003.**

The reader is asked how dinosaurs behave when they get sick, and then examples of the right way to behave and get well soon are shown.

LESSON IDEA: After reading the book, ask the students to compare how the dinosaurs behaved in the beginning of the book and at the end. Prompt the class with questions such as:

What did the dinosaur do with his tissues at first?
What was the right way to use his tissues?

SKILLS

▶ Reading for literary experience
▶ Developing compare and contrast skills
▶ Developing oral fluency
▶ Knowing how to maintain and promote personal health

Fingerplays/Rhymes

313 **I Went to the Dentist**

I went to my dentist and this is what she said:
"Brush your teeth with your hand on your head!"
Brush-a, brush-a, brush-a, brush-a, brush-a, brush-a, brush!
I went to my dentist and she said to me:
"Brush your teeth with your hand on your knee!"
Brush-a, brush-a, brush-a, brush-a, brush-a, brush-a, brush!
I went to my dentist and she said, "Oh dear!
Brush your teeth with your hand on your ear!"
Brush-a, brush-a, brush-a, brush-a, brush-a, brush-a, brush!
I went to my dentist and she said something funny:
"Brush your teeth with your hand on your tummy!"
Brush-a, brush-a, brush-a, brush-a, brush-a, brush-a, brush!
I went to my dentist and what do you suppose?
She said, "Brush your teeth with your hand on your nose!"
Brush-a, brush-a, brush-a, brush-a, brush-a, brush-a, brush!

SKILLS

▶ Recognizing rhyme
▶ Understanding the parts of the body
▶ Developing motor skills
▶ Developing oral fluency
▶ Knowing how to maintain and promote personal health

314 Teeth (to the tune of "Shake Your Sillies Out")

You gotta brush, brush, brush your teeth each day.
Brush, brush, brush your teeth each day.
Brush, brush, brush your teeth each day,
To keep them healthy and clean.

...

You gotta floss, floss, floss your teeth each day . . .
You gotta visit, visit, visit the dentist . . .

SKILLS

► Developing oral fluency
► Knowing how to maintain and promote personal health

315 Tricks to Keep You Well

5 bad germs trying to make you sick,
You washed your hands and trapped them in a bubble,
What a great trick!
4 bad germs trying to make your friends sick,
You covered your nose when you sneezed,
What a great trick!
3 bad germs trying to make you sick,
You went to bed and got extra sleep,
What a great trick!
2 bad germs trying to make you sick,
You drank extra fluids,
What a great trick!
1 bad germ trying to make you sick,
You took all your medicine,
What a great trick!
No more germs trying to make you sick,
You run and play,
That's the best trick!

SKILLS

► Counting
► Recognizing rhyme
► Knowing how to maintain and promote personal health

316 Wash Your Hands (to the tune of "Clap, Clap, Clap Your Hands")

Wash, wash, wash your hands, wash along with me.
Wash, wash, wash your hands, wash along with me.
Wash them very slowly now, wash along with me.
Wash them very slowly now, wash along with me.
Wash them very quickly now, wash along with me.
Wash them very quickly now, wash along with me.
Wash the tops and bottoms now, wash along with me.
Wash the tops and bottoms now, wash along with me.
Wash, wash, wash your hands, wash along with me.
Wash, wash, wash your hands, wash along with me.

SKILLS

► Developing motor skills
► Developing oral fluency
► Developing compare and contrast skills
► Knowing how to maintain and promote personal health

Flannelboard/Prop Stories

317 Happy Teeth Flannelboard

Place the happy and sad teeth on the top of the flannelboard and show children the pictures one at a time, asking if the items are good and healthy for their teeth or if they are bad for their teeth. *See following page for patterns.*

SKILLS

► Developing compare and contrast skills
► Developing oral fluency
► Knowing how to maintain and promote personal health

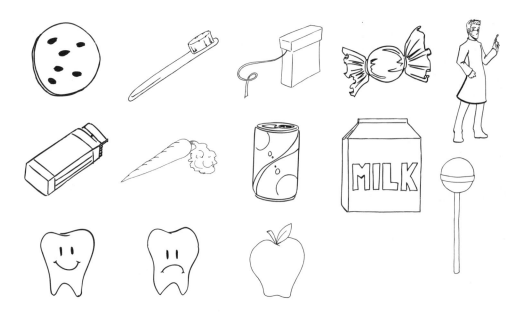

318 *Monkey Soup* **Flannelboard** (Based on the book by Louis Sachar. New York: Knopf, 1992.)

When Dad is sick, Mom decides to make him chicken soup. But his daughter wants to help him get well, too! She and her stuffed monkey decide to make their own soup to help Daddy get well. They find a laundry basket and in go all the ingredients, from bandages to tissues, that Dad needs to feel better. The little girl then stirs the soup with a wooden horse and serves it to Daddy, who loves it and feels better! Of course, when he sneezes (Aaaaahchoooo!) all the ingredients for the soup go everywhere!

SKILLS

▶ Developing text-to-self connection

▶ Understanding sequencing

Blanket

Napkin

Writing Readiness Activity

319 Washing Hands Poster

Ask the children how they can prevent the spread of germs by their hands. After discussing the steps for proper hand washing, have the children help create a poster of the steps using words or pictures or both.

Math Activity

320 Our Body Guessing Game

Ask the children to guess some fun facts about the human body. As you share each number, write it on the board. Then ask questions about which number is biggest, smallest, and so on.

How many bones are in your body? (206)
Which body part has the most bones? (hand, 27)
How many muscles are in your body? (660)
Which takes more muscles to do, smile or frown? (frown, 43; smile 17)
How many teeth will you have as an adult? (32)

Library Skill–Building Game

321 Toothbrush Call Numbers

Preparation: Copy the toothbrush pattern onto brightly colored construction paper or card stock to make enough toothbrushes for your class. Gather up nonfiction books and place them in order near your lesson area. (Make sure you have the same number of books as toothbrushes.) On each toothbrush, write a call number from the books. (If you plan to reuse this game, you may wish to laminate the toothbrushes and keep a list of the books you pull.)

Activity: Give each child a toothbrush and have him or her match it to the correct book on the cart. Guide children through the matching process by asking them what type of book the call number goes with and helping them find the numbers on the cart.

Takeaway Activity

322 Tooth Envelopes

Materials: envelopes, glue, crayons, a tooth chart for each child (available at www.ada .org/2930.aspx)

Directions:

1. Glue the chart onto the envelope.
2. Write your name on the envelope.

3. Decorate the envelope as desired.

4. Each time a tooth is lost, mark the corresponding tooth on the chart with the date it was lost.

ASL Connection

323 Staying Healthy Song (to the tune of "For He's a Jolly Good Fellow")

SKILLS

▶ Understanding basic American Sign Language

▶ Developing oral fluency

▶ Knowing how to maintain and promote personal health

We want to stay HEALTHY,
We want to stay HEALTHY,
We want to stay HEALTHY,
We don't want to get SICK.

...

We WASH OUR HANDS to stay HEALTHY . . .
We EAT good food to stay HEALTHY . . .
We get lots of SLEEP to stay HEALTHY . . .
We EXERCISE to stay HEALTHY . . .

health

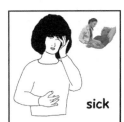
sick

wash hands

eat

sleep

exercise

Spanish Connection

324 Head, Shoulders, Knees, and Toes

SKILLS

▶ Understanding basic Spanish vocabulary

▶ Understanding the parts of the body

Introduce the vocabulary for the following body parts, and then sing the song.

Head: *cabeza* (kah-BAY-zah)
Shoulder: *hombro* (OM-bro)
Knee: *rodilla* (ro-DEE-yah)
Toe: *dedo del pie* (DAY-doh del PEE-ay)
Eye: *ojo* (O-ho)
Ear: *oreja* (o-RAY-hah)
Mouth: *boca* (BO-cah)
Nose: *nariz* (nar-EASE)

Head, Shoulders, Knees, and Toes

Cabeza, hombre, rodilla, dedo del pie, rodilla, dedo del pie,
Cabeza, hombre, rodilla, dedo del pie, rodilla, dedo del pie,
Ojo, oreja, boca, y nariz,
Cabeza, hombre, rodilla, dedo del pie, rodilla, dedo del pie.

...

Head, shoulders, knees, and toes, knees and toes,
Head, shoulders, knees, and toes, knees and toes,
Eyes and ears and mouth and nose,
Head, shoulders, knees, and toes, knees and toes.

Recommend This!

My Tooth Is About to Fall Out by Grace Maccarone. New York: Scholastic, 1995.
Germs by Judy Oetting. New York: Children's Press, 2006.
I Know Why I Brush My Teeth by Kate Rowan. Cambridge, MA: Candlewick Press, 1999.
Washing My Hands by Elizabeth Vogel. New York: PowerKids, 2001.
The Germ Busters by Rosemary Wells. New York: Hyperion, 2002.

22

Martin Luther King Jr./ Celebrating Diversity

Kindergarten Speak

What do you think diversity means? We are lucky to live in America, where people of all different colors, backgrounds, and religious beliefs are welcome. Throughout our country's history, men and women have fought to ensure freedom and rights for people of all races and religious beliefs. As a result, America has become a great "melting pot"!

Recommended Books

325 *I'm Like You, You're Like Me* by Cindy Gainer. Minneapolis, MN: Free Spirit, 1998.

Children's differences are celebrated, as well as their similarities. This book encourages tolerance and acceptance of diversity.

LESSON IDEA: Make a chart on the chalkboard and ask the children to list some of the differences and similarities mentioned in the book.

SKILLS

▶ Appreciating diversity
▶ Reading for literary experience
▶ Organizing information

326 *All the Colors of the Earth* by Sheila Hamanaka. New York: Morrow, 1994.

Children come in all the colors of the earth and sky and sea. In this celebration of our diversity, the author demonstrates that our skin and hair come in all the wonderful colors found in nature and that we love them all.

LESSON IDEA: Discuss the book's use of similes. A simile is a figure of speech comparing two unlike things, often introduced with the word "like" or "as." Have the children think of something that they can compare with one of their own characteristics (for example, "My hair is as dark as a milk chocolate candy bar"). Ask them to write down their creative expressions.

SKILLS

▶ Reading for literary experience
▶ Practicing writing
▶ Developing vocabulary
▶ Developing text-to-self connection

327 *Martin Luther King Jr. Day* **by Margaret McNamara. New York: Aladdin, 2007.**

When a class learns about Martin Luther King Jr.'s dreams for America, the teacher encourages the students to write what their dreams for the future are.

   LESSON IDEA: Discuss Martin Luther King Jr.'s "I Have a Dream" speech. Ask the children to draw a picture and write about their dreams for the world's future, too. Have the children share their dreams with the class.

SKILLS
- ▶ Reading for literary experience
- ▶ Practicing writing
- ▶ Developing text-to-self connection

328 *Singing for Dr. King* **by Angela Medearis. New York: Scholastic, 2004.**

In 1965, a little girl named Sheyann hears Dr. Martin Luther King Jr. speak and wants to help Dr. King and others as they work for equal rights for African Americans in the South.

   LESSON IDEA: Explain to the class that Dr. King and other Americans worked for civil rights. Explain that civil rights are rights of personal liberty and are based on the belief that every American, regardless of color, should have the same rights under the law. Ask the children why they think civil rights are important and how they can help ensure that all children will grow up with the same opportunities.

SKILLS
- ▶ Reading for literary experience
- ▶ Developing text-to-self connection
- ▶ Understanding how democratic values came to be and are exemplified

329 *It's Okay to Be Different* **by Todd Parr. New York: Little, Brown, 2001.**

The book stresses that it's okay to be different and uses colorful illustrations to demonstrate the many ways we are all different.

   LESSON IDEA: Ask the children if they can think of something that makes them different from their classmates. Remember to stress that *different* doesn't mean "strange" or "weird." We are all unique and have special qualities. Maybe some are really good at riding bikes or dancing or drawing. There are many wonderful things that make us different! Have the children make a picture and write about what they think makes them unique and special.

- ▶ Appreciating diversity
- ▶ Practicing writing
- ▶ Developing text-to-self connection

Fingerplays/Rhymes

330 Martin Luther King Jr. Day (to the tune of "Do You Know the Muffin Man?")

Do you know Martin Luther King? Martin Luther King? Martin Luther King?
Do you know Martin Luther King? We celebrate him today.
He believed everyone was equal, everyone was equal, everyone was equal.
He believed everyone was equal, and the world should be that way.
He said it doesn't matter if you're black or white, if you're black or white, if you're black
   or white.
He said it doesn't matter if you're black or white, we should all be friends.
Martin Luther King was a great man, a great man, a great man.
Martin Luther King was a great man, we celebrate him today.

SKILLS
- ▶ Developing oral fluency
- ▶ Understanding how democratic values came to be and are exemplified

331 Kids Around the World Wake Up (to the tune of "When Ducks Wake Up in the Morning")

When French kids wake up in the morning, they always say good day.
But when French kids wake up in the morning, they say it the French way:
"Bonjour!" (bon-JOOR) "Bonjour!" That is what they say.

...

SKILLS
- ▶ Understanding basic Spanish vocabulary
- ▶ Understanding basic French vocabulary
- ▶ Understanding basic Chinese vocabulary
- ▶ Developing oral fluency
- ▶ Appreciating diversity

When Spanish kids wake up in the morning, they always say good day.
But when Spanish kids wake up in the morning, they say it the Spanish way:
"Buenos días!" (BWAY-nos DEE-as) "Buenos días!" That is what they say.

...

When Chinese kids wake up in the morning, they always say good day.
But when Chinese kids wake up in the morning, they say it the Chinese way:
"Ni hao!" (knee how) "Ni hao!" That is what they say.

332 The World Is Like a Rainbow

SKILLS

▶ Developing oral fluency
▶ Appreciating diversity
▶ Recognizing rhyme

The world is like a rainbow
Made up of different colors.
But we are all beautiful
And should respect each other.
It doesn't matter if your skin
Is black or tan or white
Or purple polka dots or plaid
Or orange with yellow stripes!
Every person is a person,
And, in the end,
Every person is a person
Who could be your friend!

333 We Are All Different (to the tune of "Bumpin' Up and Down in My Little Red Wagon")

SKILLS

▶ Developing oral fluency
▶ Appreciating diversity

We are all different,
We are all different,
We are all different,
. . . but we're all still people.

...

Some of us have brown or white skin . . .
Some of us have straight or curly hair . . .
Some of us have blue or brown eyes . . .

Flannelboard/Prop Stories

334 "I Have a Dream" Flannelboard Game

SKILLS

▶ Developing classification and sorting skills
▶ Appreciating diversity

Discuss with the children the differences between wants and needs. We should realize what the essential needs are in order to have a good quality of life.

Show each item to the children and ask them if it is an essential need or a want.

When they've finished sorting, create a sentence using the essential needs (for example: "I have a dream that all children will learn how to read, will have enough food to eat, will have clothing, will live in good homes, and will grow up able to find a job they love.").

See following page for patterns.

335 *Lucy's Picture* **Flannelboard Story**

(Based on the book by Nicola Moon. New York: Dial, 1994.)

Lucy can't wait to see her grandfather after school, and she decides to make a special picture for him. However, her picture needs to be an extra-special one that her grandfather can see with his fingers, because he is blind. The text of the story never mentions the grandfather's blindness, allowing children to piece together the clues from the construction of Lucy's picture and the illustrations showing her grandfather with a Seeing Eye dog. This gentle story is a great way to remind students that embracing diversity means accepting people of all backgrounds and abilities. In addition to the flannelboard pieces from the patterns, cut out a large, white rectangle of felt to represent Lucy's paper (or just use paper if you are making a magnetboard). Use a variety of scraps of fabric to create the picture as Lucy does in the book.

SKILLS

▶ Appreciating diversity
▶ Developing logic

Juice cup

Writing Readiness Activity

336 Dream Quilt

Remind children that all types of people make up the world and that we each have different dreams. Ask the children to draw a picture and write about what they want to be when they grow up—what their dream is. Then put each child's picture on bulletin board paper to create a dream quilt for the class.

SKILLS
- ▶ Developing text-to-self connection
- ▶ Appreciating diversity
- ▶ Practicing writing

Math Activity

337 Signs of Inequality

Talk to the children about how they would feel if they were not allowed to go to the same schools, restaurants, swimming pools, beaches, or even restrooms as other children because of their color. Then divide the children into groups according to the color shirt they are wearing, sending them to different parts of the room. Count the students in each group and ask questions about the size of each group. Which group is largest? Which is smallest? Then ask questions about how the groupings made them feel. Were they divided from their friends? How did they feel? Were some of the groups really small? Did they feel that they were left out? Was anyone alone? If so, how did that person feel? Did the children feel it was fair to be separated based on shirt color?

SKILLS
- ▶ Appreciating diversity
- ▶ Counting
- ▶ Understanding the terms *more than, less than,* and *same as* for comparing quantity

Takeaway Activity

338 Diversity Wreath

Materials: precut hands in a variety of colors, crayons, paper plates

Directions:

1. Give each child three or four hands. On each hand the children should write something about themselves, such as "I play baseball," "I dance," or "I like to read."
2. Have the children trade hands with others in the class.
3. Glue the hands along the outside of the paper plate, fingers outward. This will help show children that people are similar in many ways, but we are also unique and enjoy different things.

SKILL
- ▶ Appreciating diversity

Library Skill–Building Game

339 Call Number Card Game

Preparation: Make five or six sets of index cards showing simple call numbers. Each set should have thirty-six cards, each with a different call number on it. On eight cards in each set, draw a star above the call number.

Activity: Review how nonfiction call numbers are formed. Write six different call numbers on the board and have the class help you put them in order. Explain that it's important to

SKILLS
- ▶ Understanding numerical order
- ▶ Developing teamwork skills
- ▶ Developing attention and response

understand how the numbers go in order because knowing this will help you find the book you are looking for more quickly.

Form teams of six students each. Give each team a set of cards. Instruct one child in each team to deal out six cards to each player. The dealer should then put a card down in the middle of the table. The student to his or her right should then put down a card showing a call number that comes *after* the dealer's. Cards with a star on them can be used at any time, and the next player must put down a card that comes after the call number on the starred card. If a player does not have a starred card or a card with a higher call number, he or she loses a turn. The first player to run out of cards wins.

ASL Connection

340 Same and Different Game

SKILLS
► Understanding basic American Sign Language
► Appreciating diversity

Teach the children the signs for SAME and DIFFERENT. (When signing SAME, the sign should be produced so that the thumb and pinkie point to the two things that are the same as the sign moves back and forth.) Then make a statement about yourself, such as "I have brown eyes," or "I am a grown-up." If the students agree that the statement is true about themselves as well, they should sign SAME. If the statement is not true, then they should sign DIFFERENT. Go around the room and have each child say something about himself or herself, and the other children should respond by signing whether that is a way they are the SAME or a way they are DIFFERENT. Statements could involve appearance, number of brothers and sisters, pets, favorite colors, activities the children like, favorite foods, or favorite stories.

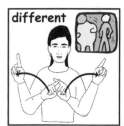

Spanish Connection

341 Population Change

SKILL
► Appreciating diversity

The United States Census Bureau projects that by the year 2042, minorities will make up more than 50 percent of the U.S. population. That means that five out of every ten people in the United States will identify themselves as Hispanic, black, Asian, American Indian, Native Hawaiian, Pacific Islander, or mixed race. Of these groups, the Hispanic population is the fastest-growing. It now makes up about 15 percent of the population, but is anticipated to become 30 percent of the population. The term *Hispanic* describes persons who came to the United States from Mexico, Puerto Rico, Cuba, or Central or South America.

Ask the children such questions as these (altering as needed based on your community's current make-up):

Can you think of ways that this change in our population will affect the area you live in?
Will the students in your school look different?

Will there be a change in your neighborhood?
Will the grocery stores carry different foods?
Will malls offer different clothes, or will entertainment change?

Recommend This!

Whoever You Are by Mem Fox. New York: Harcourt, 1997.

A Lesson for Martin Luther King, Jr. by Denise Lewis Patrick. New York: Aladdin, 2003.

What Can You Do? A Book about Discovering What You Do Well by Shelley Rotner and Sheila Kelly. Brookfield, CT: Millbrook, 2001.

The Skin You Live In by Michael Tyler. Chicago: Chicago Children's Museum, 2005.

Max Celebrates Martin Luther King Jr. Day by Adria F. Worsham. Minneapolis, MN: Picture Window, 2009.

23

The 100th Day of School

Kindergarten Speak

Remember in August when you came to school on your very first day? Can you believe 100 days have passed? One hundred seemed like such a big number when you first started to learn to count, but now you know how easy it really is. You can count by ones, fives, and tens to 100. You've finished 100 days of school, and the school year will be over in less than 100 days.

Recommended Books

342 *Henry's 100 Days of Kindergarten* **by Nancy Carlson. New York: Penguin, 2004.**

As Henry's class prepares to celebrate its 100th day of kindergarten, Henry brings in his grandmother, who is 100 years old!

    LESSON IDEA: Ask the children if they know anyone who is 100 years old. Ask them to imagine how things may have changed in 100 years. Discuss with them the changes in school: school buses, pencils, paper, and so on.

343 *The 100th Day of School* **by Brenda Haugen. New York: Picture Window, 2004.**

A class prepares to celebrate 100 days of school.

    LESSON IDEA: Host a 100th-day writing Olympics. Have the students write as many words as they can in 100 seconds.

SKILLS

▶ Reading for literary experience

▶ Counting

▶ Understanding calendar time

▶ Developing text-to-self connection

▶ Reading for literary experience

▶ Practicing writing

▶ Counting

344 *Kindergarten Count to 100* by Jacqueline Rogers. New York: Scholastic, 2004.

The children are busy counting their way through the day with a variety of activities shown.

    LESSON IDEA: Count cups in groups of five or ten, then count by fives or tens to 100. Using 100 paper cups, have the class build a cup castle, allowing each student to take a turn adding a few cups.

SKILLS

► Reading for literary experience

► Counting

345 *Miss Bindergarten Celebrates the 100th Day of Kindergarten* by Joseph Slate. New York: Puffin, 1998.

As Miss Bindergarten prepares for the 100th Day of Kindergarten, her students do, too.

    LESSON IDEA: Ask students to draw a picture of a food they could eat 100 of and write about why.

SKILLS

► Reading for literary experience

► Developing text-to-self connection

► Practicing writing

346 *Emily's First 100 Days of School* by Rosemary Wells. New York: Hyperion, 2000.

Emily and her friends describe everything they have done on each day of school, from day 1 to day 100.

    LESSON IDEA: Ask the children to share something special they remember doing since they started school. Was there a special lesson or activity? Have each child draw a picture of what he or she liked the most and write a sentence about it.

► Reading for literary experience

► Practicing writing

► Developing text-to-self connection

Fingerplays/Rhymes

347 My First 100 Days

When I first came to school,
I was so scared and shy.
Now I look back,
And can't understand why!
I've made lots of friends,
Stan and Lisa and Jay.
I've learned new things,
And still have time to play!
100 days have passed,
And I can truly say,
School is great,
Each and every day!

SKILLS

► Recognizing rhyme

► Developing oral fluency

348 One Hundred Day Shimmy

100 day shimmy
And 100 day shake. *(shake whole body)*
100 day jump
And 100 day quake. *(jump big up and down)*
100 day stretch
And 100 day yawn. *(stretch and yawn)*
100 day squat
And 100 days gone! *(sit down and cheer)*

SKILLS

► Recognizing rhyme

► Developing motor skills

► Developing oral fluency

349 One Hundred Days of School (to the tune of "Bumpin' Up and Down in My Little Red Wagon")

SKILL

▶ Developing oral fluency

We've been in school for 100 days,
We've been in school for 100 days,
We've been in school for 100 days,
Isn't that fantastic!

...

We've learned to read and write . . .
We've learned to cut and count . . .

350 We Can Count

SKILLS

▶ Recognizing rhyme
▶ Developing oral fluency

We can count to 100,
Oh what a day!
We can count to 100,
In so many ways.
We can count by 1s,
5s, and 10s,
We can count to 100,
Again and again.
We can count on our hands,
We can count on our toes,
We can count to 100
And now everyone knows.

Flannelboard/Prop Stories

351 100th Day S'mores Flannelboard

SKILL

▶ Counting

Materials: a pyramid of ten Hershey kisses, two piles of five marshmallows, two graham crackers

Directions:

1. Have children help you count to 100 using a variety of techniques. Count by ones (the graham crackers), fives (the marshmallows), and tens (Hershey kisses).
2. After doing some delicious counting, invite children to help create s'mores on the flannelboard, and count how many items make up each s'more. (Typically it would be seventeen if you use two graham crackers, ten Hershey kisses, and five marshmallows. However, if you have enough time and enough supplies, allow children to come up with their own crazy combinations and practice their adding skills.)

"S'mores, s'mores, we all need more! Count to make a treat we adore!"

352 100th Day Memories Flannelboard Story

When the bus arrived on that 1st day
We were excited and scared and some were afraid.
We entered the school
And found our desks and our teacher.
We met new friends,
And our class pet, Creature.
As the days went by, we discovered learning was fun.
The best days were when we had recess in the sun.
We learned about autumn, pumpkins, and Thanksgiving,
Gingerbread men and holiday giving.
100 days have passed; we have less left, not more.
We've learned to love school and our teacher we adore.

Writing Readiness Activity

353 100 Things to Eat

Make a list of 100 fun things to eat. Ask the children to list their favorite foods until you reach 100 items. As an extension to this activity, ask the children to write what their favorite foods are and why. Or have the children pick their favorite foods off the list to create an entirely new food. What would they name their creation?

Math Activity

354 100 Miles from Here

Go to http://maps.google.com and type in the location of your school. In the search bar, type in "100 miles north" to see what is 100 miles north of you. (Often you will have an option to select "rep0100mileradius," which will allow you to see locations 100 miles in all directions at once.) Repeat going in different directions as desired. As you discover places that are 100 miles from you, ask the children if they have been to any of those locations. This activity can also be done using a traditional map.

Takeaway Activity

355 100th Day Necklace

Materials: beads, yarn

Directions:

1. Give children a variety of colored beads and instruct each child to gather 100. Encourage them to count out the beads using one of the techniques they learned this year in school—possibly gathering different colors in groups of ten.
2. Let the children string the beads on a piece of yarn and tie securely.

Library Skill–Building Game

356 Not-So-Ordinary Ordinals

Preparation: Print out the Not-So-Ordinary Ordinals worksheet from this book's webpage. Copy one for each student. Cut the directions into strips and place the strips into envelopes, one envelope per child.

Activity: Write the following phrases on the board, and have the children help you read them. (They are purposefully presented here in a different order than they will be seen in the activity, which will help students practice using ordinal numbers.)

Nod your head.
Clap your hands.
Wiggle.
Meow like a cat.
Bark like a dog.
Touch your nose.
Fold your hands together.
Jump up and down.
Stand up.
Sit down.

Next, write the numbers 1–10 in a column on the board. Tell the children that when we are following steps in order, we use a different form of these numbers. Next to the number 1, write *1st* and then *first*. Complete the chart, asking the children to help you fill in each row.

When you have filled in the chart, pass out the envelopes. Each child should put the directions in order, using the ordinal number chart on the board as a guide if needed. Only when a child has all the directions lined up in order should he or she begin to follow them. (Prepare for a very silly school library with all the meowing and barking that is their reward for completing the activity!)

ASL Connection

357 One Hundred Days of School (to the tune of "The Farmer in the Dell")

ONE HUNDRED DAYS of SCHOOL,
ONE HUNDRED DAYS of SCHOOL,
Today's the day we celebrate
ONE HUNDRED DAYS of SCHOOL.

...

ONE HUNDRED DAYS of FRIENDS . . .
ONE HUNDRED DAYS of FUN . . .

one hundred | day | school | friend | fun

Spanish Connection

358 Going to School

Introduce the following Spanish vocabulary, and then give the clues below and ask the children which school item they refer to.

School: *escuela* (es-CWAY-la)
Desk: *el escritorio* (el es-cree-TOH-ree-oh)
Pencil: *el lapis* (el LA-pis)
Notebook: *el cuaderno* (el cwah-DAIR-no)

Clues:

I go here to learn.
This is where we sit when we go to *escuela*.
We use this to write with.
We write in these.

Recommend This!

100 Days of Fun at School by Janet Craig. New York: Scholastic, 1998.

100 Days of School by Trudy Harris. Brookfield, CT: Millbrook, 1999.

100th Day of School by Melissa Schiller. New York: Children's Press, 2003.

The 100th Day of School by Matt Mitter. Pleasantville, NY: Reader's Digest, 2003.

100 School Days by Anne Rockwell. New York: HarperCollins, 2002.

The Night Before the 100th Day of School by Natasha Wing. New York: Grosset and Dunlap, 2005.

24
Transportation

• •

Kindergarten Speak

There are a lot of different ways to get from one place to another. We can walk, and that works well for short distances. However, if you have to travel out of your neighborhood, it's often easier to get around using different types of transportation. You probably use a lot of different types of transportation depending on how far you have to go. Bikes, cars, planes, trucks, and trains are all types of transportation.

Recommended Books

359 ***Duck in the Truck*** **by Jez Alborough. New York: HarperCollins, 1999.**

This rhyming tale tells the story of Duck, who while driving his truck gets stuck in the muck, and the animals who help him.

    LESSON IDEA: Help children develop an understanding of text patterns and sequencing. Have them help you retell the story using pictures of the characters and prompting them with questions such as:

> What was Duck driving?
> Why did Duck get stuck in the muck?
> Which animal first helped Duck with the truck?
> What animal came upon them and helped next?
> Which animal approached from the water and helped them next?
> What happened when the truck got loose?

SKILLS

▶ Reading for literary experience
▶ Understanding sequencing
▶ Recognizing rhyme
▶ Developing oral fluency

360 *Dig Dig Digging* **by Margaret Mayo. New York: Henry Holt, 2002.**

A range of vehicles is explored, along with their sounds and what they do.

LESSON IDEA: Explain to the students that onomatopoeia is the use of a word or phrase that imitates the sound it is describing. Read through the story again with the children. Can they pick out the onomatopoeia on each page?

SKILLS

- ▶ Reading for literary experience
- ▶ Developing vocabulary
- ▶ Developing listening skills
- ▶ Knowing basic information about transportation

361 *Little Blue Truck* **by Alice Schertle. New York: Harcourt, 2008.**

In this rhyming tale, Little Blue Truck and the farm animals are all friendly, unlike the big dump truck. But when the dump truck gets stuck, he learns a lesson about friendship and lending a helping hand from Little Blue Truck and the animals.

LESSON IDEA: Ask the class if they can think of a time when they accomplished something because they worked together with others. Using their prior experience, have the children draw a picture and write about a time when they worked together with others to accomplish something.

- ▶ Reading for literary experience
- ▶ Developing text-to-self connection
- ▶ Practicing writing
- ▶ Developing creativity
- ▶ Knowing basic information about transportation

362 *I Love Trucks*! **by Philemon Sturges. New York: HarperCollins, 1999.**

A little boy names all of his favorite trucks, with details about what each truck does.

LESSON IDEA: Print pictures of each truck and match each to its beginning letter sound.

- ▶ Reading for literary experience
- ▶ Developing listening skills
- ▶ Associating sounds with letters
- ▶ Knowing the alphabet
- ▶ Knowing basic information about transportation

363 *Freight Train* **by Harriet Ziefert. New York: Orchard, 2000.**

A little boy shares his excitement for the train as it comes chugging through the town.

LESSON IDEA: The train in *Freight Train* carries a lot of interesting animals and items. Ask the children to draw a picture and write about what they think a train may carry.

- ▶ Reading for literary experience
- ▶ Developing logic
- ▶ Developing creativity
- ▶ Knowing basic information about transportation
- ▶ Practicing writing

Fingerplays/Rhymes

364 **At the Construction Site** (to the tune of "The Wheels on the Bus")

The hook on the crane goes up and down, up and down, up and down,
The hook on the crane goes up and down at the construction site.

...

The shovel on the digger goes dig, dig, dig . . .
The barrel on the mixer goes 'round and 'round . . .
The dumper on the dump truck goes dump, dump, dump . . .

SKILLS

- ▶ Developing oral fluency
- ▶ Developing motor skills
- ▶ Recognizing rhyme
- ▶ Knowing basic information about transportation

365 Drive the Car (to the tune of "Row, Row, Row Your Boat")

Drive, drive, drive the car,
Driving to and fro.
When the light is green we know
That now it's time to go.
Drive, drive, drive the car,
Driving through the town.
When the light is yellow we know
That it's time to slow down.
Drive, drive, drive the car,
Driving to the shop.
When the light is red we know
That now it's time to stop.

SKILLS

▶ Developing oral fluency
▶ Recognizing rhyme
▶ Developing motor skills
▶ Knowing basic information about transportation
▶ Developing compare and contrast skills

366 Helicopter

Helicopter going up, *(stand up)*
Helicopter going down, *(squat down)*
Helicopter turning, turning all around. *(turn around)*
Helicopter going left, *(move left)*
Helicopter going right, *(move right)*
Helicopter going up, out of sight. *(reach up high on tiptoes)*

SKILLS

▶ Developing oral fluency
▶ Recognizing rhyme
▶ Developing motor skills
▶ Developing compare and contrast skills

367 Vehicle Guessing Game

I have headlights and a steering wheel,
I take you near and far,
My horn says "honk!" and my engine says "vroom!"
Hop in! I am a . . . (car).

•••

I pull my cars along the rails,
I chug through sun or rain.
My smokestack lets out a "woo-woo!"
Hop aboard! I am a . . . (train).

•••

I'll take you soaring in the sky,
We'll reach the clouds and soon!
I come in bright colors, with a basket for you.
Hop in! I am a . . . (balloon).

•••

I have 2 wheels and a handlebar,
And pedals you will like.
You can ride me down the road.
Hop on! I am a . . . (bike).

•••

I have wings and an engine that roars.
My comfy cabins contain
Lots of seats where passengers sit.
Hop aboard! I am a . . . (plane).

•••

SKILLS

▶ Developing oral fluency
▶ Developing logic
▶ Developing attention and response
▶ Recognizing rhyme
▶ Knowing basic information about transportation

I have a great big cab and a loud horn,
Big wheels so I won't get stuck,
A giant trailer to carry big loads.
Hop aboard! I am a . . . (truck).

Flannelboard/Prop Stories

368 My Dump Truck, Fred Flannelboard Story

If I had a dump truck, I would name it Fred. Fred and I would go everywhere together, and everyone would get out of the way when they saw us coming! Fred would eat dinner with my family every night, and I would teach him good table manners. I'd make sure he brushed his teeth every night, and put his nightcap on, and then I'd tuck him into bed right next to me. In the morning I would make sure he ate a healthy breakfast of gravel cereal. I'd even hang a stocking up for him on Christmas Eve, but it would have to be pretty big! In the wintertime I would make sure Fred bundled up warm, and in the summer I would remind him to wear his sunglasses and hat. But no matter what, I would know that I loved Fred, and Fred loved me!

SKILLS

▶ Developing oral fluency

▶ Developing listening skills

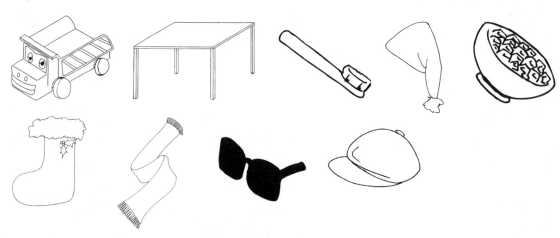

369 What Type of Transportation Do I Need? Game

SKILLS

▶ Developing oral fluency

▶ Developing logic

▶ Knowing basic information about transportation

Ask the students what type of transportation they would need if they were doing the following. (Some questions have more than one possible answer.)

I'm going to my friend Billy's. He lives two houses down from me. How should I get there?

We're going on a family vacation. I'm so excited! We're going to an island and will be crossing the ocean. How should I get there?

It's a great day and I'm going to play with my friends. We'll be going around the neighborhood. How should I get there?

I live in a city. We don't own cars here. I need to go across town. How should I get there?

We're going on vacation, but don't want to drive. How should I get there?

I live in a city. We don't own cars here. I need to go a few blocks. How should I get there?

Writing Readiness Activity

370 Transportation Imagination

Ask the children to use their imaginations and think of a new type of transportation—maybe something that doesn't use gas or something that could run on grass. Have them draw a picture of their new vehicle and write what the vehicle's name is and how it runs.

SKILLS

▶ Developing creativity
▶ Practicing writing
▶ Knowing basic information about transportation

Math Activity

371 Counting Vehicles

Make a graph of the types of vehicles children in your class have traveled in. Along the bottom of a posterboard or chalkboard, write the words *car, train, airplane, boat, truck,* and *fire engine.* After all the children have indicated which vehicles they have traveled in, fill in the columns. Ask the children which vehicle most of them have been in and which vehicle the fewest have been in.

SKILLS

▶ Developing oral fluency
▶ Understanding that graphs represent information
▶ Counting
▶ Understanding the terms more than, less than, and same as for comparing quantity
▶ Knowing basic information about transportation

Library Skill–Building Game

372 Sorting Simon Says

Preparation: Pull a variety of fiction and nonfiction books about transportation. Make sure you have enough for each child to have a book.

Activity: Review the difference between fiction and nonfiction. Show examples of call numbers of each type and ask the children to identify what kind of book they go with. Then give a book to each child. Each child should look at the call number and identify whether the book is fiction or nonfiction. Then give a series of silly directions from the following list, each preceded by "If your book is fiction . . ." or "If your book is nonfiction . . .". After every three or four directions, instruct the children to exchange books with a neighbor.

Hold your book up in the air.
Put your book on your chair.
Put your book on your head.

SKILLS

▶ Following directions
▶ Developing classification and sorting skills
▶ Developing motor skills
▶ Developing attention and response
▶ Understanding the concept of fiction
▶ Understanding the concept of nonfiction

Put your book on your belly.
Touch your book to your knee.
Wave your book above your head.
Jump up and down.
Blink your eyes quickly.
Stick out your tongue.
Twitch your nose.
Cluck like a chicken.
Wiggle your behind.
Nod your head.
Make your book dance.

Takeaway Activity

373 My Map

Materials: paper; crayons; die-cut pictures of houses, schools, cars, buses, and people; glue

Directions:

1. After showing children various maps, have them create a map of the route they take from their house to school.
2. If they ride in a school bus, have them glue a bus on the paper; if they ride in a car, glue a car on the paper; if they walk, glue a person on the paper.

SKILLS

▶ Understanding that maps can represent our surroundings

▶ Knowing basic information about transportation

▶ Developing text-to-self connection

ASL Connection

374 Bicycle Time

I have a BICYCLE, you'll see me riding past.
And whenever the light turns GREEN, I know I can ride fast! *(sign BICYCLE quickly)*
I have a BICYCLE, I'm riding, here I go!
But when the light turns YELLOW, I know I should ride slow. *(sign BICYCLE slowly)*
I have a BICYCLE, I bought it at a shop.
And whenever the light turns RED, I always know to stop.

(Follow up the rhyme with a game that encourages paying attention. The students should sign BICYCLE continuously. As they sign, you should alternate signing GREEN, YELLOW, and RED. The children need to watch to see if their bicycles should be moving quickly or slowly or stopping.)

SKILLS

▶ Understanding basic American Sign Language

▶ Recognizing colors

▶ Developing visual discrimination

▶ Developing attention and response

▶ Developing motor skills

▶ Developing compare and contrast skills

bicycle

green

yellow

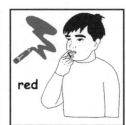

red

Spanish Connection

375 Spanish–English Soundalikes

Many Spanish words sound a lot like words in English. Share the following sentences and see if your students can guess what the Spanish words mean. Then practice saying the Spanish words together as a class.

Sean's Transportation

Some days Sean takes an *autobus* (ow-toh-BOOS).
Qué es el vehiculo? (kay ESS el vay-ee-COO-lo) Bus!
Sean likes to take an *aeroplano* (ay-ro-PLAY-no) on vacation.
Qué es el vehiculo? Airplane!
Sometimes Sean has to drive his dogs around in a *coche* (KO-che).
Qué es el vehiculo? Car!
Sean's favorite thing to ride on is a *tren* (TRAIN).
Qué es el vehiculo? Train!
When Sean's home, he rides his *bicicleta* (bee-cee-CLAY-tah) to his friend's house.
Qué es el vehiculo? Bike!

SKILLS

▶ Understanding basic Spanish vocabulary
▶ Developing logic
▶ Developing listening skills
▶ Developing attention and response
▶ Developing oral fluency

Recommend This!

Taxi Dog by Debra and Sal Barracca. New York: Dial, 1990.

Dumpy's Extra-Busy Day by Julie Andrews Edwards and Emma Walton Hamilton. New York: HarperCollins, 2006.

On the Move. New York: DK, 2007.

Train Song by Diane Siebert. New York: Crowell, 1990.

Wacky Wheelies: A Book of Transportation Jokes by Mark Ziegler. Minneapolis, MN: Picture Window, 2005.

25

Space

Kindergarten Speak

What do you think of when you think of space? The nighttime sky full of stars and the moon? The sun and other planets we can't see? All these things are right. We have learned a lot about space from NASA, the National Aeronautics and Space Administration, which is responsible for finding out what is in space and how it affects us on Earth. NASA has continued to send many shuttles and other research equipment into space to help teach us even more.

Recommended Books

376 *The Moon Over Star* **by Dianna Hutts Aston. New York: Dial, 2008.**

A young girl and her family, along with all of humankind, share the experience of the first moon landing on July 20, 1969. As the astronauts fulfill their dreams of landing on the moon, the young girl dreams of one day becoming an astronaut and following in their footsteps.

    LESSON IDEA: Help children develop an understanding of text patterns and sequencing. Have them help you retell the story, prompting them with questions such as:

> What year was the moon landing?
> Who were the astronauts involved in the first moon landing?
> What did the children do when their chores were done?
> Who was the American president who wanted to send men to the moon?
> How far away from Earth is the moon?
> What was the name of the spaceship that landed on the moon?
> What did the little girl's grandfather think of spending money on the space program?
> What did Commander Armstrong say when he stepped on the moon?

SKILLS

▶ Reading for information

▶ Understanding sequencing

▶ Developing oral fluency

▶ Understanding calendar time

▶ Understanding major discoveries in science and technology

377 *The Planets* **by Gail Gibbons. New York: Holiday House, 2008.**

This nonfiction book reveals facts about each of our eight planets and newly classified dwarf planet Pluto.

LESSON IDEA: Have the children create a poster for the planet of their choice, with pictures of the planet and a few words describing its special characteristics (for example, Saturn is known for its rings and is so light it could float in an ocean!).

SKILLS

▶ Reading for information

▶ Practicing writing

▶ Understanding major discoveries in science and technology

378 *There's No Place Like Space* **by Tish Rabe. New York: Dr. Seuss Enterprises, L.P., 1999.**

The Cat in the Hat arrives to take two children on a space adventure that they will never forget. Along the way they learn about the planets and stars, all in fun rhyming text.

LESSON IDEA: Have children create their own constellation using a spray bottle filled with yellow paint diluted with water. Give each student a piece of black construction paper and allow them to give their paper a squirt of paint. The paper will look "splattered," just like the stars in outer space. Give each student a few star stickers to place around the paper, and then have them connect stars and splatters, creating an outline for their own constellation.

SKILLS

▶ Reading for information

▶ Recognizing rhyme

▶ Developing creativity

▶ Understanding major discoveries in science and technology

379 *Space Leftovers* **by Dana Meachen Rau. Minneapolis, MN: Picture Window, 2006.**

This is a nonfiction explanation of comets, asteroids, and meteoroids.

LESSON IDEA: Create a comet tail as described at the end of the book. Follow the instructions provided.

SKILLS

▶ Reading for information

▶ Developing creativity

▶ Understanding major discoveries in science and technology

380 *Planets* **by Time For Kids Editors and Lisa Jo Rudy. New York: HarperCollins, 2005.**

This book is filled with fantastic facts and definitions of space, the planets, and more!

LESSON IDEA: One of the facts in the book is about Olympus Mons on Mars. The base of this mountain is as wide as the state of Missouri and is sixteen miles high. What points of interest are sixteen miles from your school? Ask the children if they can imagine seeing a mountain that tall.

▶ Reading for information

▶ Developing text-to-self connection

▶ Understanding major discoveries in science and technology

Fingerplays/Rhymes

381 Bumpin' Up and Down in My Space Shuttle
(to the tune of "Bumpin' Up and Down in My Little Red Wagon")

Bumpin' up and down in my space shuttle,
Bumpin' up and down in my space shuttle,
Bumpin' up and down in my space shuttle,
Won't you go to the moon with me?

...

My space suit's on and my boots are, too . . .
We step on the moon and bounce up and down . . .

SKILLS

▶ Developing oral fluency

▶ Recognizing rhyme

382 Climb Aboard

Climb aboard the spaceship, it's easy as can be,
We just need to get ready—1, 2, 3.
First we put on our space suit. *(pretend to put space suit on)*
It protects our body from the heat and cold.
Second we put on our space boots. *(pretend to put boots on)*
They protect our feet from the untold.
Third we put on our space helmet. *(pretend to put helmet on)*
It protects our head and helps us breathe.
Now we're off to outer space to visit
The places we've only dreamed.

SKILLS

▶ Recognizing rhyme
▶ Developing motor skills
▶ Developing oral fluency
▶ Understanding major discoveries in science and technology

383 Galaxy Bend and Stretch

Bend and stretch, reach for the stars,
There goes Jupiter, here comes Mars.
Bend and stretch, reach for the sky,
Stand on tiptoe, oh so high!

SKILLS

▶ Recognizing rhyme
▶ Developing motor skills
▶ Developing oral fluency

384 Orbiting the Sun (to the tune of "She'll Be Coming Around the Mountain")

Oh the Earth orbits around the sun, yes it does.
Oh the Earth orbits around the sun, yes it does.
Oh the Earth orbits around the sun,
Oh the Earth orbits around the sun,
Oh the Earth orbits around the Sun, yes it does.

...

Well it only takes 365 days, yes it does . . .

SKILLS

▶ Developing oral fluency
▶ Knowing basic patterns of the sun and moon

Flannelboard/Prop Stories

385 Rocket Ships Flannelboard

5 shiny rocket ships exploring outer space,
1 saw aliens and set off on a chase.
4 shiny rocket ships exploring outer space,
1 bumped into an asteroid and was knocked out of place.
3 shiny rocket ships exploring outer space,
1 found Jupiter first and thought he was an ace.
2 shiny rocket ships exploring outer space,
1 caught a shooting star and took off in a race.
1 shiny rocket ship left in outer space,
He wanted to go home so he headed for Earth's base.

SKILLS

▶ Recognizing rhyme
▶ Counting

386 *There Was a Bold Lady Who Wanted a Star* **Flannelboard**
(Based on the book by Charise Mericle Harper. New York: Little, Brown, 2002.)

A bold lady uses various means of transportation to capture a star in this variation on "I Know an Old Lady Who Swallowed a Fly."

SKILLS

► Developing listening skills

► Recognizing rhyme

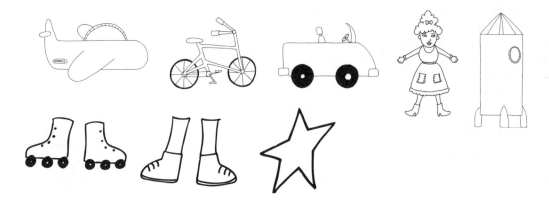

Writing Readiness Activity

387 Living on Another World

Ask the children to think about what life would be like on another planet. Using the planet, moon, or star of their choice, they can draw a picture of life there. Then have them write a description of what it would be like to live there instead of on Earth. Ask questions such as:

Would it be cold, or dark, or so sunny that everyone would need sunglasses?

SKILLS

► Developing logic

► Practicing writing

► Developing oral fluency

► Understanding major discoveries in science and technology

► Developing creativity

Math Activity

388 How Far Will Your Rocket "Fly"?

Materials: yarn or string, a balloon, tape, a straw

Directions:

1. Run a string through a drinking straw across one end of the room to another. The string can be attached to a doorknob or chairs or another common object.
2. Blow up a balloon and hold it shut while taping one side of it to the straw at one end of the string. The balloon should hang below the straw rather like a blimp.
3. Let go of the balloon. As the air is released, it will propel the balloon along the length of the string. Did the balloon fly all the way across the string? Are the results different depending on the size of balloon used or how much air is in the balloon?

SKILLS

► Understanding the nature of scientific inquiry

► Developing compare and contrast skills

Takeaway Activity

389 Telescope

Materials: paper towel tubes, black construction paper, decorating items, tape, a pin or other sharp object

Directions:

1. Have the children decorate the paper towel tube with a variety of items. Star stickers, for example, will add to the space theme of the telescope.
2. Cut squares of black construction paper big enough to wrap around the bottom of the tube.
3. Use a pin, pencil, or toothpick to punch tiny holes in the black construction paper, and then wrap the paper around the bottom end of the paper towel tube, securing it with tape or a rubber band.
4. Have children place the uncovered end of the tube up to their eye and look through. When the children look through the telescope and hold it up to a light, they will see stars!

Library Skill-Building Game

390 Create a Book

Preparation: Print out the Make a Book worksheets from this book's website. Make copies for each student. If you have limited time for the activity, choose the fill in the blanks version. If you have more time available and would like to put more emphasis on the writing component of the activity, choose the blank version. (The blank version can also be used in conjunction with the classroom teacher's lessons to provide a crosscurricular activity.) Write each of the following sentences on a large piece of paper or sentence strip:

The author writes the story.
The illustrator draws the pictures.
The publisher makes the book.
The school buys the book.
The librarian catalogs the book.
The student reads the book.

Activity: Show the students the preceding sentences out of order, and have them help you put them in order. Explain that, now that they know how a book is made, they will get to play all the parts and make their own books. Pass out the Make-a-Book handouts. (If time is limited, you may wish to have students work in groups. In this case, give one handout to each group.) Help the students put their pages in order: front cover, title page, and the six story pages. Tell the students to begin writing their stories as you go around with the stapler to staple their pages together.

When the children finish writing their stories (or filling in the blanks), they should begin on the illustrations. (Some students may wish to draw first, before writing the story. Use this as an opportunity to talk about how some stories start from words and some from pictures.) Make sure you point out the rectangle on the lower left-hand corner of the front cover and tell the students to leave it empty for now. This space is where the book's call number will go. As the students finish their books, help them write the title and author information on the front cover and title pages. You may also wish to include the year and a publisher name (perhaps your school's name) on the title page.

Review the sequence of how books are made, and ask the students which steps they have completed. At the end of the session, "buy" each student's book for the library (with payment of a bookmark or other small prize) and tell them you will work together to catalog the books during the next class (see chapter 26).

ASL Connection

391 In the Sky (to the tune of "Mary Had a Little Lamb")

In the SKY we see the SUN,
See the SUN, see the SUN.
In the SKY we see the SUN.
We know that it's DAYtime.

...

In the SKY we see the MOON,
See the MOON, see the MOON.
In the SKY we see the MOON.
We know that it's NIGHTtime.

...

In the SKY we see the STARS,
See the STARS, see the STARS.
In the SKY we see the STARS.
We know that it's NIGHTtime.

SKILLS

▶ Understanding basic American Sign Language

▶ Knowing basic patterns of the sun and moon

▶ Developing oral fluency

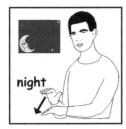

Spanish Connection

392 Blast Off!

The *astronauta* (as-TRO-nah-tah) puts on his *traje espacial* (TRAH-hay es-PAH-see-al), then climbs in his *nave espacial* (NAH-vay es-PAH-see-al) to go to the *luna* (LOO-nah). On March 30, 2006, Brazilian Air Force pilot Marcos Cesar Pontes was the first pilot from a Latin American country to go into space.

Let's help the *astronauta* count down to blast off!

Diez! (DEE-ez)
Nueve! (noo-WAY-vay)
Ocho! (OH-cho)
Siete! (see-ET-tay)
Seis! (SASE)
Cinco! (SINK-o)
Cuatro! (QUA-tro)
Tres! (TRACE)
Dos! (DOSE)
Uno! (OO-no)

Recommend This!

Minnie and Moo Go to the Moon by Denys Cazet. New York: DK, 1998.
About Space by Jana Carson. San Francisco, CA: Treasure Bay, 2001.
Night Light by Kelli C. Foster. Hauppauge, NY: Barron's, 1996.
What a Trip! by Kelli C. Foster. Hauppauge, NY: Barron's, 1994.
Doodle Dog in Space by Eric Seltzer. New York: Simon and Schuster, 2005.

SKILLS

▶ Counting
▶ Understanding basic Spanish vocabulary
▶ Understanding major discoveries in science and technology

26

Community Helpers

Kindergarten Speak

Many people in our community have jobs that help us every day. Some people have jobs that protect us, like police officers and firefighters; some have jobs that teach us, like teachers and librarians. Others have jobs that keep our community clean, like trash collectors, and some offer services that keep our community running, like mail carriers and grocers. All these people are community helpers.

Recommended Books

393 *I Know an Old Teacher* **by Anne Bowen. New York: Lerner, 2008.**

This book follows the pattern of the cumulative rhyme "I Know an Old Lady Who Swallowed a Fly." Once the old teacher starts eating class pets, the students wonder if she'll stop when she gets to them.

LESSON IDEA: Have students create their own cumulative rhyme! Students can select another community helper and, following the pattern of "I Know an Old Lady Who Swallowed a Fly," create their own crazy rhyme.

394 *My Mom Is a Firefighter* **by Lois G. Grambling. New York: HarperCollins, 2007.**

Billy has two families—his mom and dad at home and his mom and the "uncles" who work at the fire station with her. Through Billy's visits to the station, readers learn about fire safety rules and what it's like to work at the fire station.

LESSON IDEA: Have the children draw a picture of what they think is the best thing about being a firefighter and write why. Some examples could be sliding down the station pole, driving the truck, putting out the fire, and so on.

SKILLS

- ▶ Reading for literary experience
- ▶ Recognizing rhyme
- ▶ Understanding literary genres
- ▶ Practicing writing
- ▶ Knowing basic information about community helpers

- ▶ Reading for literary experience
- ▶ Practicing writing
- ▶ Knowing basic information about community helpers

395 *My New Town* by Kirsten Hall. New York: Children's Press, 2005.

When a young boy moves to a new town, he meets a variety of community helpers.

LESSON IDEA: Ask the children to name community helpers they see each week. Ask if they can think of some community helpers in your city or town that weren't mentioned in this book. Make a chart of community helpers in your community, showing where they work and what they do.

SKILLS

▶ Reading for literary experience
▶ Developing text-to-self connection
▶ Understanding that graphs represent information
▶ Knowing basic information about community helpers

396 *Library Mouse* by Daniel Kirk. New York: Abrams, 2007.

Sam, the library mouse, loves living in the library. He reads the books and begins to write his own, which he leaves for the children to enjoy. Finally the librarian leaves a note for Sam to join them on "Meet the Author" day!

LESSON IDEA: Have the children create their own picture books about community helpers. Make sure they put a title and their name on the front cover. After they share their books with the class, help them shelve their books by author's last name in your picture book section or on a cart.

▶ Reading for literary experience
▶ Practicing writing
▶ Writing one's name
▶ Understanding alphabetical order
▶ Knowing how books are made
▶ Knowing basic information about community helpers

397 *School Bus Drivers* by Dee Ready. New York: Bridgestone, 1998.

This book presents wonderful facts and details about what people must know to become a school bus driver and what school bus drivers do each day.

LESSON IDEA: Make a stop sign greeting card for your school bus driver. Provide octagon-shaped paper to the students. Have the students write STOP on one side of the paper. On the other side, have the children write a simple message such as "thank you" and draw a picture.

▶ Reading for information
▶ Developing text-to-self connection
▶ Writing one's name
▶ Practicing writing
▶ Knowing basic information about community helpers

Fingerplays/Rhymes

398 **The Firefighter**

The firefighter wears a big yellow coat *(mime putting on coat)*
And a hard hat. *(touch head)*
He pulls on 1 boot, and then the other, *(mime putting on boots)*
And sprays his fire hose like that. *(mime spraying fire hose)*

SKILLS

▶ Recognizing rhyme
▶ Developing oral fluency
▶ Developing motor skills
▶ Knowing basic information about community helpers

399 **In My Neighborhood** (to the tune of "The Wheels on the Bus")

The people in my neighborhood help me out, help me out, help me out,
The people in my neighborhood help me out all throughout my life.

...

The doctor in my neighborhood takes care of me . . . every time I'm sick.
The firefighters in my neighborhood put out fires . . . anytime there's need.
The police in my neighborhood protect me . . . every single day.
The librarian in my neighborhood finds me books . . . anytime I ask.

▶ Recognizing rhyme
▶ Developing oral fluency
▶ Knowing basic information about community helpers

400 My Teacher (to the tune of "Mary Had a Little Lamb")

At school I learn to read and write, read and write, read and write.
At school I learn to read and write, because my teacher helps me.

…

I learn math and ABCs, ABCs, ABCs.
I learn math and ABCs, because my teacher helps me.

…

I learn science and history, history, history.
I learn science and history, because my teacher helps me.

SKILLS

▶ Developing oral fluency

▶ Knowing basic information about community helpers

401 The Trash (to the tune of "The Farmer in the Dell")

We're picking up the trash,
We're picking up the trash.
The garbage truck is coming soon,
We're picking up the trash.

…

We're bagging up the trash . . .
We put it in the trash can . . .
We're putting out the trash . . .
Thank you, garbage collectors! . . .

SKILLS

▶ Recognizing rhyme

▶ Developing oral fluency

▶ Developing motor skills

▶ Knowing basic information about community helpers

▶ Understanding sequencing

Flannelboard/Prop Story

402 I Am a Grocer Flannelboard

Give out items to the children, and then ask them to bring various categories (colors, fruits, vegetables, breakfast foods, etc.) forward and place them on the board.

I am a grocer at the food store.
Every day I set out more food and more.
Do you like peaches and apples so sweet?
Bread and ice cream and broccoli and meat?
Whatever you want, go ahead and ask it,
And I will put it in your basket!

SKILLS

▶ Recognizing rhyme

▶ Developing oral fluency

▶ Knowing basic information about community helpers

Egg   Cheese

403 Community Helper Matching Game

Place each object on the flannelboard, and ask the children which helper goes with each.

Chalkboard

Writing Readiness Activity

404 Picturing Our Community Helpers

Ask the children which community helper they think is the most important and why. Have them draw a picture of what that helper does in the community and write about what he or she is doing.

Math Activity

405 Sorting the Mail Game

Show the children three baskets or mailboxes labeled "Zoo," "School," and "Jones Family." Then pass out envelopes with the following pictures pasted onto them and invite the children to help Mr. Mailman sort the mail.

Takeaway Activity

406 What Hat Should I Wear? Craft

Materials: a printout of the Community Helpers worksheet and the Community Helper Hats worksheet for each child, glue, crayons, other decorating materials

Directions:

1. Cut out the hats.
2. Match the hats with the appropriate community helpers and glue them on.
3. Color and decorate as desired.

Library Skill–Building Game

407 Classifying Books

Preparation: Gather the books your students created in chapter 25 as well as the sentence strips describing how to make a book.

Activity: Review the steps in creating a book, and ask the students where you stopped last time. Now explain that the students will play the part of your favorite community helper, the librarian, and will catalog and shelve their books. First, help the students decide whether their books are fiction or nonfiction. Then ask what kind of call number their books will have based on this information. Have the children write the letter E or the number 520 in the rectangle on the lower left-hand corner of their books. Show a book from your library, demonstrating how the second part of the call number shows the first two or three letters of the author's last name. Have the children write the first two or three letters of their own last name under the first part of the call number. Work with the class to put the books in order on a shelf or cart. If desired, add the books to your library's collection so that other students can check them out.

SKILLS

▶ Understanding the concept of fiction

▶ Understanding the concept of nonfiction

▶ Practicing writing

▶ Understanding alphabetical order

▶ Understanding numerical order

ASL Connection

408 Community Helper Guessing Game

Teach the children the following signs, and then ask the questions. The children should sign their answers.

1. Who helps us learn?
2. Who drives a fire truck?
3. Who can help us if we're lost?
4. Who can help us find just the right book?
5. Who should we visit for a check-up?
6. Who keeps us safe from fires?
7. Who knows lots of stories?
8. Who should we visit when we are sick?
9. Who catches bad guys?
10. Who can teach us about numbers and letters?

SKILLS

▶ Understanding basic American Sign Language

▶ Developing listening skills

▶ Knowing basic information about community helpers

police

fire fighter

librarian

teacher

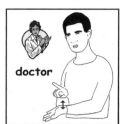
doctor

Spanish Connection

409 Community Helpers Matching Game

SKILLS

▶ Understanding basic Spanish vocabulary

▶ Understanding other cultures

▶ Developing listening skills

▶ Knowing basic information about community helpers

Teach the children the following Spanish words, and then ask the questions. The children should answer in Spanish.

Firefighter: *bombero* (bom-BAY-ro)
Police officer: *policia* (pol-ee-CEE-ah)
Doctor: *medico* (MAY-dee-co)
Trash collector: *basurero* (bah-soo-RAY-ro)
Teacher: *professor* (pro-fay-SORE)

1. Help! There's a fire! Who do I call?
2. Help! Someone stole my bike! Who do I call?
3. Help! I broke my leg! Who do I call?
4. Help! My trash is overflowing! Who do I call?
5. Help! I need to learn to read! Who do I call?

When we think of libraries, we think of buildings that have shelves and shelves of books, with librarians helping people. But you would be surprised to find that other countries have unique ways of providing books and library services for their communities. In Peru, books are delivered to families in bags. The bags usually have twenty books on various reading levels that the families can keep for a month. In even smaller communities, books are delivered in suitcases that the community can share for three months. You may even find that the books are delivered by donkey cart or wagon!

For more information on how library services and books are provided in communities around the world, check out *My Librarian Is a Camel* by Margriet Ruurs (Honesdale, PA: Boyds Mills Press, 2005).

Recommend This!

A Day in the Life of a Nurse by Connie Fluet. Mankato, MN: Capstone, 2005.

Community Helpers by Jennifer B. Gillis. Vero Beach, FL: Rourke, 2007.

Shhhhh! Everybody's Sleeping by Julie Markes. New York: HarperCollins, 2004.

The Boy Who Was Raised by Librarians by Carla Morris. Atlanta, GA: Peachtree, 2007.

Fireman Small by Wong Herbert Yee. Boston: Houghton Mifflin, 1994.

27

Valentine's Day

Kindergarten Speak

Valentine's Day is celebrated on February 14. Hearts and Cupid, with his bow and arrow, are symbols of Valentine's Day. It's most commonly celebrated by exchanging love notes or cards with people you care about. Valentine's Day is also a day to give flowers and candy to those you care about.

Recommended Books

410 *Will You Be My Valenswine?* **by Teresa Bateman. New York: Albert Whitman, 2005.**

When Polly the pig notices it's Valentine's Day, she begins to pout. She just wants someone to be her Valenswine! Luckily for Polly, her mother is waiting for her Valenswine, too!

LESSON IDEA: Make a "Guess How Much I Love You" card. For each child, cut a length of red or pink yarn that matches the distance between the fingertips of one hand and the fingertips of the other with arms stretched out. Use prepackaged blank cards or poster-board cut into rectangles and folded in half for the cards. Cut out two hearts for each child. On the first heart, have the children write "Guess how much I love you?" On the second heart, they should write "This much!" Glue one heart to the inside front of the blank card, with one end of the yarn underneath. Glue the other heart to the inside back of the blank card, with one end of the yarn underneath. Decorate the front of the card as desired.

SKILLS

▶ Reading for literary experience

▶ Practicing writing

▶ Developing text-to-self connection

▶ Developing fine motor skills

▶ Understanding basic concepts of measurement

411 *Bee My Valentine* **by Miriam Cohen. Long Island City, NY: Star Bright Books, 2009.**

As the first-grade class gets ready to celebrate Valentine's Day, the teacher reminds the students that they must make a card for each of their classmates. But when one student doesn't get cards from the whole class, the teacher and the class have to think of a way to cheer him up.

SKILLS

▶ Reading for literary experience

▶ Practicing writing

▶ Recognizing rhyme

▶ Developing oral fluency

LESSON IDEA: Cut out enough paper hearts so each child in your class will have one. Cut pictures from magazines or use clip art and glue a picture on each heart. Give each child a heart with a picture and have him or her tell you what the picture is. On the reverse side of the heart, have the child write all the words he or she can think of that rhyme with the picture (for example, a picture of a car rhymes with "star").

412 *Valentine's Day* **by Gail Gibbons. New York: Holiday House, 1996.**

This nonfiction book is full of facts and traditions about Valentine's Day.

LESSON IDEA: Ask the children what they learned about Valentine's Day. Make a list on the chalkboard of all the facts about Valentine's Day the children learned.

SKILLS
▶ Reading for information
▶ Developing oral fluency
▶ Knowing basic information about holidays

413 *Mouse's First Valentine* **by Lauren Thompson. New York: Simon and Schuster, 2002.**

Mouse watches his sister as she collects items to make something special. When she finishes the project, she gives her brother his first valentine.

LESSON IDEA: Give the children a variety of supplies to make their own special valentines to take to a family member. Supplies needed include red paper, scissors, glue, crayons, pink and red tissue paper, and stickers.

SKILLS
▶ Reading for literary experience
▶ Practicing writing
▶ Developing text-to-self connection
▶ Developing fine motor skills

414 *The Valentine Express* **by Nancy Elizabeth Wallace. Tarrytown, NY: Marshall Cavendish, 2004.**

The class learns about the origins and traditions of Valentine's Day and some ways it's celebrated around the world as well as in the United States.

LESSON IDEA: Ask the children what traditions they observe on Valentine's Day. Does anyone do something special with his or her family? What traditions did the children learn about that they would like to try?

SKILLS
▶ Reading for literary experience
▶ Developing text-to-self connection
▶ Understanding other cultures
▶ Appreciating diversity
▶ Knowing basic information about holidays

Fingerplays/Rhymes

415 **Hearts and Flowers** (to the tune of "Frère Jacques")

Hearts and flowers, hearts and flowers,
Chocolates too. Chocolates too.
A day to say I love you,
A day to say I love you.
Yes I do, yes I do.

SKILLS
▶ Developing oral fluency
▶ Recognizing rhyme
▶ Knowing basic information about holidays

416 **Oh My Darling Valentine** (to the tune of "My Darling Clementine")

Oh my darling, oh my darling,
Oh my darling Valentine,
I had hoped and I had wished
That you'd be forever mine.

...

I made a card and bought some candy,
Just for you, my Valentine,

SKILLS
▶ Developing oral fluency
▶ Recognizing rhyme
▶ Knowing basic information about holidays

I hope you like it, yes I do,
And you'll be forever mine.

...

I picked some flowers in the meadow,
For my sweet Valentine,
I'll pick you more, every day,
If you'll be forever mine.

417 Valentine's Day

I looked at the calendar and do you believe,
It's February 14th, a special day to me.
Mom makes me pancakes,
Pink and heart-shaped.
Dad gives me extra hugs,
A kiss and a cake.
I go to school and the party begins,
The box I made is filled with valentines to the rim.

SKILLS

▶ Developing oral fluency
▶ Recognizing rhyme
▶ Knowing basic information about holidays

418 Won't You Be My Valentine? (to the tune of "Do You Know the Muffin Man?")

Oh won't you be my valentine, valentine, valentine,
Oh won't you be my valentine, on this special day of the year?
I'll give you a card of red and white . . . on this special day of the year.
I'll give you a box of candy . . . on this special day of the year.

SKILLS

▶ Developing oral fluency
▶ Recognizing rhyme
▶ Knowing basic information about holidays

Flannelboard/Prop Stories

419 Five Valentines Flannelboard

5 valentine cards outside my door,
I gave 1 to my sister, and then there were 4.
4 valentine cards so beautiful to see,
I gave 1 to my brother, and then there were 3.
3 valentine cards, lovely and new,
I gave 1 to my mother, and then there were 2.
2 valentine cards, isn't this fun?
I gave 1 to my father, and then there was 1.
1 valentine card, and I will say,
As I give it to you, "Happy Valentine's Day!"

SKILLS

▶ Developing oral fluency
▶ Recognizing rhyme
▶ Knowing basic information about holidays
▶ Counting

420 Matching Hearts Magnetboard (to the tune of "Happy Birthday")

(Cut out at least ten hearts from white posterboard. If you will have a large group, cut out two for each child. Using magic markers, design the hearts with stripes, polka dots, and other designs. Make two hearts with each design. You may wish to laminate the hearts so you can reuse them. Place adhesive magnets on the back of each heart. Place the hearts on the magnetboard. Use the following song to invite each child to the magnetboard to find a match.)

> Which 2 hearts are the same?
> Which 2 hearts are the same?
> (Child's name), please show me
> Which 2 hearts are the same?

Writing Readiness Activity

421 Valentine Postcard

Materials: posterboard, doily, sponge, paint

Directions:

1. Cut postcard-sized rectangles from posterboard.
2. Give each child a postcard, a doily, a piece of sponge, and paint.
3. Have the children cover the postcard with the doily and dab paint on with a sponge.
4. Remove and throw away the doily and let the postcard dry.
5. Have the children write a valentine message to someone special.

Math Activity

422 Heart Matching Game

Cut several large hearts in a variety of colors. Cut the hearts in half from top to bottom. Then put a number on one half of the heart and a corresponding number of dots or heart stickers on the other side of the heart. Have the children match the heart halves.

Takeaway Activity

423 Valentine Tic-Tac-Toe

Materials: a paper square for each child, two strips of pink paper for each child, two strips of purple paper for each child, five pink hearts and five purple hearts for each child

Directions:

1. Have the children divide the square paper into nine small squares by gluing two strips of pink paper vertically and two strips of purple paper horizontally.
2. The children can use the five pink hearts and five purple hearts to play tic-tac-toe with someone they love.

Library Skill–Building Game

424 Cumulative Tales

Read the book *This Is the Bird* by George Shannon (Houghton Mifflin, 1997). Ask the students what they noticed about the story. Point out that the story not only repeats but also adds new information with each repetition. Explain that this type of story is called a cumulative tale. (As this is a difficult word for young children to pronounce, you may wish to use the term *add-and-repeat tale* instead.) Ask the children if they know any other examples of cumulative tales. Make a list of their examples on the board.

Next, explain that you will play a Valentine's Day game that will tell a cumulative story. Have the children sit in a circle. Begin the story, "Once upon a time there was a little boy named Billy. On Valentine's Day, he decided to make valentines for all his favorite people in the community. First he made a valentine for his neighbor. He gave it to his neighbor and said, 'My name is Billy, and maybe it's silly, but I made a valentine for my neighbor.' Then he made a valentine for his teacher. He said, 'My name is Billy, and maybe it's silly, but I made a valentine for my teacher and my neighbor.'" Let the child to your right say the next part, adding on to the story. Each repetition should use the following pattern:

"Then he made a valentine for _____. He said, 'My name is Billy, and maybe it's silly, but I made a valentine for _____ and _____ and _____.'"

If you have a larger class, you may wish to start a new round about halfway through. For the second round, use the following pattern: "My name is Sunny, and maybe it's funny . . . ."

End the story as follows:

"And then (repeat entire list of people) came to Billy and said, 'Your name is Billy, and you're not silly! Thank you, and happy Valentine's Day to you!'"

SKILLS

▶ Recognizing rhyme

▶ Knowing basic information about community helpers

▶ Developing memory

▶ Developing attention and response

▶ Developing oral fluency

▶ Understanding literary genres

ASL Connection

425 I-LOVE-YOU Song (to the tune of "Bumpin' Up and Down in My Little Red Wagon")

(This song explains the origin of the sign I-LOVE-YOU, which combines the signs for the letters I, L, and Y. Be sure to demonstrate each letter individually as you teach the song, and then show how we put up all three letters at the same time to make the sign I-LOVE-YOU.)

I is for I, that's ME, ME, ME, ME.
L is for LOVE, that's LOVE, LOVE, LOVE, LOVE.
Y is for YOU, that's YOU, YOU, YOU, YOU.
I, L, Y, I-LOVE-YOU.
On VALENTINE'S DAY we say I-LOVE-YOU.
It's a great day to say I-LOVE-YOU.
Let's all say it again, I-LOVE-YOU,
HAPPY VALENTINE'S DAY!

SKILLS

▶ Understanding basic American Sign Language

▶ Associating sounds with letters

▶ Developing oral fluency

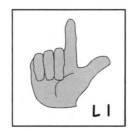

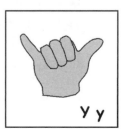

Signs continue on following page.

Spanish Connection

426 **Valentine Colors**

Show a variety of heart shapes in different colors. Introduce the Spanish words for the colors as you place the hearts on the board, then recite the following rhyme and invite the children to respond in Spanish.

White: *blanco* (BLAHN-ko)

Red: *rojo* (ROH-ho)

Pink: *rosa* (RO-sa)

Blue: *azul* (ah-ZOOL)

Green: *verde* (VAIR-day)

Yellow: *amarillo* (ah-mah-REE-yo)

Orange: *naranja* (na-RAHN-ha)

Purple: *morado* (mo-RAH-doh)

SKILLS

▶ Recognizing rhyme

▶ Recognizing colors

▶ Understanding basic Spanish vocabulary

▶ Understanding other cultures

James's Valentines

James made a valentine for his friend, and it was fine.

It was the color of sheep and clouds and more. Do you know? *De qué color?*
    (day KAY co-LORE)

It was the color of apples and roses and more. Do you know? *De qué color?*

It was the color of bubblegum and flowers and more. Do you know? *De qué color?*

It was the color of the sky and sea and more. Do you know? *De qué color?*

It was the color of grass and trees and more. Do you know? *De qué color?*

It was the color of the sun and bananas and more. Do you know? *De qué color?*

It was the color of oranges and clownfish and more. Do you know? *De qué color?*

It was the color of grapes and flowers and more. Do you know? *De qué color?*

In Brazil, there is no Valentine's Day. Instead, *Día dos Namorados,* "Day of the Enamored" or "Boyfriend's/Girlfriend's Day," is celebrated on June 12, when couples exchange gifts such as chocolates, cards, and flower bouquets. This day is chosen because it is the day before the feast day of St. Anthony, who is known as the marriage saint. Many single women search for a boyfriend or a husband on that day.

In Colombia, the *Día del amor y la amistad,* "Love and Friendship Day," is celebrated on the third Friday and Saturday in September. The *amigo secreto* ("secret friend") tradition is quite popular, where friends give anonymous gifts.

Recommend This!

Dumpy's Valentine by Julie Andrews Edwards and Emma Walton Hamilton. New York: HarperCollins, 2006.

Love, Ruby Valentine by Laurie Friedman. Minneapolis, MN: Carolrhoda, 2006.

Little Bear's Valentine by Else Holmelund Minarik. New York: HarperCollins, 2003.

1 2 3 Valentine's Day by Jeanne Modesitt. Honesdale, PA: Caroline House, 2002.

Be My Valentine by Rosemary Wells. New York: Hyperion, 2001.

28

Presidents' Day

Kindergarten Speak

Presidents' Day was first celebrated to honor President George Washington's birthday on February 22. Washington's birthday first became a federal holiday in 1880. Eventually, Presidents' Day was celebrated on the third Monday in February and is generally thought to be a celebration of all presidents who have served our country.

Recommended Books

427 ***Duck for President* by Doreen Cronin. New York: Simon and Schuster, 2004.**

Duck is tired of doing his chores and begins to question why Farmer Brown is in charge. He decides to hold an election and run against Farmer Brown. But once Duck wins, he quickly discovers how hard it is to run a farm, and eventually his political career leads him to become president.

 LESSON IDEA: Help children develop an understanding of text patterns and sequencing. Have them help you retell the story, prompting them with questions such as:

> Why did Duck want to have an election at the farm?
> What were some of the voter registration requirements for the animals?
> How did Duck feel about running the farm?
> When Duck realized running the farm was hard, what job did he decide to run for next?
> How did Duck feel about running the state?
> When Duck realized running the state was hard, what job did he decide to run for next?
> How did Duck feel about running the country?
> What did Duck finally decide to do?

428 *Max for President* by Jarrett J. Krosoczka. New York: Random House, 2004.

Max and Kelly are both running for class president. This great book shows the process of elections and campaigns.

LESSON IDEA: Ask the children to pretend they are running for president and need an election poster. Ask them to draw a picture of themselves and think of what they would do if they were elected. Then have them write that on the poster!

SKILLS

► Reading for literary experience
► Developing text-to-self connection
► Developing creativity
► Practicing writing
► Understanding how democratic values came to be and are exemplified

429 *Presidents' Day* by Anne Rockwell. New York: HarperCollins, 2008.

As a class learns about why we celebrate Presidents' Day, they decide to put on a play for the whole school so they can share some amazing things our presidents have done.

LESSON IDEA: Learn more about Mount Rushmore. Visit www.nps.gov/moru/.

How big are the faces on Mount Rushmore? Visit www.nps.gov/moru/forkids/upload/washmeas2.pdf.

Use lengths of rope to demonstrate how big President Washington is on Mount Rushmore!

► Reading for literary experience
► Understanding basic concepts of measurement
► Knowing why important buildings, statues, and monuments are associated with national history

430 *Let's Celebrate Presidents' Day* by Connie and Peter Roop. Brookfield, CT: Millbrook, 2001.

This book is loaded with facts about many of our presidents and first ladies, along with other information about why we celebrate Presidents' Day, which president was the first to live in the White House, why Washington, D.C., is the capital of the United States, and more.

LESSON IDEA: Follow the instructions for the George Washington Button activity suggested at the end of the book.

SKILLS

► Reading for information
► Understanding how democratic values came to be and are exemplified

431 *My Teacher for President* by Kay Winters. New York: Scholastic, 2004.

A little boy nominates his teacher for president, as she has all the requisite skills: she's used to leading meetings, making people pay attention, and keeping the peace, among other things. Each two-page spread shows the teacher's everyday job on one side and compares it to the president's on the other. This story is a great way to bring the presidency down to kindergartners' level.

LESSON IDEA: After reading the story, make a chart on the board with three columns labeled "Job," "Teacher," and "President." Go through the story again and have the children identify each job, then fill in the chart to show how the teacher and the president each completed it. Then add a fourth column labeled "Kids." Go through each job and ask the children to come up with ways they get people to pay attention, sign important papers, show health care is important, and do the other things in the book. (For example, they might show health care is important by always remembering to wash their hands after using the toilet.)

SKILLS

► Reading for literary experience
► Organizing information
► Developing text-to-self connection
► Knowing basic information about community helpers
► Developing compare and contrast skills

Fingerplays/Rhymes

432 Honest Abe

Abe Lincoln was a tall, tall man, *(reach high above head)*
And honest as could be.
He lived during the Civil War,

SKILLS

► Recognizing rhyme
► Understanding how democratic values came to be and are exemplified
► Developing oral fluency
► Developing motor skills

And set all the slaves free. *(join wrists, then move them apart as if breaking shackles)*
We look back now and we can see
How much he gave and gave
As president of the U.S.A.
Thank you, Honest Abe!

433 **Do You Know George Washington?** (to the tune of "Do You Know the Muffin Man?")

Do you know George Washington, George Washington, George Washington,
Do you know George Washington, our country's first president?
He led our country's fight for freedom, fight for freedom, fight for freedom,
He led our country's fight for freedom, in the Revolutionary War.
He was president for 2 terms, 2 terms, 2 terms,
He was president for 2 terms, 8 years in all.
He is called the Father of Our Country, Father of Our Country, Father of Our Country,
He is called the Father of Our Country, because he served our nation well.

SKILLS

▶ Recognizing rhyme
▶ Understanding how democratic values came to be and are exemplified
▶ Developing oral fluency

434 **Mr. President** (to the tune of "Rockin' Robin")

He works in the White House all day long,
Leading our country and keeping it strong.
All of the people in the U.S.A.
Watch what he does every single day.
Mr. President,
Mr. President,
He's the one we elect to run our country right.

SKILLS

▶ Recognizing rhyme
▶ Knowing basic information about community helpers
▶ Developing oral fluency

435 **The President Says**

Play this variation on "Simon Says" using simple actions such as turning around, walking in place, standing, sitting, waving, and so on. When the leader prefaces the directions with "The President says . . . ," the class should follow the directions. When the leader does not say "The President says . . . ," the class should do nothing.

SKILLS

▶ Developing listening skills
▶ Developing attention and response
▶ Developing motor skills

Flannelboard/Prop Stories

436 **Election in the Library! A Prop Story**

(Materials: cow puppet, pig puppet, ballot sheets [from pattern], ballot box for students to put votes in)

Once upon a time in the (insert your school's name here) library, Cow and Pig decided they wanted to run for President of the Library. They filled out lots of paperwork to get on the official ballot, and then they had a debate so all the children could hear how they would run the library.

Pig: "A vote for Pig is a vote for change! Who can find anything in the library now, with its alphabetical order? Vote for me and I will rearrange the library so that all the books are grouped by color! From now on, any time you want to find a purple book, it will be easy! Oh, and free ice cream with every book you check out!"

Cow: "Why change a system that works well? Our alphabetical system now makes it easy to find all the books by the same author in one place, because they are all on the shelf together."

SKILLS

▶ Understanding how democratic values came to be and are exemplified
▶ Developing critical thinking skills
▶ Developing compare and contrast skills
▶ Developing prediction skills

Pig: "But she's not offering free ice cream! Vote for me!"

Cow: "Ice cream in the library would be too messy! It would get all over the books! If I were Library President, I would make sure that everyone had lots of choices for fun books to read."

Pig: "But no ice cream! Do you hear her? How unreasonable!"

Cow: "No, no ice cream. But maybe we could have treats once in awhile. Neat treats that wouldn't mess up the books."

Then it was time for the children to vote. (Pass out the ballots and pencils, and remind children of the two candidates' positions. Ask the children to put a check mark in the box next to the animal they want to vote for, then fold their papers and put them into the ballot box. When everyone has voted, count the votes together, tallying the numbers on the board. Let the winning animal make a brief victory speech, and then ask the children what they think the library would be like with that animal as president. If they elected Pig, for instance, what might the library look like in a few months?)

I vote for:
☐ **Cow**
☐ **Pig**

437 National Images Flannelboard Game

Ask the children if they can name the items as you place them on the flannelboard, and then share a little bit of information about each monument and what it represents.

SKILLS

▶ Knowing why important buildings, statues, and monuments are associated with national history

▶ Developing oral fluency

Writing Readiness Activity

438 Favorite Presidents

Talk to the children about the presidents they have learned about. Ask them to draw a picture of their favorite president and write why that president is their favorite.

SKILLS

▶ Developing text-to-self connection

▶ Developing creativity

▶ Practicing writing

Math Activity

439 Counting Pennies

Using the pictures of bills and coins in various denominations, have the children identify the presidents on United States currency. Abraham Lincoln is on the penny and five dollar bill, Thomas Jefferson is on the nickel, Franklin D. Roosevelt is on the dime, George Washington is on the quarter and one dollar bill, Andrew Jackson is on the twenty dollar bill, and Ulysses

SKILLS

▶ Counting

▶ Knowing why important buildings, statues, and monuments are associated with national history

▶ Developing teamwork skills

S. Grant is on the fifty dollar bill. Then divide the class into groups and give each group a bag of five to ten pennies. The group should count the pennies. Have each group report how many pennies it has, and then count how many pennies the whole class has.

Takeaway Activity

440 Lincoln's Log Cabin

Materials: construction paper, craft sticks, a penny for each child, glue, crayons

Directions:

1. Glue the craft sticks on the paper to make the outline of a log cabin.
2. Color a roof on the paper and add windows and a door to the cabin as desired.
3. Glue the penny onto the cabin, Lincoln's face side up.

SKILL

▶ Developing fine motor skills

Library Skill-Building Game

441 Sequencing

Preparation: Print out the Presidential Sequencing Cards from this book's webpage.

Activity: Show the presidential sequencing cards out of order and ask the children to help you put them in order. Point out the clues in each sentence that help the children place the cards in the correct order: the years and the ordinal numbers.

Next, explain that the class just put the cards in sequence, or in order by time. Now explain that the president is just waking up in the morning and is getting ready to meet with other leaders. Have the children help you make a sequence of the things he needs to do to get ready, such as brush his teeth, get dressed, and so on. Write their suggestions on the board in the form of sentences using ordinals (for example, "First, he gets out of bed.").

SKILLS

▶ Understanding sequencing
▶ Developing text-to-self connection
▶ Recognizing and ordering ordinal numbers

ASL Connection

442 It's Presidents' Day (to the tune of "Happy Birthday")

It's PRESIDENTS' DAY, it's PRESIDENTS' DAY.
THANK YOU, George Washington.
It's PRESIDENTS' DAY.

(Repeat, inviting the children to name other presidents.)

SKILLS

▶ Understanding basic American Sign Language
▶ Developing oral fluency

Spanish Connection

443 Presidents' Day Greetings

On Presidents' Day we must remember to say *hola* (OH-la), Mr. President.

When the president is near, we must remember to say *gracias* (GRAH-cee-as), Mr. President.

As the president leaves, we must remember to say *adios* (ah-di-OSE), Mr. President.

Presidential elections in Mexico are held every six years, unlike in the United States, where they are held every four years. Also, Mexican presidents can only serve one six-year term. In the United States, presidents can run for reelection, but they cannot serve more than two consecutive terms.

Recommend This!

Abe Lincoln's Hat by Martha Brenner. New York: Random House, 1994.

Mount Rushmore by Judith Jango-Cohen. Minneapolis, MN: Lerner, 2004.

Presidents' Day by David F. Marx. New York: Children's Press, 2002.

George Washington and the General's Dog by Frank Murphy. New York: Random House, 2002.

The Impossible Patriotism Project by Linda Skeers. New York: Dial, 2007.

29

Fairy Tales and Folktales

• •

Kindergarten Speak

People used to tell stories instead of writing them, and many of those stories have survived to this day. Folktales are stories that were told orally, or out loud, from one person to another. Folktales typically have themes of good winning over evil. Fairy tales are like folktales, although they often have an element of magic to make sure that good wins over evil.

Recommended Books

444 *The Little Red Hen* by Paul Galdone. New York: Clarion, 1973.

When the Little Red Hen asks for help from the dog, the cat, and the mouse, she is repeatedly turned down. But when the animals smell the cake the Little Red Hen baked, they all want some. The Little Red Hen instead eats the entire cake herself, since the other animals didn't help her with any work. From then on, the other animals always help with the work to be done.

LESSON IDEA: Ask the children if they think the Little Red Hen was right not to let the dog, the cat, and the mouse eat any cake. Do they think it is fair that only one person would do the chores at home? Ask if they help with the chores that need to be done at home. Print out the Will Work for _____ worksheet from this book's webpage and instruct the children to draw pictures and make a list of chores they are willing to do to help at home. Make sure the children fill in the blank with what they are willing to work for (cookies, kisses, cake, etc.).

SKILLS

▶ Reading for literary experience

▶ Developing text-to-self connection

▶ Developing teamwork skills

▶ Practicing writing

▶ Understanding literary genres

445 *Fairytale News* by Colin and Jacqui Hawkins. Cambridge, MA: Candlewick Press, 2004.

When Mother Hubbard discovers her cupboard is bare, she asks her son Jack to find a job. Jack quickly becomes a paperboy, delivering the *Fairytale News*. While delivering the paper, Jack gets to know many of the fairy tale characters we are all familiar with.

LESSON IDEA: Have the children create their own newspaper. Choose a story or fairy tale and work with the students to summarize the main points of the story. Write them on the board. Have the children complete the pictures to go with the story.

SKILLS

▶ Reading for literary experience
▶ Developing text-to-self connection
▶ Understanding literary genres
▶ Developing creativity

446 *The Kiss That Missed* by David Melling. Hauppauge, NY: Barron's, 2002.

When the King's bedtime kiss misses his son, it rattles around the room and escapes out the window. Soon the spooky and scary things in the forest are tamed with the kiss, which is finally rescued by a brave Knight and returned to the young Prince.

LESSON IDEA: Help the children develop an understanding of text patterns and sequencing. Have them help you retell the story, prompting them with questions such as:

Why did the King's kiss miss his son?
Where did the kiss go?
Who did the Prince tell about the kiss missing?
Who was ordered to follow the kiss?
What was in the forest when the Knight arrived?
What happened when the kiss floated by the forest animals?
What was the Knight sitting on?
Did the Dragon eat the Knight and his horse? Why not?
What does the King promise to do?

SKILLS

▶ Reading for literary experience
▶ Understanding sequencing
▶ Developing comprehension strategies

447 *Kate and the Beanstalk* by Mary Pope Osborne. New York: Atheneum, 2000.

In this adapted retelling of the classic story "Jack and the Beanstalk," Kate and her mother are poor and struggling to survive. Kate must confront a giant who killed a brave knight and stole his riches. As Kate recovers the riches and kills the giant, she finds that she has been tested to see if she is worthy of her inheritance, as she is the knight's daughter.

LESSON IDEA: Ask the children if they can think of another way to tell the story of Jack and the Beanstalk. Have the children work together to create a new character and situation where the main character has to recover riches and confront a giant. Write the story the children create on the board and read it aloud to them at the end. It is fine to prompt the children to follow the format of the story to keep them on task: "Who is our main character and who does he or she live with?" "What is the first item the character has to recover?"

This activity can work with any fairy tale you choose!

SKILLS

▶ Reading for literary experience
▶ Understanding sequencing
▶ Developing creativity
▶ Understanding literary genres
▶ Developing teamwork skills

448 *The Three Pigs* by David Wiesner. New York: Clarion, 2001.

This is the classic tale of the three pigs, with a twist. As the wolf attempts to huff and puff, the pigs decide to jump out of the story and drop into different fairy tales.

LESSON IDEA: Ask the children if they recognized some of the stories the three pigs dropped into. What are some other ways David Wiesner's version of the three pigs differs from the traditional tale they know? In what ways is it the same? Write the children's answers on the board.

SKILLS

▶ Reading for literary experience
▶ Developing compare and contrast skills
▶ Understanding literary genres

Fingerplays/Rhymes

449 Castle Capers

I am the king of running,
I run and run and run.
My subjects all run with me,
And we have so much fun!

...

I am the queen of jumping,
I jump and jump and jump.
My subjects all jump with me,
And fall down with a bump.

...

I am the prince of turning,
I turn and turn and turn.
My subjects all turn with me,
It's an easy thing to learn!

...

I am the princess of dancing,
I dance and dance and dance.
My subjects all dance with me,
And sit when they get the chance!

SKILLS

▶ Recognizing rhyme
▶ Developing motor skills
▶ Developing oral fluency

450 Dragon, Dragon

Dragon, dragon, swoop and sway,
Dragon, dragon, fly away.
Dragon, dragon, fly even higher,
Dragon, dragon, breathe your fire!

SKILLS

▶ Recognizing rhyme
▶ Developing motor skills
▶ Developing oral fluency

451 My Castle

4 stone walls on my castle tall, *(use flat hands to show walls)*
A tower, a garden, and a garden wall. *(mold a tower in the air and point to indicate garden)*
Down goes the drawbridge over the moat so wide, *(move flat hands down and away from you)*
Hello, my friends! Please come inside! *(wave and gesture friends inside)*

SKILLS

▶ Recognizing rhyme
▶ Developing motor skills
▶ Developing oral fluency

452 To Win a Prince

1 sweet princess trying to win her prince
Slept on a bed of peas that made her wince.
The princess tossed and turned all through the night,
When she appeared for breakfast she was quite a sight.
Her delicate skin was black and blue,
For the peas had turned her pale skin an ugly hue.
But the prince knew she was fit to be a queen,
All because the peas had left something to be seen.

SKILLS

▶ Recognizing rhyme
▶ Developing oral fluency

Flannelboard/Prop Stories

453 Five Little Dragons Flannelboard

5 little dragons with great big scales,
1 lost his balance and bumped his tail.
He cried "Ouch!" and breathed some fire,
And then he flew away, higher and higher.

...

4 little dragons . . .
3 little dragons . . .
2 little dragons . . .
1 little dragon . . .

SKILLS

▶ Recognizing rhyme
▶ Developing motor skills
▶ Developing oral fluency
▶ Counting

454 Three Billy Goats Gruff Flannelboard Story (adapted traditional)

SKILLS

▶ Understanding sequencing
▶ Developing listening skills
▶ Comparing size and volume
▶ Understanding literary genres

Once upon a time, there were 3 billy goats: a little billy goat, a medium-sized billy goat, and a big billy goat. Every day they grazed on a field of lovely grass. But one day, the little billy goat said, "I am tired of grazing in this same field every day. I want to see what's down the road."

"You go on," said the other two billy goats. "We will come in a while." So the little billy goat set off down the road. Well, soon he came to a bridge. And this wasn't any ordinary bridge, because there was a troll living underneath it. The little billy goat started across the bridge, trip-trap, trip-trap.

The troll was a grumpy fellow. You see, he hadn't had any breakfast that morning. So he snarled, "Who's that tripping over my bridge?"

"It's only me, the littlest Billy Goat Gruff," said the little billy goat in a tiny voice.

"Well, I am coming to gobble you up!" said the troll.

"Oh no, I would barely be a mouthful," said the clever little billy goat. "You had better wait until my big brother comes."

The troll thought about that. It seemed sensible. "Well, be off with you," he said.

And the little billy goat crossed the bridge and found a hillside full of delicious grass on the other side.

A little while later, the medium-sized billy goat set off down the road and started to cross the bridge, trip-trap, trip-trap.

"Who's that tripping over my bridge?" snarled the troll.

"It's only me, the medium-sized Billy Goat Gruff," said the medium-sized billy goat in a medium-sized voice.

"Well, I am coming to gobble you up!" said the troll.

"Oh no, you'd still be hungry," said the clever medium-sized billy goat. "You had better wait until my big brother comes."

The troll thought about that. It seemed sensible. "Well, be off with you," he said.

A little while later, the big billy goat set off down the road and started to cross the bridge, trip-trap, trip-trap.

"Who's that tripping over my bridge?" snarled the troll.

"It's only me, the big Billy Goat Gruff," said the big billy goat in a big voice.

"Well, I am coming to gobble you up!" said the troll.

And the big billy goat laughed. The troll jumped up onto the bridge, and the big billy goat ran at him with his huge horns. He tossed the troll right off the bridge and into a berry bush on the other side. The troll tasted one of those berries and decided that they were much tastier than goat meat anyway.

And the big billy goat went to join his brothers in the field, and they had a wonderful time eating and playing there all day long.

Writing Readiness Activity

455 The Class Beanstalk

Materials: leaves cut from green construction paper, crayons, other decorating materials, tape, a cord hanging from the ceiling to the floor

Directions:

1. Hang a cord or rope from the ceiling that touches the floor.
2. Have the children decorate leaves for the beanstalk with their favorite fairy tale title, a picture from the fairy tale, and their name.
3. Tape the leaves to the cord to build a beanstalk.
4. If you cannot hang the beanstalk from the ceiling, tape the leaves on the wall, growing a beanstalk to the ceiling.

SKILLS

▶ Practicing writing
▶ Writing one's name
▶ Developing creativity
▶ Developing text-to-self connection

Math Activity

456 Building a Castle

Display pictures of castles for the children to see. Using blocks of various shapes or paper cutouts of geometric shapes (triangle, square, rectangle, etc.), have the children create their own castles by fitting the pieces together. If you are using paper shapes, allow the children to glue their shapes onto a piece of construction paper so they can take their newly "built" castle home.

SKILLS

▶ Recognizing shapes
▶ Developing creativity

Takeaway Activity

457 Grow Your Own Beanstalk

Materials: soil, a cup for each child, a sugar snap bean seed for each child

Directions:

1. Give each child a cup and enough soil to fill half the cup.
2. Give each child a seed and have the children plant their own magic bean. They will have fun watching it grow!

SKILLS

▶ Appreciating nature
▶ Knowing that living things go through a process of growth and change

Library Skill–Building Game

458 Giant Footprints Review Game

Preparation: Trace and cut out "Giant Footprints" from construction paper. You will need one footprint for each question. Next, develop a list of questions. This game can be used to review a specific skill or a combination of skills that have been taught throughout the year. Examples:

> Where do you go to check out your books?
> Where can you find the title of a book?
> Do fiction books have just letters or numbers and letters in their call
>   numbers?
> Which word comes first in alphabetical order: bat or cat?
> What number comes after nine?

Activity: Divide the class into two teams. Line each team up on opposite sides of the room. Ask each team a question in turn, going down the lines of students. Each time a team answers correctly, place a giant footprint on the ground in front of that team, so that the footprints make a path on the floor. When the game is over, ask the students to guess which team has more footprints. Then count the footprints on each side and see if their guess was correct.

ASL Connection

459 The King Says/The Queen Says

Teach the following signs, and then play a variation on "Simon Says." Start by signing instructions, such as "The king says jump" or "The queen says turn." The children should only do the action if you sign "The king says" or "The queen says" first. After you have signed a few directions, allow the children to take turns being the leader.

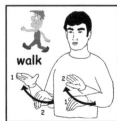
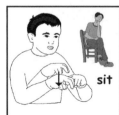

king queen say jump turn run walk sit

Spanish Connection

460 *Cinco Verde Dragónes* (Five Green Dragons) (to the tune of "Ten Green Bottles")

SKILLS

▶ Counting to 5
▶ Developing oral fluency
▶ Understanding basic Spanish vocabulary

Uno verde dragón (OO-no VAIR-day drag-OWN) flying in the sky.
Uno verde dragón (OO-no VAIR-day drag-OWN) flying in the sky.
And if *uno más* (OO-no mahs) dragon should happen to fly by,
There'll be *dos* (DOSE) *verde dragónes* flying in the sky.

...

Dos verde dragónes flying in the sky . . .
Tres (TRACE) *verde dragónes* flying in the sky . . .
Cuatro (QUA-tro) *verde dragónes* flying in the sky . . .
Cinco (SINK-o) *verde dragónes* flying in the sky . . .

Folktales and fairy tales are told around the world. Many of the tales we are familiar with originated in different countries. For a comprehensive look at folktales around the world, including many from South and Central America, check out *Best-Loved Folktales of the World* by Joanna Cole (Anchor, 1982). Some favorites to explore are "Señor Coyote and the Dogs" (from Mexico) and "Three Magic Oranges" (from Costa Rica).

Recommend This!

Snog the Frog by Tony Bonning. Hauppauge, NY: Barron's, 2005.
The Missing Tarts by B. G. Hennessy. New York: Viking Penguin, 1989.
Dragon Pizzeria by Mary Morgan. New York: Knopf, 2008.
Good Night, Good Knight by Shelley Moore Thomas. New York: Dutton, 2000.
Boogie Knights by Lisa Wheeler. New York: Atheneum Books for Young Readers, 2008.

30

St. Patrick's Day

Kindergarten Speak

St. Patrick's Day is a celebration of the patron saint of Ireland, Saint Patrick. People celebrate St. Patrick's Day in many places around the world, whether they are Irish or not. A lot of fun customs are associated with St. Patrick's Day, including wearing green. Those caught not wearing green are pinched! This is also the day to be on the lookout for shamrocks, leprechauns, and pots of gold.

Recommended Books

461 *St. Patrick's Day Shamrocks* **by Mary Berendes. Chanhassen, MN: Child's World, 2000.**

This nonfiction book explains why shamrocks are the symbol of Ireland, why they are believed to be lucky, who St. Patrick was, and how St. Patrick's Day is celebrated.

LESSON IDEA: Ask the children to share some of the things they learned about St. Patrick, St. Patrick's Day, and shamrocks. Create a chart on the chalkboard of their responses in each category.

462 *St. Patrick's Day* **by Brenda Haugen. Minneapolis, MN: Picture Window, 2004.**

This informative nonfiction book explains the origins of St. Patrick's Day and the traditions and customs observed.

LESSON IDEA: Follow the directions in the back of the book to make a shamrock shaker.

SKILLS

▶ Reading for information

▶ Developing oral fluency

▶ Organizing information

▶ Knowing basic information about holidays

SKILLS

▶ Reading for information

▶ Developing creativity

▶ Developing fine motor skills

▶ Knowing basic information about holidays

463 *Good Luck! A St. Patrick's Day Story* by Joan Holub. New York: Aladdin, 2007.

This rhyming story is about a group of ants trying to find their treasure: a bounty of crackers.

LESSON IDEA: Review the rhyming chunks in this story and make a list on the board. Ask the children to think of other words that may rhyme and have the same chunk ending.

SKILLS

► Reading for literary experience
► Recognizing rhyme

464 *Jeremy Bean's St. Patrick's Day* by Alice Schertle. New York: Morrow, 1987.

When Jeremy Bean forgets to wear green on St. Patrick's Day, all his classmates tease him. Luckily Mr. Dudley, the school principal, is able to share a bit of green with Jeremy.

LESSON IDEA: Have each child create a shamrock pin so each is guaranteed to have something green to wear for St. Patrick's Day. Give each child a green shamrock shape to decorate with crayons, green tissue, and glitter. To create a sturdier pin, use card stock rather than construction paper. To finish, hot-glue a pin back to each shamrock or attach a safety pin.

SKILLS

► Reading for literary experience
► Developing creativity

465 *The Night Before St. Patrick's Day* by Natasha Wing. New York: Penguin, 2009.

'Twas the night before St. Patrick's Day, and Tim and Maureen were spending the night setting traps to catch a leprechaun. Even though they catch a leprechaun, they don't manage to get his gold!

LESSON IDEA: Ask the children to help you retell the story.

SKILLS

► Reading for literary experience
► Developing oral fluency
► Understanding sequencing
► Developing listening skills

Fingerplays/Rhymes

466 Leprechaun

Oh little leprechaun, all dressed in green,
You're the silliest man I've ever seen.
I'd like to find your secret hole,
Where you've buried all that gold.

SKILLS

► Recognizing rhyme
► Developing oral fluency

467 Leprechaun Stretch

Leprechaun, leprechaun, turn around.
Leprechaun, leprechaun, touch the ground.
Leprechaun, leprechaun, reach up high.
Leprechaun, leprechaun, touch the sky.
Leprechaun, leprechaun, hide your gold.
Leprechaun, leprechaun, sit as you're told.

SKILLS

► Recognizing rhyme
► Developing oral fluency
► Developing motor skills

468 Shamrock Song

1 little, 2 little, 3 little shamrocks,
4 little, 5 little, 6 little shamrocks,
7 little, 8 little, 9 little shamrocks,
On St. Patrick's Day.

SKILLS

► Counting
► Recognizing rhyme
► Developing oral fluency

469 **Green Grow the Clovers** (to the tune of "Trot Trot to Boston")

Green grow the clovers, green grow the trees, *(start squatting on the floor, then grow to standing tall with arms above head)*
Green grow the shamrocks blowing in the breeze. *(sway arms and body)*
Green on the leprechauns as you hear them say, *(cup hand to ear)*
"Wear something green, for it's St. Patrick's Day!" *(wave hands joyfully)*

SKILLS

▶ Recognizing rhyme
▶ Developing oral fluency
▶ Developing motor skills

Flannelboard/Prop Stories

470 **Five Pots of Gold Flannelboard**

5 pots of gold on St. Patrick's Day,
Oh me, oh my, the leprechauns are hiding them away.
1 pot of gold is hidden underneath the floor,
Oh me, oh my, that leaves only 4.
1 pot of gold is hidden behind the tree,
Oh me, oh my, that leaves only 3.
1 pot of gold is hidden in a large green shoe,
Oh me, oh my, that leaves only 2.
1 pot of gold is hidden near a sticky bun,
Oh me, oh my, that leaves only 1.
The last pot of gold is hidden underneath the sun,
Oh me, oh my, to find it I'd better run.

SKILLS

▶ Counting
▶ Developing oral fluency
▶ Recognizing rhyme

471 **Five Leprechauns Flannelboard**

1 little leprechaun alone with nothing to do,
Along came another and then there were 2.
2 little leprechauns telling tales near a tree,
Along came another and then there were 3.
3 little leprechauns danced a jig out the door,
Along came another and then there were 4.
4 little leprechauns hiding their gold near a hive,
Along came another and then there were 5.

SKILLS

▶ Counting
▶ Developing oral fluency
▶ Recognizing rhyme

Writing Readiness Activity

472 **Catch a Leprechaun**

Have the children draw a picture and write about how they would catch a leprechaun and steal his gold.

SKILLS

▶ Practicing writing
▶ Developing creativity

Math Activity

473 Match the Shamrock Game

Using the shamrock pattern, cut out enough shamrocks for each child to have one. Then draw patterns such as stripes, polka dots, and triangles on the shamrocks. Draw two of each pattern. (You may also use letters, numbers, or simple words instead of patterns, if you wish to emphasize a different skill.) One at a time, each child should come up to the board, describe the pattern on his or her shamrock, and then show it. The child who has the matching shamrock should come up and put both shamrocks side by side on the board. Continue until all shamrocks have been matched.

Takeaway Activity

474 Shamrock Craft

Materials: three or four hearts for each child cut from green paper, a green pipe cleaner or straw for each child, glue, crayons, other decorating materials

Directions:

1. Glue edges of three hearts together to make a three-leaf shamrock or four hearts for a four-leaf clover.
2. Decorate as desired.
3. Tape a green pipe cleaner or straw stem to the decorated shamrock.

Library Skill–Building Game

475 Character Coins

Preparation: Cut out twenty to thirty circles from yellow paper. On each of these "coins," write a word or phrase that describes a personality trait or physical characteristic of one of the main characters from the following story. You may wish to leave some coins blank so you can incorporate additional suggestions from the class. Then cut out two large pots from black construction paper. Here are some suggestions to get you started:

lazy	wears aprons
has red hair	sneaky
whiny	easily fooled
complains a lot	boastful
hardworking	smart
has curly hair	kind
has brown hair	

Activity: Read *Jamie O'Rourke and the Big Potato* by Tomie dePaola (New York: Putnam, 1997). Ask the children to identify the two main people in the story (Jamie and his wife, Eileen), and then explain that the people in the story are called *characters*. The most important people in the story are the main characters. Write "Jamie" on one of the pots and "Eileen" on the other, and place them on the board.

Next, explain that the author tells you about the characters by describing:

> how they look
> what they do
> what they are like

Give examples by sharing sentences describing members of the class, such as "Sarah has blonde hair" or "Billy always sits up straight" or "Jennifer is friendly." Then ask the class to describe Jamie's and Eileen's characters. If they pick words or phrases that you have on your coins, attach those coins to the top of the appropriate pot. Write any new suggestions on the blank coins. Ask prompting questions until the class runs out of ideas, and then present any remaining coins and ask the class to determine which pot they belong to.

ASL Connection

476 We're All Wearing Green (to the tune of "The Wearing of the Green")

Oh, we're all WEARING GREEN.
Oh, we're all WEARING GREEN.
Because it is ST. PATRICK'S DAY,
We are all WEARING GREEN.

...

Oh, we're all doing a DANCE . . .
Oh, we're celebrating IRELAND . . .

SKILLS

▶ Understanding basic American Sign Language
▶ Developing oral fluency

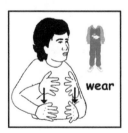

wear

green

St. Patrick's Day

dance

Irish

Spanish Connection

SKILLS

▶ Understanding basic Spanish vocabulary

▶ Recognizing colors

▶ Counting

▶ Developing oral fluency

▶ Developing memory

▶ Developing attention and response

▶ Understanding other cultures

477 *Cinco Verde* **Shamrocks**

Introduce or reinforce the Spanish words for colors by showing five shamrocks in the following colors and saying their Spanish names. Then count the shamrocks in Spanish. Finally, play a memory game: Instruct the children to look at the colors carefully and then close their eyes. Remove a shamrock from the board, count to three, and tell the children to open their eyes. They should identify which color was taken away by telling you the Spanish word. Count the shamrocks in Spanish, and then repeat the game until all the shamrocks are gone.

Green: *verde* (VAIR-day)
Blue: *azul* (ah-ZOOL)
Red: *rojo* (ROH-ho)
Yellow: *amarillo* (ah-mah-REE-yo)
White: *blanco* (BLAHN-ko)

1: *uno* (OO-no)
2: *dos* (DOSE)
3: *tres* (TRACE)
4: *cuatro* (QUA-tro)
5: *cinco* (SINK-o)

The tiny island of Montserrat is known as the Emerald Island of the Caribbean. Montserrat is the only country in the world outside Ireland where St. Patrick's Day is a public holiday. On March 17, celebrations are staged across the island, consisting of special events, concerts, and performances. The festivities now spread over a week, taking on a distinctly Caribbean flavor with blends of calypso, reggae, and iron band music. During the week, islanders observe the custom of wearing green.

To learn more about the Irish history of Montserrat, visit its website at www.visitmont serrat.com/St_Patricks_Festival.

Recommend This!

St. Patrick's Day by Carmen Bredeson. New York: Children's Press, 2003.

Lucky Tucker by Leslie McGuirk. Cambridge, MA: Candlewick Press, 2008.

Mary McLean and the St. Patrick's Day Parade by Steven Kroll. New York: Scholastic, 1991.

The Luck of the Irish by Margaret McNamara. New York: Aladdin, 2007.

St. Patrick's Day by Mari C. Schuh. Mankato, MN: Capstone, 2003.

31
Dinosaurs

Kindergarten Speak

Dinosaurs lived between 230 and 65 million years ago—millions of years before people ever lived on Earth. Dinosaurs are extinct, which means there are no more of their species left on Earth. When a dinosaur died, sometimes the remains of the animal were covered by things like mud and sand, which made fossils. Paleontologists are scientists who study fossils and try to learn as much about the dinosaurs as they can.

Recommended Books

478 *Dinosaurs* by Gail Gibbons. New York: Holiday House, 2008.

This nonfiction book describes what paleontologists do, how they use fossils to gain information about the dinosaurs, and facts about the dinosaurs discovered.

LESSON IDEA: Paleontologists have divided the nonbird dinosaurs into seven main groups: prosauropods, theropods, sauropods, stegosaurs, ankylosaurs, ceratopsians, and ornithopods. After reading the book, use pictures of the dinosaurs discussed and ask the children if they can remember which category the dinosaur belongs in and what some of the characteristics of the dinosaurs are within the categories.

479 *If the Dinosaurs Came Back* by Bernard Most. New York: Harcourt, 1978.

A little boy who loves dinosaurs imagines what life would be like if they came back.

LESSON IDEA: Discuss the ways the boy imagined dinosaurs helped people when they came back. Then ask the children if they can think of some more ways dinosaurs would be helpful if they came back or ways they would like to play with the dinosaurs.

480 *How Big Were the Dinosaurs* by Bernard Most. New York: Harcourt Brace, 1996.

It's hard to imagine just how big the dinosaurs really were. This book compares dinosaurs to everyday objects all kids will recognize.

LESSON IDEA: Bring in some of the items listed in the book (a toothbrush, a stuffed hen) and have lengths of rope available for the really large dinosaurs. Have the children compare the size of a T. rex's teeth to their teeth, and so on. Stretch the rope out on the floor, have the children lie head-to-toe along the length of the rope, and then count how many children it takes to be as long as a dinosaur.

SKILLS

▶ Reading for information

▶ Understanding basic concepts of measurement

▶ Developing text-to-self connection

▶ Understanding biological evolution and the diversity of life

481 *Bizarre Dinosaurs* by Christopher Sloan. Washington, DC: National Geographic, 2008.

Descriptions and facts about the lesser known and more unusual dinosaurs are included in this book.

LESSON IDEA: Place a map of the world on the board. Discuss which continent each dinosaur in the book came from and mark it with a tack or flag. Ask the children if they notice any one area that had more dinosaurs.

SKILLS

▶ Reading for information

▶ Understanding that maps can represent our surroundings

▶ Understanding the terms *more than, less than,* and *same as* for comparing quantity

▶ Understanding biological evolution and the diversity of life

482 *How Do Dinosaurs Go to School?* by Jane Yolen. New York: Blue Sky, 2007.

The reader is asked how dinosaurs behave when they go to school, and then examples of the right way to behave are shown.

LESSON IDEA: After reading the book, ask the students to compare how the dinosaurs behaved in the beginning of the book and at the end. Prompt them with questions such as:

Was the dinosaur a bully on the playground in the beginning of the book?
How did he change?
What did the dinosaur do when he lost his tooth?

SKILLS

▶ Reading for literary experience

▶ Developing compare and contrast skills

▶ Developing oral fluency

Fingerplays/Rhymes

483 Dinosaur Romp

(Print pictures of the dinosaurs from the Internet to show what type of dinosaur you're describing.)

Can you stretch your neck like an apatosaurus? *(stretch neck)*
Can you run fast like an ostrich mimic ornithomimid? *(run in place)*
Can you roar like a T. rex? *(roar)*
Can you stomp like an ultrasaurus? *(stomp)*
Can you get real small like a compsognathus? *(sit down)*

SKILLS

▶ Developing vocabulary

▶ Developing motor skills

▶ Understanding biological evolution and the diversity of life

484 Five Dinosaurs

5 enormous dinosaurs let out a huge ROAR,
1 ran away, and then there were 4.
4 enormous dinosaurs munching on a tree,
1 walked away, and then there were 3.

SKILLS

▶ Developing oral fluency

▶ Counting

3 enormous dinosaurs looking for something to do,
1 fell asleep, and then there were 2.
2 enormous dinosaurs going for a run,
1 couldn't keep up, so then there was 1.
1 enormous dinosaur all alone in the setting sun,
He decided to go home, so now there are none.

485 I Am a T. Rex (to the tune of "I'm a Little Teapot")

I am a T. rex on the hunt.
I've got a tail in back and sharp claws up front.
When I am hungry, hear me roar.
I'm a ferocious dinosaur!

SKILL

▶ Developing oral fluency

486 If You're a Dinosaur (to the tune of "If You're Happy and You Know It")

If you're a dinosaur and you know it, stomp your feet.
If you're a dinosaur and you know it, stomp your feet.
If you're a dinosaur and you know it, then you really ought to show it.
If you're a dinosaur and you know it, stomp your feet.

...

. . . swing your tail.
. . . show your teeth.
. . . let out a roar.

SKILLS

▶ Developing oral fluency
▶ Developing motor skills

Flannelboard/Prop Stories

487 Dinosaur, Dinosaur, What Do You Eat? Flannelboard Game

Discuss with your students the fact that some dinosaurs were carnivores (meat eaters) and some were herbivores (plant eaters). Paleontologists study dinosaur fossils and can tell by their teeth whether they were plant eaters or meat eaters. Meat eaters had sharp teeth and claws, whereas plant eaters had blunt teeth, and many had cheek pouches where they could store food for a while.

Play a guessing game with your students to see if they can tell which dinosaurs were the plant eaters and which were the meat eaters. Place the picture of the steak at the top of one side of the flannelboard and the picture of the plant on the other. After saying the chant "Dinosaur, dinosaur, what do you eat?" show the dinosaur pictures one at a time and see if the children can guess which column they go into.

SKILLS

▶ Developing classification and sorting skills

▶ Understanding biological evolution and the diversity of life

▶ Developing attention and response

▶ Developing logic

488 Five Dinosaurs Flannelboard (to the tune of "One Elephant Went Out to Play")

1 dinosaur went out to play,
Over the hills and far away.
He had such enormous fun, he called for another dinosaur to come.

...

2 dinosaurs . . .
3 dinosaurs . . .
4 dinosaurs . . .
5 dinosaurs . . . They had such enormous fun, and then went home when the day was done.

SKILLS

► Counting
► Developing oral fluency

Writing Readiness Activity

489 How Does a Dinosaur Spell?

Preparation: Cut out the letters of the word *dinosaur* from construction paper. Make them large enough to be seen from the back of the class.

Activity: Attach the mixed-up letters to the board with magnets, and have the children help you spell the word *dinosaur* by sounding out the word. When you are finished, invite the children to stand up and write the word *dinosaur* in the air with their fingers.

SKILLS

► Practicing writing
► Associating sounds with letters
► Knowing the alphabet

Math Activity

490 How Big Was T. Rex?

Help the children visualize just how big the dinosaurs really were. Have children measure out a dinosaur's length using yardsticks and string. Select a variety of dinosaurs both large and small. This assortment will help the children realize that there were many sizes of dinosaurs, some much bigger and smaller than they are. Stretch a string the length of each dinosaur. Get your class to lie down head-to-toe along the measured area. Count how many children it takes to make a dinosaur's length.

SKILLS

► Understanding basic concepts of measurement
► Comparing size and volume
► Understanding biological evolution and the diversity of life

Takeaway Activity

491 Dino Skeleton

Materials: outline picture of various dinosaurs, glue, pasta in different shapes

Directions:

1. Pretend you are paleontologists discovering the fossils of a dinosaur or, rather, creating the fossils.
2. Glue various shapes of pasta into a dinosaur outline to create a skeleton of a dinosaur!

SKILL

► Developing creativity

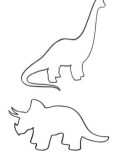

Library Skill–Building Game

492 Setting Toss

Preparation: Obtain a soft ball that can be thrown indoors.

Activity: Read a book about dinosaurs. Explain that one important element of a story is its setting, or where the story takes place. Ask the students to help you describe the setting of the book you just read. Was the setting a swamp? A mountain? A house? Explain that setting also means *when* the story takes place. Ask them to talk about when your story occurred. Discuss some of the other books you have read with the class and describe their settings.

Next, have the class sit in a circle. Hold up the ball and name a possible setting for a story (such as "a library" or "the Wild West"), then say a child's name and toss or roll the ball to that child. That child should name another setting, and then pass the ball to another child. Continue until every child has had a turn. If a child has difficulty thinking of a setting, name a book that the class has read to prompt him or her.

ASL Connection

493 Dinosaur, Dinosaur

DINOSAUR, DINOSAUR, TURN around.
DINOSAUR, DINOSAUR, touch the ground.
DINOSAUR, DINOSAUR, JUMP up high.
Now be a DINOSAUR that can FLY!

Spanish Connection

494 Dinosaur Run, Roar, and Snore

Dinosaur RUN on the count of 5 *(everyone run on* cinco*)*
uno, dos, tres, quatro, cinco! (OO-no, DOSE, TRACE, QUA-tro, SINK-o)
Dinosaur ROAR on the count of 5 *(everyone roar on* cinco*)*
uno, dos, tres, quatro, cinco!
Dinosaur SNORE on the count of 5 *(everyone snore on* cinco*)*
uno, dos, tres, quatro, cinco!

On a map of South America, show the children Argentina. Tell the children that a four-legged, plant-eating dinosaur was recently found in Argentina, and scientists named it the argentinasaurus. It may have been even heavier than the ultrasauros. The ultrasauros was a plant eater from Colorado, with bones that indicate the animal was six stories high and may have weighed more than fifty tons! A ton equals 2,000 pounds! A full-grown male elephant weighs between 9,000 and 13,000 pounds! Can you imagine how big a dinosaur is that weighs fifty tons? Ask children how much they weigh as a comparison.

SKILLS

▶ Understanding basic Spanish vocabulary
▶ Counting
▶ Developing attention and response
▶ Understanding other cultures

Recommend This!

Dinosaurs That Ate Plants by Leonie Bennett. New York: Bearport, 2006.
Dino Rib Ticklers by Michael Dahl. Minneapolis, MN: Picture Window, 2003.
Ask Dr. K. Fisher about Dinosaurs by Claire Llewellyn. Boston, MA: Kingfisher, 2007.
Meet the Dinosaurs. New York: DK, 2006.
Oh Say Can You Say Di-no-saur? by Bonnie Worth. New York: Random House, 1999.

32 Weather

· ·

Kindergarten Speak

We experience weather every day! Sometimes we can tell the weather just by looking outside. We can see rain, snow, and fog. Some weather we don't know about until we're outside. We feel the wind and how hot or cold it is.

Recommended Books

495 *Like a Windy Day* **by Frank Asch. New York: Harcourt Books, 2002.**

A girl imagines all she would do if she were the wind.
> **LESSON IDEA:** Ask the children what they would do if they were the wind. After discussing how the wind moves the clouds, let the children have cloud races by pretending they are the wind while blowing into straws to move "cloud" cotton balls.

496 *If Frogs Made Weather* **by Marion Dane Bauer. New York: Holiday House, 2005.**

A child describes the weather various animals would make and the weather he would make.
> **LESSON IDEA:** Create a chart on the chalkboard. Have the children name the animals in the book and the weather associated with them.

SKILLS

- ▶ Reading for literary experience
- ▶ Developing text-to-self connection
- ▶ Developing motor skills
- ▶ Knowing that short-term weather conditions can change daily and that weather patterns change over the seasons
- ▶ Knowing vocabulary for different types of weather
- ▶ Appreciating nature

- ▶ Reading for literary experience
- ▶ Knowing that short-term weather conditions can change daily and that weather patterns change over the seasons
- ▶ Knowing vocabulary for different types of weather
- ▶ Appreciating nature
- ▶ Organizing information

497 *One Hot Summer Day* by Nina Crews. New York: Greenwillow, 1995.

This nonfiction book describes all the things a little girl can do on a hot summer's day.

LESSON IDEA: Have the children name some of the things they like to do on a hot summer's day. Make a list on the chalkboard. Then have the children raise their hands to vote for their favorite thing to do. Which activity is the most popular?

SKILLS

▶ Reading for literary experience
▶ Developing text-to-self connection
▶ Developing oral fluency
▶ Knowing vocabulary for different types of weather
▶ Organizing information
▶ Counting

498 *Snip, Snip . . . Snow!* by Nancy Poydar. New York: Holiday House, 1997.

Sophie and her friends are looking forward to the forecasted snow, but when the storm stalls they decide they need to make their own snow!

LESSON IDEA: Following the directions at the end of the book, teach the children how to make their own snowflakes.

▶ Reading for literary experience
▶ Knowing vocabulary for different types of weather
▶ Developing fine motor skills
▶ Developing creativity

499 *Wet World* by Norma Simon. Cambridge, MA: Candlewick Press, 1995.

This book uses alliteration to demonstrate a girl's experiences on a wet day.

LESSON IDEA: Explain to the students that alliteration is the repeated use of a consonant sound at the beginning of neighboring words or syllables. Read through the story again with the children, and ask them to touch their noses every time they hear alliteration.

▶ Reading for literary experience
▶ Knowing vocabulary for different types of weather
▶ Developing vocabulary
▶ Developing listening skills
▶ Associating sounds with letters

Fingerplays/Rhymes

500 I Love Sunshine (to the tune of "Frère Jacques")

I love sunshine, I love sunshine,
Yes I do, yes I do.
Whether in the morning, whether in the morning,
Or afternoon, afternoon.

...

I love sunshine, I love sunshine,
Yes I do, yes I do.
We can play outside, we can play outside.
Do you want to? Do you want to?

▶ Developing oral fluency
▶ Recognizing rhyme

501 Seasons

I love the seasons for so many reasons!
Autumn's air is crisp and the leaves are too,
Listen to them crunch when you squish them with your shoe.
Winter is cold, with holidays and cheer,
It's the best time of all when the snow is here.
Spring is beautiful, with all the flowers blooming,
Kids are outside playing, their voices booming.
Summer is fun, even with the heat,
The pool is great and so are icy treats!

SKILLS

▶ Developing oral fluency
▶ Knowing that short-term weather conditions can change daily and that weather patterns change over the seasons
▶ Knowing vocabulary for different types of weather
▶ Recognizing rhyme

502 Splash! Crash! Flash!

Down comes the rain!
Splash, splash, splash!
Now comes the thunder!
Crash, crash, crash!
Lightning sizzles!
Flash! Flash! Flash!

SKILLS

▶ Developing oral fluency
▶ Recognizing rhyme
▶ Knowing vocabulary for different types of weather

503 Weather Song (to the tune of "If You're Happy and You Know It")

If it's raining and you know it, put on your boots.
If it's raining and you know it, put on your boots.
If it's raining and you know it, then what you wear will show it.
If it's raining and you know it, put on your boots.

…

If it's snowing and you know it, put on your coat . . .
If it's sunny and you know it, put on your sunglasses . . .
If it's windy and you know it, hold on to your hat . . .

SKILLS

▶ Developing oral fluency
▶ Recognizing rhyme
▶ Knowing vocabulary for different types of weather
▶ Developing motor skills

Flannelboard/Prop Stories

504 Five Snowflakes Flannelboard

1 little snowflake falls on a shoe,
He calls for a friend and then there are 2.
2 little snowflakes hanging in a tree,
Another drops in and then there are 3.
3 little snowflakes stuck to the door,
The wind blows again and then there are 4.
4 little snowflakes, through the air they dive.
But it's still snowing, and then there are 5.
5 little snowflakes having lots of fun,
Playing hide-and-seek from the morning sun.

SKILLS

▶ Developing oral fluency
▶ Recognizing rhyme
▶ Knowing vocabulary for different types of weather
▶ Counting

505 Seasons Game

Write the names of the seasons on the board, then show pictures of various seasonal activities and ask the children if the activities are done in the winter, spring, summer, or fall. To make it more challenging, include activities that can be done all year long, like playing with a ball.

SKILLS

▶ Developing classification and sorting skills
▶ Knowing vocabulary for different types of weather
▶ Knowing that short-term weather conditions can change daily and that weather patterns change over the seasons

Writing Readiness Activity

506 Weather Words

Write the following words on the board:

    snow   wind   rain   sun

Then invite the children to imagine they are snowmen and to write the word *snow* in the air with their fingers, using cold, crisp lines.

Next, tell the children to imagine they are the wind, blowing through the trees. Ask them how the wind would write. Have them use blowy, squiggly lines to write the word *wind* in the air.

Now, have the children imagine they are rain clouds and write *rain* in the air in a wet and squishy way.

Last, ask the children to stand up straight and imagine they are shining like the sun. Have them write *sun* in the air using bold strokes.

As you do this activity, lead the children through the letters one at a time, describing each line (for example, "The letter S starts up top and then curves like a snake").

SKILLS

► Developing spelling knowledge

► Developing creativity

► Practicing writing

► Appreciating nature

► Knowing vocabulary for different types of weather

► Knowing that short-term weather conditions can change daily and that weather patterns change over the seasons

Math Activity

507 Library Temps

What's the weather in your school library? Have a thermometer that the children can easily read. If there is time, begin a chart that allows you to track the temperature in your school library over several weeks or months.

SKILLS

► Understanding basic concepts of measurement

► Knowing that short-term weather conditions can change daily and that weather patterns change over the seasons

► Organizing information

► Understanding that graphs represent information

Takeaway Activity

508 Weather Wheel

Materials: paper plates, crayons, glue, scissors, magazines, paper fasteners, paper arrows

Directions:

1. Divide a paper plate into four equal sections. Mark each section with a different type of weather: sunny, windy, rainy, snowing.
2. Draw a picture of the type of weather described in each section.
3. Attach a paper arrow to the plate with a paper fastener and point to the type of weather you're having.

SKILLS

► Developing creativity

► Practicing writing

► Knowing vocabulary for different types of weather

► Knowing that short-term weather conditions can change daily and that weather patterns change over the seasons

► Developing text-to-self connection

Library Skill–Building Game

509 Story Elements—Problems and Solutions

Preparation: Make enough weather cards for each member of your class. On each card, write the name of a kind of weather. You may also include pictures to make this activity easier for prereaders. Repeat weather types as many times as needed. Some suggestions are:

rainy	snowy	cold
windy	icy	stormy
sunny	hot	foggy

Activity: Read the book *Hello, Sun!* by Dayle Ann Dodds (Dial, 2005). Then explain that every story has a problem, or something that the main character wants, and a solution, which is the way the main character either gets what he or she wants or accepts that he or she can't have it. Ask the children to identify the main problem in *Hello, Sun!* (the girl wants to dress to match the weather, but the weather keeps changing). Then make a chart on the board with the class, listing the problems (each change in weather) and the solutions (what kinds of clothes she puts on).

Then play a game using the weather cards and a ball. Have the children sit on the floor in a circle. Select a weather card and say, "I'd like to go outside and play on this very _____ day" (filling in the weather from your card). Then say a child's name and roll the ball to him or her. That child should identify a "solution" to the weather "problem" you posed (for example, if you said "rainy," the child might say "put up an umbrella"). Then that child selects a card, reads it, and rolls the ball to another child who has not yet had a turn. Even if the weather "problems" repeat, the children should identify new "solutions." (For example, other solutions to "rainy" could be "wear galoshes," "put on your raincoat," or "stay inside.") After their turns, the children should place their cards on the floor in front of them so everyone can see who has had a turn and who hasn't. If a child gets stuck, let him or her pick a friend to help.

SKILLS

▶ Knowing the elements of a story

▶ Knowing vocabulary for different types of weather

▶ Developing oral fluency

▶ Developing problem-solving skills

▶ Developing teamwork skills

ASL Connection

510 See the Weather (to the tune of "London Bridge")

See the RAIN come falling down,
Falling down, falling down.
See the RAIN come falling down
On this RAINY day.

...

See the SUN come shining through . . .
Feel the way the WIND does blow . . .
See the SNOW come falling down . . .

SKILLS

▶ Understanding basic American Sign Language

▶ Knowing vocabulary for different types of weather

▶ Developing oral fluency

Spanish Connection

511 Weather Words

Introduce the following vocabulary, and then ask the children to respond in Spanish to the questions.

Windy: *viento* (vee-EN-toh)
Sunny: *soleado* (so-lay-AH-doh)
Cloudy: *nuboso* (NOO-bo-so)

Snowy: *cubierto de nieve*
(coo-be-ERR-toh day nee-AY-vay)

What Is the Weather?

What is the weather? *Cual es el tiempo?* (COO-ahl ES el tee-EM-po)
I need to hold onto my hat today! *Cual es el tiempo?* Windy!
Whew! It's hot! *Cual es el tiempo?* Sunny!
It looks like it might rain today. *Cual es el tiempo?* Cloudy!
It's very cold and white stuff is falling from the sky. *Cual es el tiempo?* Snowy!

Recommend This!

Snow in July by Kelli C. Foster and Gina Clegg Erickson. New York: Barron's, 1996.

Un-brella by Scott E. Franson. New Milford, CT: Roaring Brook, 2007.

Who Likes the Snow? by Etta Kaner. New York: Kids Can Press, 2006.

About the Seasons by Sindy McKay. San Anselmo, CA: Treasure Bay, 2000.

Sunny Weather Days by Pam Rosenberg. New York: Scholastic, 2007.

33 Spring

Kindergarten Speak

Spring in the United States happens during the months of March, April, and May. During these months, we have different kinds of weather. Some days might be cold and even snowy, but usually by May it's hot and sunny. Trees and flowers begin blooming again, and gardens are planted. It is a wonderful time to go outside and ride your bike! What are some activities you do with your family in the spring?

Recommended Books

512 *Rabbit's Good News* by Ruth Lercher Bornstein. New York: Clarion, 2008.

When Rabbit hears something calling her, she climbs out of her hole to discover everyone experiencing spring.

    LESSON IDEA: Ask the children to name some signs of spring in your area. Have them make a collage with magazine pictures of things that remind them of spring. Garden and seed catalogs, as well as wildlife magazines, are wonderful for this activity.

513 *Splish, Splash, Spring* by Jan Carr. New York: Holiday House, 2001.

Rhyming text describes some of the delights of spring.

    LESSON IDEA: Practice sequencing. Using the flannelboard pieces, place the items in the order they appear in the story. *See following page for patterns.*

SKILLS

▶ Reading for literary experience

▶ Developing text-to-self connection

▶ Knowing that short-term weather conditions can change daily and that weather patterns change over the seasons

▶ Developing creativity

SKILLS

▶ Reading for literary experience

▶ Understanding sequencing

514 *Hurray for Spring* by Patricia Hubbell. Minnetonka, MN: NorthWord, 2005.

Rhyming text describes the activities a boy experiences in spring.

    LESSON IDEA: Ask the children to draw a picture of what they do in spring and then describe what they have drawn.

▶ Reading for literary experience

▶ Developing text-to-self connection

▶ Knowing that short-term weather conditions can change daily and that weather patterns change over the seasons

515 *Spring Song* by Barbara Seuling. San Diego, CA: Gulliver Books, 2001.

This book describes what a variety of animals do as spring begins.

    LESSON IDEA: Discuss the concept of cause and effect as demonstrated in the book. On the chalkboard make two columns, one titled "Cause" and the other titled "Effect." Read the book again and have the children tell you which items are the cause and which are the effect (for example, the snow melting and rushing down the mountainside is a cause; the black bear being able to catch the swimming treat is the effect).

▶ Reading for literary experience

▶ Appreciating nature

▶ Knowing that short-term weather conditions can change daily and that weather patterns change over the seasons

▶ Understanding simple cause-and-effect relationships

516 *Do Zebras Bloom in the Spring?* by Viki Woodworth. Plymouth, MN: Child's World, 1998.

Using rhymes, this book asks the reader a series of questions about things that appear in the spring.

    LESSON IDEA: While reading this book, pause to allow the children to answer the questions. Print pictures of the animals and items in the book, and ask the students to match each picture to its beginning letter sound.

▶ Reading for information

▶ Developing logic

▶ Knowing that short-term weather conditions can change daily and that weather patterns change over the seasons

▶ Developing oral fluency

▶ Associating sounds with letters

▶ Knowing the alphabet

Fingerplays/Rhymes

517 Be a Tree

See, see, see the trees
Sway, sway in the breeze.
Reach up high and you will see
It's easy to pretend that you're a tree!

▶ Developing oral fluency

▶ Recognizing rhyme

▶ Developing motor skills

518 Butterfly

Crawling along on the ground *(hunch on the floor)*
A caterpillar could be found.
He munched and munched a leaf he tore *(mime eating)*
And ate 'til he could eat no more. *(pat stomach)*
He spun himself in a tight cocoon, *(turn in a circle)*
While we waited, would it be soon?
It shook and shimmied before our eyes, *(shake and shimmy)*
And out popped a beautiful butterfly. *(spread arms out like wings)*

SKILLS

▶ Developing oral fluency
▶ Recognizing rhyme
▶ Developing motor skills
▶ Knowing that living things go through a process of growth and change

519 In the Spring (to the tune of "Mary Had a Little Lamb")

In the spring the sun does shine, sun does shine, sun does shine,
In the spring the sun does shine. That's how we know it's spring.

...

. . . rain does fall . . .
. . . wind does blow . . .
. . . flowers grow . . .
. . . birds build nests . . .
. . . sun does shine . . .

SKILLS

▶ Developing oral fluency
▶ Knowing that short-term weather conditions can change daily and that weather patterns change over the seasons
▶ Appreciating nature

520 Spring Dance

Can't you hear? Spring is here.
Let's all dance to a springtime beat!
Down fall the raindrops *(wiggle fingers)*
With a splat, splat, splat. *(tap feet)*
Up sprout the seeds *(pop up)*
With a snap, snap, snap. *(tap feet)*
Flowers burst open, *(open hands)*
With a pop, pop, pop. *(tap feet)*
Birds make their nests, *(pretend to build nests)*
With a plop, plop, plop! *(tap feet)*

SKILLS

▶ Developing oral fluency
▶ Knowing that short-term weather conditions can change daily and that weather patterns change over the seasons
▶ Appreciating nature
▶ Developing motor skills
▶ Recognizing rhyme

Flannelboard/Prop Stories

521 *Mouse's First Spring* Flannelboard (Based on the book by Lauren Thompson. New York: Simon and Schuster, 2005.)

A mouse discovers all the wonders of spring as he explores nature with his mother. Hide each piece until you read the text describing it, and encourage the children to guess what the object is.

SKILLS

▶ Developing listening skills
▶ Knowing that short-term weather conditions can change daily and that weather patterns change over the seasons
▶ Appreciating nature

Patterns continue on following page.

522 Matching Kites Flannelboard

Using felt, create a variety of kite pairs with different designs. Pass out the kites to the children. Then place a kite on the flannelboard and say the following chant to invite the child with the matching kite to come up and place it on the board. Continue until all kites are matched.

> The spring wind blew the kites away.
> Can you find your match today?

Writing Readiness Activity

523 Spring Acrostic **WEB**

Write the letters of the word *spring* along the top of the board. Then invite the children to think of as many spring-related words as they can that start with each letter. Write the words under the appropriate letters. Then give each child a copy of the Spring Acrostic worksheet from this book's webpage. Invite them to select their favorite word from each list to make their own poems about spring.

Math Activity

524 Flower Power

Make a variety of "flowers" from craft sticks and construction paper or card stock cut into flower shapes and glued onto the sticks. Place flowerpots around the room with different numbers on them. Have the children work in groups to count out the appropriate number of flowers and place them in the appropriate pots.

Takeaway Activity

525 **Buggy Day**

Materials: large butterfly shapes (from pattern) cut from white construction paper, large butterfly shapes (from pattern) cut from clear contact paper, small butterfly shapes (from pattern) cut from colored construction paper, glitter, small squares of tissue paper, glue, crayons, other decorating materials

Directions:

1. Decorate the colored butterfly shape with tissue paper, glitter, and crayons as desired.
2. Center the decorated butterfly over the large white construction paper butterfly.
3. Place the contact paper over the top to seal the decorations in.

Library Skill–Building Game

526 **Story Elements Review Game**

SKILLS

▶ Knowing the elements of a story
▶ Counting
▶ Developing teamwork skills
▶ Developing attention and response
▶ Developing listening skills

Preparation: Develop a list of questions about story elements based on books your class has read in recent months and on well-known stories. Examples:

Name a character in "The Three Bears."
What is the setting of *Rabbit's Good News?*
In *The Snowy Day,* Peter wants to save his snowball, but it melts. Is the snowball melting an example of a character, the setting, or a problem in the story?
What is the problem in "The Little Red Hen"?
What solution does the Little Red Hen come up with?
Tell me a word to describe the character of Goldilocks.

Activity: Begin by writing the terms *character, setting,* and *problem and solution* on the board and reviewing what they mean. Draw two trees on the blackboard, and then divide the class into two teams. Have the teams line up on opposite sides of the room. Ask each team a question in turn, going down the lines of students. (If a student is unsure, he or she should ask teammates for help.) Each time a team answers correctly, draw a flower on that team's tree. When the game is over, ask the students to guess which team has more flowers. Then count the flowers on each tree and see if their guess was correct.

ASL Connection

527 Little Caterpillar (to the tune of "The Itsy Bitsy Spider")

Little CATERPILLAR went LOOKING FOR some lunch (FOOD).
She FOUND a LEAF, crunch, crunch, crunch.
She made a little cocoon and she HID herself inside,
And when she WOKE UP, she was a beautiful BUTTERFLY.

Spanish Connection

528 Flower Rainbow

Introduce or review the following vocabulary, and then ask the questions to elicit responses in Spanish.

Yellow: *amarillo* (ah-mah-REE-yo)
Red: *rojo* (ROH-ho)
Orange: *naranja* (na-RAHN-ha)
Pink: *rosa* (RO-sa)
White: *blanco* (BLAHN-ko)

A Rainbow of Flores

Ashleigh's garden is *bonita* (bo-NEE-ta) today. She has so many flowers blooming in different colors.

There are tulips the color of the sun. *De qué color?* (day KAY co-LORE)

Ashleigh's roses are the color of fire trucks. *De qué color?*

The marigolds are the color of a juicy orange. *De qué color?*

Ashleigh's zinnias are the color of strawberry ice cream. *De qué color?*

The impatiens is the color of snow. *De qué color?*

South America experiences a wide range of weather and conditions depending on the region. Due to their proximity to the equator, many of the countries in South America experience their seasons opposite what we experience in the United States. To see what temperature various countries are experiencing while we are having springtime here, check out the Weather Channel's site: www.weather.com/common/drilldown/SAMER .html?from=searchbox_typeahead&lswe=South%20America.

Recommend This!

Goose Moon by Carolyn Arden. Honesdale, PA: Boyds Mills Press, 2004.

My Spring Robin by Anne Rockwell. New York: Macmillan, 1989.

Poppleton in Spring by Cynthia Rylant. New York: Scholastic, 1999.

Spring: A Haiku Story by George Shannon. New York: Greenwillow, 1996.

Bear Wants More by Karma Wilson. New York: Simon and Schuster, 2003.

34
Zoo Animals

Kindergarten Speak

How many of you have visited a zoo? It's a wonderful place to go where you can see all types of animals. The animals are often those that are not from where you live. Animals that are usually found in a zoo include elephants, lions, giraffes, and tigers. Zookeepers work at the zoo and take care of the animals. Sometimes zookeepers offer programs that you can attend to learn more about the animals.

Recommended Books

529 ***Dear Zoo* by Rod Campbell. New York: Simon and Schuster, 1982.**

A child writes the zoo because he desperately wants a pet. The zoo sends the child a variety of pets, but he sends most back because they aren't quite right.

LESSON IDEA: The story uses a series of adjectives (such as "big," "jumpy," and "naughty") to describe the reasons why the child sends the animals back. Introduce the term *adjective* and make a chart with the children showing the animals and the words used to describe them. Ask the children if they can think of other words to describe those animals. Then add other animals to the chart and come up with words to describe them.

530 ***Pssst!* by Adam Rex. New York: Harcourt, 2007.**

When a little girl goes to the zoo, the animals start requesting items from her. After she returns with the items, the animals set off on an adventure of their own.

LESSON IDEA: Ask the children to think about what the zoo animals may ask them for. On the chalkboard, create your own list of items the animals would ask for. Then, as a group, decide what the animals want to build with their items.

SKILLS

▶ Reading for literary experience
▶ Understanding biological evolution and the diversity of life
▶ Developing vocabulary
▶ Developing spelling knowledge
▶ Using adjectives
▶ Recognizing animal characteristics

SKILLS

▶ Reading for literary experience
▶ Understanding biological evolution and the diversity of life
▶ Developing logic
▶ Developing creativity
▶ Developing vocabulary

531 *Panda Bear, Panda Bear, What Do You See?* **by Bill Martin Jr. New York: Henry Holt, 2003.**

A variety of endangered animals and their characteristics are explored in this colorful book illustrated by Eric Carle.

LESSON IDEA: Discuss the idea of endangered animals with the children. Visit the Kids Planet Especies website for more information on endangered animals around the world: www.kidsplanet.org/factsheets/map.html. Focusing on animals in your area, ask the children to make a poster of an animal of their choice. Have them write the animal's name and any ideas for ways we can protect the animal.

SKILLS

- ▶ Reading for literary experience
- ▶ Understanding biological evolution and the diversity of life
- ▶ Developing vocabulary
- ▶ Practicing writing
- ▶ Developing creativity
- ▶ Developing text-to-self connection

532 *The Baby BeeBee Bird* **by Diane Redfield Massie. New York: HarperCollins, 2000.**

When the baby beebee bird stays up all night singing, the animals in the zoo can't sleep. The next day, the animals try to keep the baby beebee bird awake all day so they can all sleep at night!

LESSON IDEA: Help children develop an understanding of text patterns and sequencing. Have them help you retell the story, prompting them with questions such as:

Why couldn't the animals sleep at night?
How did the animals react to the noise?
What did the zookeeper see the animals doing in the morning?
What was the lion's plan?
How did the beebee bird react to the noise?
Did the plan work? What was everyone doing at night?

SKILLS

- ▶ Reading for literary experience
- ▶ Understanding sequencing
- ▶ Knowing the elements of a story

533 *Wild about Books* **by Judy Sierra. New York: Knopf, 2004.**

When librarian Molly McGrew visits the zoo, all the animals become wild for books.

LESSON IDEA: Have the children write their own zoo book! Ask them to think of their favorite animal in the zoo and write and illustrate a book about that animal's adventures.

SKILLS

- ▶ Reading for literary experience
- ▶ Understanding biological evolution and the diversity of life
- ▶ Practicing writing

Fingerplays/Rhymes

534 Alligator, Alligator Recognizing Rhyme

Alligator, alligator, swim around, *(mime swimming)*
Alligator, alligator, don't make a sound. *(hold finger to lips)*
Alligator, alligator, if we tap, *(tap fist with index finger of other hand)*
You open your jaws with a great big snap! *(open and close hands like an alligator's jaw)*

SKILLS

- ▶ Recognizing rhyme
- ▶ Developing oral fluency
- ▶ Developing motor skills

535 I'm a Giraffe (traditional)

I'm a big tall giraffe stretching way up high, *(stretch arms up over head)*
A big tall giraffe, I almost reach the sky. *(stand on tiptoes)*
I eat the leaves from the tallest trees, *(pretend to pull leaves from the trees)*
And when I run, I move with ease. *(run in place)*
I'm a big tall giraffe stretching way up high, *(stretch arms up over head)*
A big tall giraffe, I almost reach the sky. *(stand on tiptoes)*

SKILLS

- ▶ Recognizing rhyme
- ▶ Developing oral fluency
- ▶ Developing motor skills

536 **Kangaroo Baby**

If I were a kangaroo baby, *(curl up in a ball, and gradually uncurl over the first 6 lines)*
I'd stay with my mommy all day,
Curled up in her little pouch
As we hopped along our way.
Everyone would call me joey
Until I got bigger, then they'd stop,
Because I would come out of my mommy's pouch *(jump up)*
With a hop, hop, hop, hop, hop! *(hop)*

537 **The Animals at the Zoo** (to the tune of "The Wheels on the Bus")

The lions at the zoo go roar roar roar,
Roar roar roar, roar roar roar.
The lions at the zoo go roar roar roar,
All day long!

...

The snakes at the zoo go hiss hiss hiss . . .
The hyenas at the zoo go ha ha ha . . .
The monkeys at the zoo go eee-eee-eee . . .

Flannelboard/Prop Stories

538 **Five Little Snakes Flannelboard**

1 little snake looking for something to do,
He finds another and that makes 2.
2 little snakes wrapped around a tree,
Another slithers up and that makes 3.
3 little snakes by the garden door,
They see another and that makes 4.
4 little snakes notice 1 more arrive,
Basking in the sun, the snakes make 5.
5 little snakes, having quite a day,
Shh, let's leave them alone, and tiptoe away!

539 **Lion Hide-and-Seek Flannelboard**

(For each place the cub hides, place the cub under the item on the flannelboard with its tail or nose or ear sticking out so the children can see it.)

Lucy Lion was looking for her cub. But he wanted to play hide-and-seek! Can you see him? Yes, he's there behind the tree! Oh no, he's hidden again. Can you see him? Yes, there he is, behind that rock! *(Repeat with other hiding places.)*

Lucy couldn't find her cub anywhere! Finally she called, "Suppertime!" and her cub popped out and said, "Here I am, Mama!"

See following page for patterns.

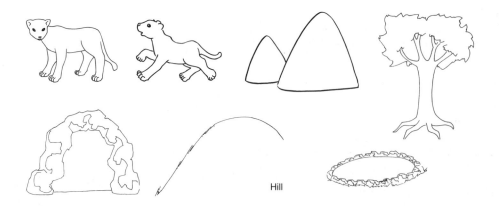

Hill

Writing Readiness Activity

540 **Dear Zoo Letter**

Have the children write a letter to the zoo asking the zookeepers to send them a pet. The children should draw a picture and write which pet they want. They can also list ways in which they would take care of the pet.

SKILLS

- ► Practicing writing
- ► Developing text-to-self connection
- ► Writing one's name

Math Activity

541 **Zoo Graph**

Prepare a graph with a few zoo animal names, or pictures of the animals, at the bottom. Discuss zoo animals and ask each child to place an X in the column of his or her favorite animal. This activity allows the children to easily see which animals are more favored and which animals are less favored. When the graph is done, ask the children which animal was the favorite and which was the least favorite.

SKILLS

- ► Understanding that graphs represent information
- ► Counting
- ► Understanding the terms *more than, less than,* and *same as* for comparing quantity

---

Takeaway Activity

542 **Zebra Habitat**

Materials: zebra shape, construction paper, crayons, markers, glue, scissors, leaves, twigs, grass

Directions:

1. Glue the zebra shape to the construction paper and decorate as desired.
2. Glue leaves, twigs, and grass to the picture for the zebra to graze on.

SKILLS

- ► Developing creativity
- ► Understanding biological evolution and the diversity of life
- ► Developing fine motor skills
- ► Appreciating nature

Library Skill–Building Game

543 Searching Shimmy Shake

▶ Understanding the nature and uses of different forms of technology

▶ Knowing basic strategies for searching for information

▶ Organizing information

▶ Developing logic

▶ Developing motor skills

Preparation: Set up a projector and screen so that everyone can see your online catalog. If your school does not have an online catalog, use your local public library's catalog on the Internet. If you do not have an LCD projector, print screenshots from the catalog and copy them onto transparency film to use with an overhead projector.

Activity: Begin by asking the children the different ways that one can find what one is looking for in the library, and list the ways on the board:

1. Ask the librarian.
2. Use the signs/call numbers to figure out where the book would be.
3. Use the catalog.

Explain that there are two ways to search when using the catalog:

Keyword searching finds the words you search for anywhere in the book's record.

Browsing takes you to a specific spot in an index (or alphabetical list). When you browse, you are looking *only* at a list of authors, titles, or words that describe the subject, depending on which kind of index you are browsing.

As you explain the two types, show children sample searches for zoo animals and point out where your search terms appear. Ask them which type of searching they think would be better, and then explain that each is a good way to search, depending on what you are looking for. If you want to find everything that even mentions a certain word, then keyword searching is better. If you are looking for a certain author's books, or a certain title, or books on a very specific topic, then browsing is better.

Next, play the Searching Shimmy Shake game. Read each of the following sentences. If the children think that a keyword search would be best for that search, they should shimmy and grasp with their hands at the air (as if picking all the keywords out of the air). If they think a browse would be best, they should jump up and put their arms in the air one time (because browsing is best for finding one specific title, author, or subject).

1. I want to find the book *Brown Bear, Brown Bear, What Do You See?*
2. I need to find all kinds of information about zoo animals.
3. I want to find a book about Koko, the chimpanzee who knows sign language.
4. I want to find books about zoos all over the world.
5. I need to find a book by Cynthia Rylant.
6. I want to find a book about giant pandas.
7. I need to find a book about all kinds of jungle animals, but I don't know the names of the animals.
8. I want to find the book *I Am Going to the Zoo.*
9. I want to find books about all the different people who work with animals.
10. I want to find a book by Eric Carle.

ASL Connection: Animal Count

544 *1, 2, 3 to the Zoo!* **by Eric Carle. New York: Philomel, 1968.**

This wordless picture book is an excellent way to introduce animal signs, as well as the signs for numbers 1–10. After reading the story, sign questions to the children about the animals, such as "HOW MANY BIRDS?" Ask for a volunteer to come up and count, then sign the answer. Then have the volunteer sign a question for the class.

one

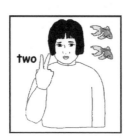
two

three

four

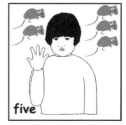
five

six

seven

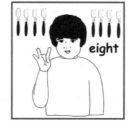
eight

nine

ten

how many

elephant

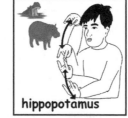
hippopotamus

giraffe

lion

bear

alligator

seal

monkey

snake

bird

Spanish Connection

SKILLS

► Understanding basic Spanish vocabulary

► Counting

► Understanding other cultures

► Appreciating nature

► Developing oral fluency

545 *Cinco Monos Pequeños* **(Five Little Monkeys)**

Cinco monos pequeños (SINK-o MO-nos pay-KAY-nios) swinging in the tree,
Teasing Mr. Alligator, "You can't catch me."
Along came Mr. Alligator quiet as can be,
And SNAPPED that *mono* (MO-no) out of the tree.

...

Cuatro (QUA-tro) *monos pequeños* . . .
Tres (TRACE) *monos pequeños* . . .
Dos (DOSE) *monos pequeños* . . .
Uno (OO-no) *mono pequeño* (pay-KAY-nio) . . .

Belize is one of the smallest countries in Central America, but it has one of the greatest zoos in the world. The Belize Zoo and Tropical Education Center was started in 1983. The zoo keeps only animals native to Belize, animals which much of the local population had not even seen until the zoo opened.

Check out the Belize Zoo at www.belizezoo.org. Be sure to watch the video about how the Belize Zoo was created.

Recommend This!

If a Monkey Jumps Onto Your School Bus by Jean M. Cochran. Raynham Center, MA: Pleasant St., 2008.

New at the Zoo by Frank B. Edwards. Buffalo, NY: Firefly, 1998.

Let's Go to the Zoo by Cate Foley. New York: Children's Press, 2001.

Sammy the Seal by Syd Hoff. New York: HarperCollins, 2000.

The Class Trip by Grace Maccarone. New York: Scholastic, 1999.

At the Zoo by Dana Meachen Rau. New York: Marshall Cavendish, 2008.

A Trip to the Zoo by Karen Wallace. New York: DK, 2003.

35

Farm Animals

Kindergarten Speak

A farm is a large area of land that is mainly used to produce food. That food can be in the form of crops like corn, wheat, or soybeans, or it can be used for animals that give us food, such as cows or chickens.

Recommended Books

546 *Book! Book! Book!* **by Deborah Bruss. New York: Scholastic, 2001.**

When the children return to school, the farm animals get bored. Soon they discover the joys of the local library and reading.

    LESSON IDEA: Have the children retell the story with the pieces for the flannelboard.

SKILLS

▶ Reading for literary experience

▶ Recognizing animals and their sounds

▶ Understanding sequencing

▶ Knowing the elements of a story

547 *Thump, Quack, Moo* by Doreen Cronin. New York: Atheneum, 2008.

When Farmer Brown begins to transform his farm for the annual Corn Maze Festival, his maze masterpiece isn't exactly what he anticipated. A ride in the hot air balloon lets Farmer Brown know that Duck was involved in an unexpected way.

LESSON IDEA: Give each student a piece of graph paper and let the children plan out and design a maze of their choice.

SKILLS

- ► Reading for literary experience
- ► Developing creativity
- ► Understanding sequencing
- ► Understanding that maps can represent our surroundings

548 *Barnyard Banter* by Denise Fleming. New York: Henry Holt, 1994.

The farm animals are all busy making their noises, and one goose is on the loose.

LESSON IDEA: Before reading the story, ask the children if they know what the word *banter* means. When you've finished reading the story, discuss *banter* again. Then have the children make a chart showing the animals in the story and the sound each animal made.

- ► Reading for literary experience
- ► Developing vocabulary
- ► Understanding biological evolution and the diversity of life
- ► Recognizing animals and their sounds
- ► Organizing information

549 *The Perfect Nest* by Catherine Friend. Cambridge, MA: Candlewick Press, 2007.

Jack the cat builds the perfect nest in hopes of attracting the perfect chicken, who will lay the perfect egg, so that he can make the perfect omelet. But when a chicken, a duck, and a goose all claim the nest, Jack doesn't get what he hoped for.

LESSON IDEA: Ask the children to think of what their perfect food is and what they would do to get it. Then have them draw a picture of the food and write what they would do.

- ► Reading for literary experience
- ► Developing text-to-self connection
- ► Practicing writing

550 *Punk Farm* by Jarrett Krosoczka. New York: Knopf, 2005.

As the farmer gets ready for bed, the animals get ready for their nighttime concert!

LESSON IDEA: What do animals do for entertainment when the people aren't looking? Create a story with the children about what animals might do for fun when we're asleep. Start with the sentence, "Fred the cow made sure there were no people nearby." Then ask each child to contribute a sentence to make a story. When you are getting to the last few children, remind them they need to create an ending to the story. Write down the story and read it aloud to the class once all the children have taken a turn. Then work with the class to describe the characters, setting, and problem/solution in your story.

SKILLS

- ► Reading for literary experience
- ► Developing creativity
- ► Knowing the elements of a story

Fingerplays/Rhymes/Songs

551 Farm Yard Fun

Working on the farm was hard work today,
I used my pitchfork to spread the hay. *(pretend to pick up hay with pitchfork)*
I fed the chickens, *(feed chickens)*
And gathered eggs from the hens. *(pick up eggs)*
I milked the cows, *(milk cows)*
Then cleaned the muck from the pigpen. *(hold nose)*
I was happy to see the setting sun,
Because I knew my day was done. *(head on hands pretending to sleep)*

SKILLS

- ► Developing oral fluency
- ► Recognizing rhyme
- ► Developing motor skills

552 How Much Is That Piggy? (to the tune of "How Much Is That Doggy in the Window?")

How much is that piggy in the pigsty? (Oink oink!)
The one with the curly tail. (Oink oink!)
How much is that piggy in the pigsty? (Oink oink!)
I do hope that piggy's for sale.

553 This Is the Way (to the tune of "Here We Go 'Round the Mulberry Bush")

This is the way the rooster calls,
The rooster calls, the rooster calls,
This is the way the rooster calls, so early in the morning. (Cock-a-doodle-doo!)

…

This is the way the hens wake up . . . (Cluck, cluck, cluck!)
This is the way the cows say hello . . . (MOO!)

(Continue with more animals as desired.)

554 Farm Song (to the tune of "The Wheels on the Bus")

The tractor on the farm goes vroom, vroom, vroom,
Vroom, vroom, vroom, vroom, vroom, vroom.
The tractor on the farm goes vroom, vroom, vroom, all day long.

…

The horses on the farm go neigh, neigh, neigh . . .
The cows on the farm go moo, moo, moo . . .
The ducks on the farm go quack, quack, quack . . .
The hens on the farm go cluck, cluck, cluck . . .
The pigs on the farm go oink, oink, oink . . .

…

The farmer on the farm says time for bed,
Time for bed, time for bed.
The farmer on the farm says time for bed, after all the work is done!

Flannelboard/Prop Stories

555 Five Silly Pigs Flannelboard

5 silly pigs dancing a jig,
The farmer was coming and 1 went a-running,
Right out the barnyard door.
Now we're left with 4!
4 silly pigs dancing a jig,
The farmer was coming and 1 went a-running,
And bumped right into a tree.
Now we're left with 3!
3 silly pigs dancing a jig,
The farmer was coming and 1 went a-running,
And hid under the cow who said MOO!
Now we're left with 2!

2 silly pigs dancing a jig,
The farmer was coming and 1 went a-running,
Right out into the blinding sun.
Now we're left with 1!
1 silly pig dancing a jig,
The farmer was coming and he went a-running,
Knowing the dancing was done.
Because now we're left with none!

556 Rooster's Feathers Flannelboard

(Cut feathers [from pattern] out of different colors of felt. Place the rooster on the flannelboard. Hand out the feathers to the children. Have the children decorate the rooster as you sing the following song to the tune of "Do You Know the Muffin Man?")

> Do you have a red feather, a red feather, a red feather?
> If you have a red feather, bring it up here now.

(Repeat with other colors.)

SKILLS
- ▶ Recognizing colors
- ▶ Developing attention and response
- ▶ Developing oral fluency

Writing Readiness Activity

557 Down on the Farm

Ask if any of the children live on a farm or have visited a farm or a fair where there were lots of farm animals. Have the children draw a picture of their favorite farm animal and write why that animal is their favorite. Ask if they know what sound their animal makes. If so, have them write that on their paper, too!

SKILLS
- ▶ Practicing writing
- ▶ Developing text-to-self connection
- ▶ Understanding biological evolution and the diversity of life
- ▶ Recognizing animals and their sounds

Math Activity

558 Egg Carton Counting

Divide the children into groups and give each group an old egg container with the cups labeled 1–12. Provide a variety of materials, such as marbles, seeds, small erasers, and so on, for them to count into the egg cups, filling each cup with the appropriate number of items.

SKILL
- ▶ Counting

Takeaway Activity

559 What a Pig!

Materials: a pig picture for each child, pink and brown tissue paper, pink pipe cleaners, glue, crayons

SKILLS
- ▶ Developing creativity
- ▶ Developing fine motor skills

Directions:

1. Decorate the pig picture using pink tissue paper for the body and brown tissue paper for the mud puddle.
2. Curl a piece of pink pipe cleaner and glue it on to create a curly tail.

Library Skill–Building Game

560 Search Term Race

Preparation: Set up a projector and screen to show your online catalog or your local public library's catalog. If you do not have an LCD projector, print out screenshots of sample searches and copy them onto overhead transparency film.

Activity: Review the two types of searching (keyword and browsing). Explain that it's important to find the right words to search for. Lead children through some sample searches to demonstrate. For example, "If I want to find a book about pigs, but I search for the term *farm animals,* I will find too many books, and many of them won't be what I am looking for."

Next, divide the class into groups of three or four students. Write the word *cows* on the board and give the groups three to five minutes to brainstorm as many words as they can about cows (examples might be *milk, calf, moo*). Then have the groups report and make a list of the words on the board. As you write each word, discuss the kinds of books that are likely to result from a search using that word. Discuss how one can combine search words to find more specific items (for example, *America* and *cows* would result in books about cows in America only). Repeat the activity using a broader term: *farms.* Have the children brainstorm words again, and this time when you list the words, emphasize which are *general* and which are *specific.*

SKILLS

▶ Knowing basic strategies for searching for information

▶ Developing vocabulary

▶ Developing oral fluency

▶ Developing spelling knowledge

▶ Developing teamwork skills

ASL Connection

561 Old MacDonald

Old MacDonald had a FARM, E-I-E-I-O.
And on that farm he had a COW, E-I-E-I-O.
With a moo-moo here and a moo-moo there,
Here a moo, there a moo, everywhere a moo-moo.
Old MacDonald had a FARM, E-I-E-I-O.
(Repeat with other animals.)

SKILLS

▶ Understanding basic American Sign Language

▶ Developing oral fluency

▶ Recognizing animals and their sounds

Signs continue on following page.

Spanish Connection

562 Farm Animals

Using pictures, introduce the Spanish vocabulary for the following farm animals:

Cow: *vaca* (VAH-cah)
Piglet: *cerdito* (sair-DEE-toh)
Sheep: *oveja* (o-VAY-hah)
Duck: *pato* (PAH-toh)
Dog: *perro* (PAIR-ro)
Horse: *caballo* (cah-BY-yo)

Down on Grandpa's Farm (traditional)

Down on Grandpa's farm there is a big brown *vaca.*
Down on Grandpa's farm there is a big brown *vaca.*
The *vaca,* she makes a sound like this: MOO MOO!
The *vaca,* she makes a sound like this: MOO MOO!

(Repeat with other animals.)

When we think of crops that come from our farms, we think of corn and wheat. But South America's principle crop is coffee! The word for "coffee" in Spanish is *café.* Farmers carefully tend the coffee trees, which take two or three years to produce their first crop. Corn, or maize, is also a basic food in Mexico and Central America, and *masa* is the basis for most of the corn foods. *Masa* is made by soaking or cooking corn in lime and water until it is softened, and then the corn is ground.

Recommend This!

Cock-a-doodle-doo! Barnyard Hullabaloo by Giles Andreae. Wilton, CT: Tiger Tales, 1999.
The Farm Team by Linda Bailey. Tonawanda, NY: Kids Can Press, 2008.
Chicken Said, "Cluck!" by Judyann Ackerman Grant. New York: HarperCollins, 2008.
A Day at Greenhill Farm by Sue Nicholson. New York: DK, 1998.
On a Farm by Dana Meachen Rau. Tarrytown, NY: Marshall Cavendish, 2008.

36
Sea Animals

Kindergarten Speak

Animals that live in the ocean are called marine animals. *Marine* is a fancy word that means "ocean." Can you think of another word that means "ocean"? How about *sea*? Oceans have saltwater in them and are home to lots of different kinds of animals. Do you like to play in the ocean?

Recommended Books

563 *Commotion in the Ocean* by Giles Andreae. Wilton, CT: Little Tiger, 1998.

Through humorous poems, readers will discover various animals found in the ocean and some of their more unusual characteristics.

LESSON IDEA: Read the book a second time, asking the children to identify rhyming words. On the chalkboard, make a list of rhyming words they find. Once you've made your list, ask children if they can think of any other words that rhyme with the ones listed.

SKILLS

▶ Reading for literary experience
▶ Recognizing rhyme
▶ Developing vocabulary
▶ Developing spelling knowledge

564 *Sea Creatures* by Sue Malyan. New York: DK, 2005.

This nonfiction book with fantastic photos and facts features some of the more unusual animals in the ocean.

LESSON IDEA: Discuss with the children how some animals live near the top of the ocean where the water is warmer (fish), while others live lower where it is cooler (whales). Then show them that hot water rises by filling a clear container with cold water. Next add blue hot water (dyed with blue food coloring). The blue hot water will rise to the top of the container.

▶ Reading for information
▶ Understanding biological evolution and the diversity of life
▶ Knowing properties of water

565 *Way Down Deep in the Deep Blue Sea* by Jan Peck. New York: Simon and Schuster, 2004.

A boy uses his imagination to dive for buried treasure in his bathtub. Along the way he meets a variety of sea animals.

LESSON IDEA: Help children develop an understanding of text patterns and sequencing. Have them help you retell the story, prompting them with questions such as:

What was the first sea animal the boy met?
Which animal did the boy play peek-a-boo with?
Which animal did the boy dance with?
Which animal did the boy play tag with?
Who waved to the boy with his eight arms?
Which animal did the boy fence with?
Which animal did the boy swim away from?

SKILLS

▶ Reading for literary experience
▶ Understanding sequencing
▶ Knowing the elements of a story
▶ Developing oral fluency

566 *One Nighttime Sea* by Deborah Lee Rose. New York: Scholastic, 2003.

This counting book examines nocturnal sea animals.

LESSON IDEA: Ask the children if they know what the largest creature in the world is and how long they think it is. The answer is a blue whale. Get a long rope (about 100 feet) and have them unwind it. They will be amazed at how long a blue whale is. Next ask them how many of their lengths it would take to make a blue whale. If time allows, let the children lie along the length of the rope to see if their entire class could fit in a blue whale.

SKILLS

▶ Counting
▶ Reading for information
▶ Understanding basic concepts of measurement
▶ Developing text-to-self connection
▶ Understanding biological evolution and the diversity of life

567 *What the Sea Saw* by Stephanie St. Pierre. Atlanta, GA: Peachtree, 2006.

This book provides a wonderful introduction to the relationship between sea creatures, other animals, plants, and the ecosystems where they live.

LESSON IDEA: Ask the children to discuss the similarities and differences of animals in the book. What are the needs of animals that live in different areas? Compare land and ocean animals. Are some needs the same regardless of where the animal lives?

SKILLS

▶ Reading for information
▶ Developing compare and contrast skills
▶ Understanding biological evolution and the diversity of life

Fingerplays/Rhymes

568 Five Clownfish

5 clownfish swimming in the sea, *(make 5 fingers wiggle for the fish)*
Teasing Mr. Shark, "You can't catch me!"
Along comes Mr. Shark
As quiet as can be,
When SNAP . . . *(clap hands)*

...

4 clownfish . . .
3 clownfish . . .
2 clownfish . . .
1 clownfish . . .

SKILLS

▶ Counting
▶ Developing oral fluency
▶ Developing motor skills
▶ Recognizing rhyme

569 Gone Fishing

Maxwell the fisherman floats on the sea,
Sitting in his boat is where he really loves to be. *(make boat with cupped hands)*
He throws in his line and makes a little wish, *(mime throwing fishing line)*
Hoping that maybe today he'll catch a fish. *(cross fingers)*
When he reels it in from the water cold and black, *(mime reeling in fishing pole)*
He gives that little fish a little kiss, *(mime kissing fish)*
And then he throws it back. *(mime throwing it back)*

SKILLS

▶ Developing oral fluency
▶ Developing motor skills
▶ Recognizing rhyme

570 Octopus, Octopus

Octopus, octopus, turn around.
Octopus, octopus, touch the ground.
Octopus, octopus, reach up high.
Octopus, octopus, wave goodbye. *(wave good-bye with arms and legs)*

SKILLS

▶ Developing oral fluency
▶ Developing motor skills
▶ Recognizing rhyme

571 Sea Animal Walk

Wiggle your tail with a swish like a fish.
Jump up high like a dolphin saying hi.
Scuttle side to side like a crab in the tide.
Get real low like a snail moving slow.

SKILLS

▶ Developing oral fluency
▶ Developing motor skills

Flannelboard/Prop Stories

572 *Blue Sea* Flannelboard (Based on the book by Robert Kalan. New York: Greenwillow, 1979.)

In this simple classic, a small fish escapes from a larger fish, the larger fish escapes from an even larger fish, and so on. Use a piece of netting to create a net and a piece of felt with various-sized holes to trap the bigger fish.

SKILLS

▶ Developing listening skills
▶ Comparing size and volume

 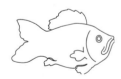  

573 Five Fish Flannelboard

1 lonely fish, with fins of blue,
Met another in the ocean and that makes 2.
2 fish swimming through the sea,
Met another by the reef and that makes 3.
3 striped fish, looking for some more,
Met another at school and that makes 4.
4 fish practicing their dives,
Met another in the deep and that makes 5.
5 happy fish, swimming off to play,
Then swimming home at the end of the day.

SKILLS

▶ Counting
▶ Developing oral fluency
▶ Recognizing rhyme
▶ Understanding biological evolution and the diversity of life

Writing Readiness Activity

574 Sea Animals

Ask the children to think of an animal they have seen at the beach or an aquarium. Ask them to draw a picture of the animal and write the name of the animal underneath the picture. Work together as a class to write the name of each animal on the board.

SKILLS

▶ Practicing writing
▶ Developing text-to-self connection
▶ Understanding biological evolution and the diversity of life

Math Activity

575 Create a Fish

Provide a piece of construction paper and a variety of precut shapes for each child. Let the children create a fish from the shapes and glue it onto the paper.

SKILLS

▶ Recognizing shapes
▶ Developing creativity

Takeaway Activity

576 Paper Plate Portholes

Materials: colored tissue paper, crayons or markers, stickers, yarn, construction paper, two paper plates for each child, tape, scissors

Directions:

1. Fold one paper plate in half. Carefully cut out the center circle and put the plate aside.
2. Create an ocean scene on the other plate using crayons, markers, yarn, stickers, tissue paper, and other materials.
3. Lay the first paper plate (with the center cut out) over the second plate (with the ocean scene). Tape the edges together.
4. Hold the plate up and look out through your "porthole."

SKILLS

▶ Developing creativity
▶ Developing fine motor skills

Library Skill–Building Game

577 Fishing for Call Numbers

Preparation: Copy the fish pattern onto brightly colored construction paper or card stock to make enough fish for your class. Gather up books in the areas whose call numbers you want to reinforce and place them in order near your lesson area. (Make sure you have the same number of books as fish.) Write one call number on each fish. (If you plan to reuse this game, you may wish to laminate the fish and keep a list of the books you pull.) Put a paper clip on each fish. Make simple fishing rods using sticks or dowel rods with yarn and a magnet tied to the end.

Activity: Place the fish on the floor. Give each child a turn to catch a fish using the fishing rod, and then match it to the correct book on the cart. Guide the children through the

SKILLS

▶ Developing motor skills
▶ Understanding the parts of the library
▶ Understanding the concept of fiction
▶ Understanding the concept of nonfiction

matching process by asking what type of book the call number goes with or by helping them identify the letters if you are sticking with picture books. You may also wish to use small fish stickers or a hand stamp to reward correct answers.

ASL Connection

578 Fish Dance

Show the children the sign for FISH. Using a freeze dance such as "Rock and Roll Freeze Dance" by Hap Palmer (on *So Big: Activity Songs for Little Ones,* Hap-Pal Music, 2001), encourage the children to make the FISH sign swim up, down, and in circles while the music is playing, and freeze when it stops. Then explain that in American Sign Language, we listen with our eyes, not our ears. Do a "listening with your eyes" freeze dance, where the children must watch your FISH sign to know when theirs should swim or stop.

fish

SKILLS

▶ Understanding basic American Sign Language

▶ Developing visual discrimination

▶ Developing attention and response

▶ Developing listening skills

Spanish Connection

579 *Pez* Poem

In the ocean you will find
An assortment of *pez* (PACE), more than one kind!
Pez is the Spanish word for "fish."

The second-largest coral reef in the world lies off the coast of Belize, in Central America, and is home to over 500 species of fish. Coral reefs are among the most biologically diverse ecosystems on earth. Second only to tropical rain forests in the number of species they harbor, they are sometimes called the rain forests of the sea.

For more information on Belize's coral reef, visit the National Geographic website, which discusses the threats to the reef: http://video.nationalgeographic.com/video/player/environment/habitats-environment/oceans/belize-coral.html.

SKILLS

▶ Understanding basic Spanish vocabulary

▶ Understanding biological evolution and the diversity of life

Recommend This!

A House for Hermit Crab by Eric Carle. Saxonville, MA: Picture Book Studio, 1987.

Sometimes I Wish by Kelli C. Foster. New York: Barron's, 1991.

I'm the Biggest Thing in the Ocean by Kevin Sherry. New York: Dial, 2007.

I'm the Best Artist in the Ocean by Kevin Sherry. New York: Dial, 2008.

I Saw the Sea and the Sea Saw Me by Megan Montague Cash. New York: Viking, 2001.

37

In the Garden

Kindergarten Speak

How many of you have a garden at home? Some gardens have fruits and vegetables, while others have flowers. Even if you don't have a lot of space, you can have a garden using different pots and containers. It's even possible to grow some vegetables, like tomatoes and cucumbers, in pots on a sunny balcony, deck, or front porch. Gardens make it possible for families to have food and flowers all summer long.

Recommended Books

580 *Up, Down and Around* by Katherine Ayres. Cambridge, MA: Candlewick Press, 2007.

The children discover that some plants grow up, some grow down, and some grow around and around.

    LESSON IDEA: Follow up the story with a sorting game. Pass out pictures of various vegetables. Write the headings "Above the Ground" and "Below the Ground" on the board and invite the children to place their vegetables in the appropriate category.

581 *Planting a Rainbow* by Lois Ehlert. New York: Harcourt Brace, 1988.

Each year, a child and his mother plant a garden with a variety of flowers in every color of the rainbow.

    LESSON IDEA: Make your own rainbow. Provide a piece of construction paper for each child. Have the children glue some store-bought Easter grass at the bottom of their paper. Then have them draw a stem and leaves for one or two flowers. Give each child a paper muffin cup liner to glue to the stem, creating a personal rainbow garden.

SKILLS

▶ Reading for information

▶ Developing classification and sorting skills

▶ Appreciating nature

▶ Knowing that living things go through a process of growth and change

SKILLS

▶ Reading for literary experience

▶ Developing creativity

▶ Appreciating nature

▶ Knowing that living things go through a process of growth and change

582 *Whose Garden Is It?* **by Mary Ann Hoberman. New York: Harcourt, 2004.**

When Mrs. McGee goes walking one day, she discovers a beautiful garden and wonders whose garden it is. Suddenly the animals, bugs, plants, dirt, rain, and sun all claim ownership of the garden. This book is a wonderful example of how things in life are interconnected and dependent on one another.

    LESSON IDEA: Ask the children whose garden they think it was and why. Does any one person, animal, bug, or element have a better claim to the garden?

SKILLS

▶ Reading for literary experience
▶ Appreciating nature
▶ Knowing that living things go through a process of growth and change

583 *One Hundred Hungry Ants* **by Elinor J. Pinczes. New York: Houghton Mifflin, 1993.**

When 100 ants smell a picnic, they rush in the direction of the food. But one little ant discovers they can all get to the picnic faster if they organize themselves in rows, first two rows of fifty, then four rows of twenty-five, and so on.

    LESSON IDEA: This is a wonderful book to reinforce the different ways you can count to 100! Using various manipulatives (pickup sticks, marbles, etc.) have the children work in groups to practice the different ways to count to 100 explored in the book.

SKILLS

▶ Reading for literary experience
▶ Reading for information
▶ Counting

584 *Carrot Soup* **by John Segal. New York: Simon and Schuster, 2006.**

Rabbit's favorite season is spring, and he is excited to plant many different types of carrots so that he can have carrot soup. But when his carrots disappear, Rabbit gets a surprise.

    LESSON IDEA: Give each child a cup with some dirt and carrot seeds to plant! They will enjoy watching the carrots grow. Include a carrot soup recipe of your choice for the children to take home, or print the following recipe: http://allrecipes.com/Recipe/Creamy-Carrot-Soup-2/Detail.aspx.

SKILLS

▶ Reading for information
▶ Developing text-to-self connection
▶ Appreciating nature
▶ Knowing that living things go through a process of growth and change

Fingerplays/Rhymes

585 Five Green Peas (adapted traditional)

5 green peas in a pea pod pressed, *(make fist)*
1, 2, 3, 4, 5. *(lift fingers one at a time)*
They grew and grew and did not stop *(stretch fingers out)*
Till 1 day that pea pod popped! *(clap hands)*

SKILLS

▶ Recognizing rhyme
▶ Developing motor skills
▶ Developing oral fluency
▶ Knowing that living things go through a process of growth and change

586 Garden Stretch

I reach high for the apples *(reach high on tiptoes)*
And low for the peas. *(squat low)*
I eat too many strawberries, *(pretend to eat)*
But stop when Mom sees. *(stop eating)*
With a snap, snap, snap *(snap)*
I pick the tomatoes. *(pretend to pick)*
With a grunt, grunt, grunt *(grunt)*
I pull the potatoes. *(pretend to pull)*
I work all day with the sun in the sky, *(pretend to dig)*
But when the moon rises, I say goodbye. *(wave)*

SKILLS

▶ Recognizing rhyme
▶ Developing motor skills
▶ Developing oral fluency

587 I Love . . .

I love broccoli,
I love peas,
I love carrots,
If you please.
I love lettuce,
And one thing more,
Tomatoes make
A salad I adore.

SKILLS

▶ Recognizing rhyme
▶ Developing oral fluency

588 I'm a Little Seed (to the tune of "I'm a Little Teapot")

I'm a little seed growing in the ground *(huddle on the floor)*
Deep beneath the soil, without a sound.
Now the rain is falling down just so. *(reach arms up to show rain falling)*
The sun shines on me, and up I grow! *(grow to standing)*

SKILLS

▶ Developing oral fluency
▶ Recognizing rhyme
▶ Developing motor skills
▶ Knowing that living things go through a process of growth and change

Flannelboard/Prop Stories

589 Picking Fruits and Vegetables Flannelboard

Monday is my apple day,
I pick apples from the tree this way.
Tuesday is my blueberry day,
I pick blueberries from the bush this way.
Wednesday is my raspberry day,
I pick raspberries from the bramble this way.
Thursday is my strawberry day,
I pick strawberries from the plant this way.
Friday is my sweet potato day,
I pick sweet potatoes from the ground this way.
Saturday is my pumpkin day,
I pick pumpkins from the vine this way.
Sunday is my pie-making day,
I eat all my pies this way!

SKILLS

▶ Recognizing days of the week
▶ Understanding biological evolution and the diversity of life
▶ Recognizing rhyme
▶ Developing oral fluency

590 Seeds

(Match the seed/fruit/vegetable with the plant it comes from.)

Seeds, seeds, that's what I need! What do I get from this seed?

Acorn   Sunflower seed   Tomato

Tomato plant   Blueberrry   Sunflower   Apple tree

Oak tree

Watermelon vine   Strawberry plant   Berry bushes   Watermelon

SKILLS

▶ Understanding biological evolution and the diversity of life

▶ Recognizing rhyme

▶ Developing classification and sorting skills

Writing Readiness Activity

591 Picturing Pie

Pies are made from all types of fruits and vegetables. Have the children draw a picture of their favorite pie and list the ingredients that they need to make it. Or have them create a new recipe for a pie of their choice!

SKILLS

▶ Developing creativity

▶ Developing text-to-self connection

▶ Practicing writing

Math Activity

592 Sorting Veggies

Glue pictures of vegetables to index cards. Divide the children into groups and give each group eight cards. The groups should work together to sort their vegetables in different ways (by color, by size, by type, etc.). How many different ways can they find to sort?

SKILLS

▶ Developing classification and sorting skills

▶ Understanding biological evolution and the diversity of life

▶ Understanding patterns

▶ Developing teamwork skills

▶ Developing visual discrimination

Takeaway Activity

SKILLS

593 Pea Pod Craft

Materials: a printout of a pea pod for each child (from pattern), green tissue paper, glue, crayons, other decorating materials

► Developing creativity
► Developing fine motor skills

Directions:

1. Color the pea pod.
2. Squish small pieces of green tissue into balls to make peas for your pod.
3. Glue the tissue "peas" to the pod.
4. Decorate as desired.

Library Skill–Building Game

594 Library Vocabulary Bingo

SKILLS

Preparation: Create a list of up to thirty library-related vocabulary words you want to reinforce. (Your list might include names of areas of the school library, as well as words like *fiction, nonfiction, character.*) Create bingo cards featuring these vocabulary words. You can find a wonderfully easy, free way to make bingo cards online at DLTK's Custom Bingo Cards (www.dltk-cards.com/bingo/bingo1.asp). If you have fewer than thirty vocabulary words, then select a theme from the list on the DLTK website, and the program will fill in the extra spaces with pictures. Make sure that you select the vocabulary option so that you can input your list. In the final step, you can print both a callout sheet containing all the words and pictures as well as bingo cards with the words and pictures randomly distributed. Cut the callout sheet into squares and place the squares in an envelope.

► Developing vocabulary
► Developing attention and response
► Understanding the parts of the library
► Developing listening skills

Activity: Provide a bingo card and objects to mark it with (such as small candies or stickers) for each child. As you pull each word out of the envelope, give clues about what it is and see if the children can guess it. Let the children try to find the word themselves, and then write it on the board.

ASL Connection

595 Flowers for My Family

SKILLS

FIVE pretty FLOWERS in my garden by the door.
I picked one for my MOTHER, and then there were FOUR.
FOUR pretty FLOWERS underneath the tree.
I picked one for my FATHER, and then there were THREE.
THREE pretty FLOWERS growing like flowers do.
I picked one for my SISTER, and then there were TWO.
TWO pretty FLOWERS growing in the sun.
I picked one for my BROTHER, and then there was ONE.
ONE pretty FLOWER, and I thought it would be fun
To pick that one for YOU, and then there were NONE.

► Understanding basic American Sign Language
► Counting
► Recognizing rhyme
► Developing oral fluency

See following page for signs.

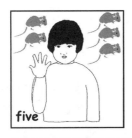

five

flower

mother

four

father

three

sister

two

brother

one

you

Spanish Connection

596 *Cinco Verde Guisantes* **(Five Peas)** (adapted traditional)

Cinco (SINK-o) *verde guisantes* (VAIR-day gee-SAHN-tays) in a pea pod pressed,
   (make fist)
Uno, dos, tres, cuatro, cinco. (OO-no, DOSE, TRACE, QUA-tro, SINK-o)
   (lift fingers one at a time)
They grew and grew and did not stop *(stretch fingers out)*
Till 1 day that pea pod popped! *(clap hands)*

SKILLS

- ▶ Understanding basic Spanish vocabulary
- ▶ Counting
- ▶ Developing oral fluency
- ▶ Developing motor skills
- ▶ Recognizing rhyme

Recommend This!

Jasper's Beanstalk by Nick Butterworth. New York: Bradbury, 1993.
Garden Friends. New York: DK, 2003.
Flowers and Friends by Anita Holmes. New York: Marshall Cavendish, 2001.
Harvey the Gardener by Lars Klinting. Boston: Houghton Mifflin, 1997.
Watch Me Plant a Garden by Jack Otten. New York: Children's Press, 2002.

38 Summer

· ·

Kindergarten Speak

Summer in the United States is during the months of June, July, and August. It's often when schools are on break. The summer is usually hot and sunny, and it's a terrific time to do all sorts of outdoor activities. What are some of your favorite activities? Camping, picnicking, and swimming are some summer favorites.

Recommended Books

597 *One Summery Day* **by Larry Dane Brimmer. New York: Child's World, 2006.**

This family explores many of the activities you can do during summer, when there is no school.

LESSON IDEA: Ask students how they knew the story took place in the summer. Write what the students say on the board under the label "We know the setting is summer because . . . ."

598 *Ants at the Picnic* **by Michael Dahl. Minneapolis, MN: Picture Window, 2006.**

One hundred ants find the perfect picnic with lots of food and begin carrying it off, ten ants at a time, until all the food and ants are gone.

LESSON IDEA: This is a great book to practice counting in tens. Have the students practice counting by tens up to 100 and back down to zero. Give the students craft sticks or other items to help them count.

SKILLS

▶ Reading for literary experience

▶ Knowing that short-term weather conditions can change daily and that weather patterns change over the seasons

▶ Differentiating between text and pictures

▶ Knowing the elements of a story

▶ Developing oral fluency

SKILLS

▶ Reading for literary experience

▶ Counting

599 *Sea, Sand, Me!* **by Patricia Hubbell. New York: HarperCollins, 2001.**

A girl experiences the joy of spending the day at the beach.

LESSON IDEA: Ask the children if they have visited the beach. Ask what they need to pack to prepare for the beach. What do they like to do at the beach? For those children who haven't gone to the beach, ask them to imagine how they would spend the day. How would the sand feel? What would the ocean be like?

SKILLS
- ► Reading for literary experience
- ► Developing text-to-self connection
- ► Developing oral fluency

600 *Beach Day* **by Karen Roosa. New York: Clarion, 2001.**

A family spends the day playing at the beach, enjoying all the activities and other children there.

LESSON IDEA: Ask the children if they collect seashells when they go to the beach. Show a variety of shells. Hand out magnifying glasses so the students can closely examine the shells. What things did they notice about the shells with the magnifying glass that they didn't see when they looked without it?

SKILLS
- ► Reading for literary experience
- ► Developing visual discrimination
- ► Using simple tools to gather information

601 *The Night Before Summer Vacation* **by Natasha Wing.** 【WEB】 **New York: Grosset and Dunlap, 2007.**

In this variation of the classic tale, a family races to get packed the night before summer vacation.

LESSON IDEA: Print the Summer Vacation Suitcase worksheet from this book's webpage. Ask the children to think about where they want to go on vacation. Ask the children to fill their suitcases with items they need for vacation. They can either draw pictures or write the words.

SKILLS
- ► Reading for literary experience
- ► Recognizing rhyme
- ► Developing text-to-self connection
- ► Developing creativity
- ► Practicing writing

Fingerplays/Rhymes

602 Hot

It's so hot, I don't know what to do.
I think I need an ice cream, what about you?
It's so hot, help me please,
We'll have to stay in the shade of the green trees.
It's so hot, how can we stay cool?
Oh I know, let's jump in the pool!

SKILLS
- ► Recognizing rhyme
- ► Developing oral fluency

603 O-C-E-A-N (to the tune of "B-I-N-G-O")

There is a place we like to swim,
The ocean is its name, oh.
O-C-E-A-N, O-C-E-A-N, O-C-E-A-N,
The ocean is its name, oh.

(Repeat, gradually replacing letters with claps.)

SKILLS
- ► Developing oral fluency
- ► Developing spelling knowledge

604 **Sand Between My Toes Call-and-Response Chant**

I love to feel the sand between my toes.
I dig in it.
I scoop it up.
Let it fall.
Pour on some water.
Mound it up.
A sand castle tall!

SKILLS

▶ Recognizing rhyme
▶ Developing oral fluency
▶ Developing attention and response
▶ Developing listening skills

605 **Sand on My Head** (to the tune of "Spider on the Floor")

There's sand on my head, on my head,
There's sand on my head, on my head,
Oh how I dread this sand on my head,
There's sand on my head, on my head.

...

There's sand up my nose . . . How do you suppose this sand got up my nose . . .
There's sand in my ear . . . I really, really fear there's sand in my ear . . .
There's sand in my shorts . . . This sand in my shorts is making me out of sorts . . .
There's sand down my leg . . . Oh help me, I beg . . .
There's sand in my sandal . . . I don't know how to handle . . .

SKILLS

▶ Recognizing rhyme
▶ Developing oral fluency
▶ Developing motor skills

Flannelboard/Prop Stories

606 **Ant Picnic Flannelboard**

The ants came to the park today,
Hoping to find a luncheon buffet.
1 ant found a basket of cherries,
The 2nd ant found some delicious strawberries.
A 3rd ant found a piece of bread,
The 4th ant found some cheese to spread.
The 5th ant was as lazy as could be.
While the others worked, he napped in a tree.

SKILLS

▶ Recognizing rhyme
▶ Developing oral fluency
▶ Counting

607 We're Going on Vacation

Place a variety of pictures on the flannelboard and ask the children if the items are something they would need for vacation at the beach, the mountains, or both.

Writing Readiness Activity

608 Summer Collage

Collect different magazines with pictures related to summer. Have the children cut out pictures of what they like about summer. Have them glue their pictures to a bright piece of paper and write their favorite things about summer under the collage.

Math Activity

609 Shell Match

From the pattern, cut out seashells from construction paper or card stock. Create a pair of seashells. On one shell, write a number. On the second shell of the pair, draw that number of dots. Have the children match the written number to the correct number of dots.

Takeaway Activity

SKILLS

▶ Developing creativity

▶ Developing fine motor skills

610 Sun Catcher

Materials: plastic deli lids, paint, glitter, sand, glue, yarn

Directions:

1. Punch a small hole near the edge of the lid so that you can later add yarn to hang it.
2. Decorate the lid using paint, glitter, and sand.
3. Tie a length of yarn to the hole.
4. Hang the lid in the window to catch the light.

Library Skill–Building Game

SKILLS

▶ Understanding the parts of a library

▶ Knowing t he elements of a story

▶ Developing oral fluency

▶ Developing attention and response

611 Summer Reading Time/Librarian Says

Preparation: Ask your local public library for information about its summer reading program. Find a book relating to the summer reading program theme.

Activity: Read a book relating to the summer reading program theme, then introduce the summer reading program and explain how it works. Finish by playing "Librarian Says" to review major concepts from the year. Some suggested commands:

Point to the easy fiction books (and other areas of the library).
Show how we sit while listening to a story.
Pretend you are reading a book.
Show how we hold a book.
Show how we move in the library.
Say the name of a character.
Touch your nose if you can think of a setting.
Turn to your neighbor and tell him or her the name of your favorite book.

ASL Connection

SKILLS

▶ Understanding basic American Sign Language

▶ Recognizing rhyme

▶ Developing oral fluency

612 Chocolate Ice Cream Cone (to the tune of "Baby Bumblebee")

I'm licking up my chocolate ICE CREAM cone.
I'm so GLAD I've got my very own.
I'm licking up my chocolate ICE CREAM cone.
Ouch! Brain freeze!

...

I'm crunching up my chocolate ICE CREAM cone.
I'm so GLAD I've got my very own.
I'm crunching up my chocolate ICE CREAM cone.
Now it's all over my hands! MESSY!

...

I'm CLEANING up my chocolate ICE CREAM cone.
I'm so GLAD I had my very own.
I'm CLEANING up my chocolate ICE CREAM cone.
ALL DONE!

  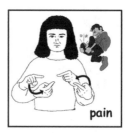 

Spanish Connection: It's Hot!

613 ***Hace Calor!* (ah-SAY kah-LORE) (Hot!)**

Hace calor, I don't know what to do,
I think I need an ice cream, what about you?
Hace calor, help me please,
We'll have to stay in the shade of the trees.
Hace calor, how can we stay cool?
Oh I know, let's jump in the pool!

SKILLS

► Understanding basic Spanish vocabulary
► Recognizing rhyme
► Developing oral fluency

Recommend This!

Out of the Ocean by Debra Frasier. New York: Harcourt, 1998.

Sun Dance Water Dance by Jonathan London. New York: Dutton, 2001.

Picnic Farm by Christine Morton. New York: Holiday House, 1998.

Katie Discovers Summer by Liesbet Slegers. New York: Clavis, 2009.

We Had a Picnic This Sunday Past by Jacqueline Woodson. New York: Hyperion, 1997.

APPENDIX A

Further Resources for Lesson Planning

Resource Books

Baltuck, Naomi. *Crazy Gibberish and Other Story Hour Stretches*. Hamden, CT: Linnet Books, 1993.

Benton, Gail, and Tricia Waichulaitis. *Ready-to-Go Storytimes: Fingerplays, Scripts, Patterns, Music, and More*. New York: Neal-Schuman, 2003.

Briggs, Diane. *101 Fingerplays, Stories, and Songs to Use with Finger Puppets*. Chicago: American Library Association, 1999.

_____. *Preschool Favorites: 35 Storytimes Kids Love*. Chicago: American Library Association, 2007.

Castellano, Marie. *Simply Super Storytimes: Programming Ideas for Ages 3–6*. Fort Atkinson, WI: Upstart Books, 2003.

Christel, Mary. *Lesson Plans for Creating Media-Rich Classrooms*. Urbana, IL: National Council of Teachers of English, 2007.

Chupela, Dolores C. *Once Upon a Childhood: Fingerplays, Action Rhymes, and Fun Times for the Very Young*. Lanham, MD: Scarecrow Press, 1998.

Cooper, Cathie Hilterbran. *The Storyteller's Cornucopia*. Fort Atkinson, WI: Alleyside Press, 1998.

Cullum, Carolyn N. *The Storytime Sourcebook: A Compendium of Ideas and Resources for Storytellers*. New York: Neal-Schuman, 1999.

_____. *The Storytime Sourcebook II: A Compendium of 3,500+ New Ideas and Resources for Storytellers*. New York: Neal-Schuman, 2007.

Dowell, Ruth E. *Move Over, Mother Goose! Finger Plays, Action Verses, and Funny Rhymes*. Mt. Rainier, MD: Gryphon House, 1987.

Esche, Maria Bonfanti, and Clare Bonfanti Braham. *Kids Celebrate! Activities for Special Days Throughout the Year*. Chicago: Chicago Review Press, 1998.

Faurot, Kimberly K. *Books in Bloom: Creative Patterns and Props That Bring Stories to Life*. Chicago: American Library Association, 2003.

Fox, Kathleen. *Fun-Brarian: Games, Activities, and Ideas to Liven Up Your Library!* Janesville, WI: Upstart Books, 2007.

Frey, Yvonne Awar. *One-Person Puppetry Streamlined and Simplified*. Chicago: American Library Association, 2005.

Fujita, Hiroko. *Stories to Play With: Kids' Tales Told with Puppets, Paper, Toys, and Imagination*. Little Rock, AR: August House, 1999.

Hamilton, Leslie. *Child's Play: 200 Instant Crafts and Activities for Preschoolers*. New York: Crown, 1989.

_____. *Child's Play Around the World: 170 Crafts, Games, and Projects for Two-to-Six-Year-Olds*. New York: Perigee, 1996.

Keeling, Joyce. *Lesson Plans for the Busy Librarian: A Standards-Based Approach for the Elementary Library Media Center*, Volume 2. Santa Barbara, CA: Libraries Unlimited, 2005.

Lima, Carolyn and John. *A to Zoo: Subject Access to Children's Picture Books.* Westport, CT: Libraries Unlimited, 2001.

MacDonald, Margaret Read. *Bookplay: 101 Creative Themes to Share with Young Children.* North Haven, CT: Library Professional Publications, 1995.

_____. *Twenty Tellable Tales.* Chicago: American Library Association, 2005.

MacMillan, Kathy. *A Box Full of Tales: Easy Ways to Share Library Resources through Story Boxes.* Chicago: ALA Editions, 2008.

_____. *Try Your Hand at This: Easy Ways to Incorporate Sign Language into Your Programs.* Lanham, MD: Scarecrow Press, 2005.

MacMillan, Kathy, and Christine Kirker. *Storytime Magic: 400 Fingerplays, Flannelboards, and Other Activities.* Chicago: ALA Editions, 2009.

Reid, Rob. *Children's Jukebox, Second Edition: The Select Subject Guide to Children's Musical Recording.* Chicago: American Library Association, 2007.

_____. *Family Storytime: Twenty-four Creative Programs for All Ages.* Chicago: American Library Association, 1999.

_____. *Storytime Slam! 15 Lesson Plans for Preschool and Primary Story Programs.* Bt Bound, 2006.

Schiller, Pam, and Jackie Silberg. *The Complete Book of Activities, Games, Stories, Props, Recipes, and Dances for Young Children.* Beltsville, MD: Gryphon House, 2003.

Sierra, Judy. *The Flannelboard Storytelling Book.* New York: H. W. Wilson, 1997.

Silberg, Jackie, and Pam Schiller. *The Complete Book of Rhymes, Songs, Poems, Fingerplays, and Chants.* Beltsville, MD: Gryphon House, 2002.

Stangle, Jean. *Is Your Storytale Dragging?* Belmont, CA: Fearon Teacher Aids, 1989.

Story-Hoffman, Ru. *Nursery Rhyme Time.* Fort Atkinson, WI: Alleyside Press, 1996.

Trevino, Rose Zertuche. *Read Me a Rhyme in Spanish and English.* Chicago: ALA Editions, 2009.

Warren, Jean, ed. *Nursery Rhyme Theme-a-Saurus.* Torrance, CA: Totline Publications, 1993.

_____. *Storytime Theme-a-Saurus.* Everett, WA: Warren Publishing House, 1993.

Wilmes, Liz and Dick. *Felt Board Fingerplays with Patterns and Activities.* Elgin, IL: Building Blocks, 1997.

Software

American Sign Language Clip and Create 5. Institute for Disabilities Research and Training (www.idrt.com), 2009.

Websites

ASL Pro (American Sign Language video dictionary): www.aslpro.com

Best Kids Book Site (thematic book recommendations, crafts, fingerplays): www.thebestkidsbooksite.com/storytimes.htm

Child Care Lounge (fingerplays): www.childcarelounge.com/activity/finger-plays.php

ChildFun (fingerplays, crafts, and activities): www.childfun.com

DLTK Kids (crafts and fingerplays): www.dltk-kids.com

Enchanted Learning (crafts and fingerplays): www.enchantedlearning.com (A paid subscription is required to print craft patterns and coloring pages.)

First-School (crafts and fingerplays): www.first-school.ws

Gayle's Preschool Rainbow (crafts and fingerplays): www.preschoolrainbow.org

The Idea Box (activities and crafts): www.theideabox.com

Kids' Chalkboard (crafts and fingerplays): www.kidschalkboard.com

Songs for Teaching (fingerplays and songs): www.songsforteaching.com

Storytime Stuff (fingerplays, flannelboards, book recommendations): www.storytimestuff.net

Vendors of Prepackaged Flannelboards, Big Books, and Other Props

Book Props, LLC: www.bookprops.com

Brodart: www.shopbrodart.com

Demco: www.demco.com

The Felt Source: www.thefeltsource.com

Folkmanis Puppets: www.folkmanis.com

Highsmith: www.highsmith.com

Lakeshore Learning: www.lakeshorelearning.com

The Library Store: www.thelibrarystore.com

MerryMakers: www.merrymakersinc.com

School Specialty: www.schoolspecialtyonline.net

Teacher's Paradise: www.teachersparadise.com

Making Flannelboards, Stick Puppets, and More

Flannelboards/Magnetboards

Every theme in this book features flannelboard rhymes or stories. Flannelboards are a wonderful addition to all storytimes. If you don't own a large flannelboard, you can make your own by covering the inside of a metal cookie sheet (where cookies normally go) with felt. This homemade flannelboard can travel anywhere with you and can also serve as a magnetboard! Any metal surface can be made into a magnetboard, and magnetboard story pieces are easy to make by adding an adhesive magnet to the back.

You can buy premade flannelboard pictures, or you can make your own. There are several easy ways to make your own. If you don't feel you are artistic, clip art is readily available online or on many common computer packages such as Microsoft Word. Print out the pictures you need, trim, and mount on a piece of construction paper. Laminate the clip art for durability. If you don't have a laminating machine, use clear contact paper to seal the picture. Then glue a piece of felt or a magnet to the back of the picture, and you're done!

When making your own flannelboard pieces with felt, you can use any of the patterns included in this book or one of your own creations. Patterns can be enlarged or reduced on a copy machine to fit your specific needs. When tracing the pattern on felt, use a Sharpie or other marker. Use a good pair of scissors to cut the felt. Be creative! Decorate the felt pieces with fabric paint, feathers, sequins, and so on. Wiggly eyes can be used on animals and people to give a more animated appearance.

If you have a scanner, you can scan characters and items directly from books and magazines, and then print them on fusible fabric. The fusible fabric can then be mounted on felt. When creating a flannelboard activity based on a book, remember to cite the book title and author.

Stick Puppets

Stick puppets are a fun addition to storytimes. Most of the flannelboards and rhymes in this book can be converted to use with stick puppets, and stories often lend themselves to being told with stick puppets. You can make stick puppets with clip art, hand-drawn illustrations, or pictures cut from books or magazines. Laminate the pictures for durability. If you don't have a laminating machine, use clear contact paper to seal the picture. Glue the laminated picture to a craft stick. When using stick puppets with a lap theater, add a square of Velcro to the stick, about an inch from the bottom. This will allow you to secure the stick puppet to the lap theater. If you will have a large audience, use large images glued to paint sticks so the entire crowd can see.

Paint sticks can also be used as props. With Velcro attached to the paint stick, you can attach and detach various clip art pieces and tell many rhymes and stories. For example, you can attach five monkeys to a paint stick with Velcro. While chanting the "Five Little Monkeys" rhyme, bounce the stick up and down. Every time a monkey falls off the tree, remove the monkey from the stick.

Die-Cutting Machines and Laminators

Make use of the equipment the school owns. Many schools own die-cutting machines and a variety of die-cuts. Use die-cuts to make a variety of items for flannel, chalk, or magnet boards, in various colors. The die-cutting machine will save you from having to hand cut many of the basic items you need to create a wonderful media experience. Also, if you need a heavier weight paper to create die-cuts, index cards often fit the machine perfectly and provide a sturdier option. Index cards are available in a variety of colors, and they come unlined.

To ensure the durability of paper items you create, use the school's laminating machine. Often the school's laminating machine will allow you to laminate many items at once, which you can then cut out.

Lap Theater

Lap theaters are a wonderful way to tell your stick puppet stories. They provide a storage spot for your puppet pieces, allowing you to unveil the story slowly and surprise the audience. To create a lap theater, find a box big enough to accommodate a puppet show, but still fits easily on your lap. Cut off the top of the box as well as the back "wall" of the box. Decorate the remaining three sides of the box as desired, or create a curtain for the box. The curtain need not be fancy; you could just use a piece of material glued to the walls of the box. Along the inside top edges of the walls add a Velcro strip. This will give you the option of securing your stick puppets to the walls during your puppet show, allowing your hands to be free to introduce and move other characters.

Glove Puppets

Glove puppets are a great way to tell a story or rhyme. Inexpensive cotton garden gloves work well. Rhymes and stories with five characters or pieces are ideal, but others can be done as well if you attach more than one item to the fingers of the glove. Create the animals or pieces of the rhyme with felt, pom-poms, or clip art. If the story has a constant, such as the tree in the "Five Little Monkeys" rhyme, you can attach that piece to the center of the glove. Use Velcro to attach the pieces to each finger of the glove.

Read-Alongs

A wonderful way to involve your audience in storytime is to use read-alongs. Pass out a copy of the book you are reading to each participant so everyone can follow along while you read. This technique works really well if you have an oversized book to read from that has simple text.

Costumed Stories

Have fun telling your stories and show your multiple personalities. With each new character introduced, add a headband or other identifying item. Each time that character is speaking, make sure to add the item. Animal stories and rhymes are an easy option to do this activity with, as there are inexpensive premade animal headbands available for purchase. You could also invite the audience to participate by wearing the costumes and playing the parts in the story.

Manipulatives for Storytime

Bubbles: Invest in a bubble gun; they are a great source of fun and will save you from trying to blow bubbles manually for an entire song. Pop on a bath or summer fun song and blow the bubbles around the crowd, while encouraging the children to clap and stomp them.

Rhythm sticks: Rhythm sticks can be made by cutting wooden dowels and sanding the rough edge. They really keep the beat while marching around, make excellent spider legs during rhymes, and easily demonstrate the different sounds things make in the room when you drum with them.

Scarves: Scarves are inexpensive to buy. Purchase them in a rainbow of colors. They make great kites and wonderful dancing partners, and you can use them to play peek-a-boo!

Shakers: Shakers can be made by filling plastic eggs with beans or rice and sealing the eggs with tape. Shakers are fantastic background instruments for any rockin' song.

Streamers: Streamers can be made with crepe paper, old plastic bags, wrapping paper, or wide ribbon cut into strips. Streamers are fun to dance with, can be used with rhymes to represent wind, and make great ticklers.

Index of Names and Titles

Titles of books are in italic. Titles of stories, songs, rhymes, and other activities are in roman.

Index of Topics, Themes, and Skills

You may also be interested in

Storytime Magic: 400 Fingerplays, Flannelboards, and Other Activities

Kathy MacMillan and Christine Kirker

"Both new and veteran storytellers will appreciate this book."
—*School Library Journal*

"There are lots of ideas here on common themes both in the real world and the world of imagination."—*Teacher Librarian*

PRINT: 978-0-8389-0977-5
152 PGS / 8.5 x 11

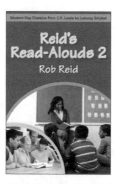

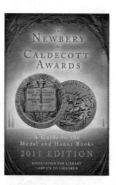

Order today at **alastore.ala.org** or **866-746-7252!**
ALA Store purchases fund advocacy, awareness, and accreditation programs for library professionals worldwide.